W

AND WHAT YOU CAN DO ABOUT IT

WHEN PARENTS DISAGREE AND WHAT YOU CAN DO ABOUT IT

RON TAFFEL, PhD

with ROBERTA ISRAELOFF

THE GUILFORD PRESS
New York   London

Copyright © 1994 by Ron Taffel
Revisions © 2003 The Guilford Press
A Division of Guilford Publications, Inc.
72 Spring Street, New York, NY 10012
www.guilford.com

Printed in the United States of America

This book is printed on acid-free paper.

Last digit is print number: 9   8   7   6   5   4   3   2   1

Library of Congress Cataloging-in-Publication Data

Taffel, Ron.
   When parents disagree and what you can do about it /
Ron Taffel, with Roberta Israeloff.
     p. cm.
   Rev. ed. of: Why parents disagree. 1st ed. c1994.
   Includes index.
   ISBN 1-57230-796-X (pbk.)
    1. Parenting—United States. 2. Child rearing—United States.
3. Sex role—United States. 4. Marital conflict.   I. Israeloff, Roberta,
1952– II. Taffel, Ron. Why parents disagree, 1994. III. Title.
HQ755.83 .T34   2003
649′.1—dc21   2002011816

Originally published in hardcover by William Morrow and Co., Inc., as *Why Parents
Disagree: How Women and Men Parent Differently and How We Can Work Together*

Originally published in paperback by Avon Books, as *Why Parents Disagree and What
You Can Do About It: How to Raise Great Kids While You Strengthen Your Marriage*

The excerpt on page 130 from *Meet Samantha* by Susan Adler is reproduced with the
permission of Pleasant Company, Inc., Middleton, Wisconsin.

To my wife, Stacey,
and my two children, Leah and Sammy,
whose tenderness, fire, and love
found their way into these pages.

—R. T.

For David, Ben, and Jacob:
in disagreement and in harmony,
always with love.

—R. I.

ACKNOWLEDGMENTS

People help with the process of creativity in ways they can't imagine and often don't realize. This is my chance to thank them.

First of all, a brief conversation with Arlie Hochschild, author of *The Second Shift*, reassured me about the direction this book was taking. She probably doesn't realize how much I needed her support at that exact moment.

My years of work with Betty Carter, whose guidance and clinical acumen, especially regarding gender, helped me put abstract ideas into concrete practice. Although we get to see each other too rarely these days, hers is a voice I will never forget.

Thanks also to:

My colleague and literary agent, Jim Levine, who got involved in the "hot" topic of fathering over twenty-five years before it became fashionable. Early on, he validated the unanticipated direction this book was taking.

Kitty Moore, my editor at The Guilford Press, who had the foresight to see the merit in this material.

My coauthor on *When Parents Disagree*, Roberta Israeloff, who worked with me as a real partner—struggling together over and over and over again until we got it "good enough." Her combination of logic and lyricism moved us past the seemingly endless problems one must face in a process like this. And, in the end, a soulmate and loyal friend to boot.

My father, Leo, who, in what was unusual for the fifties, put in enough "mommy" time to help me see things just a little differently. He sat with me when I was sick, studied with me for those endless tests, came into my room to kiss me and say prayers at bedtime every single night of my growing up.

My mother, Lottie, who, once when I was fourteen years old, went with the "girls" to Atlantic City on money from the canasta club—leaving the men of the family to fend for themselves. Despite neatly packaged and labeled meals, and her 101 other preparations, we wandered around the house that evening more than a little lost. One night over thirty-five years ago taught me how much we can all take for granted who does what around the house.

I am deeply grateful to both my parents for having said over so many years, "Ronnie, pick a profession when you grow up that you'll love. And if you're lucky, it will also do good for other people." Unfortunately, they never got to see how much I took their values to heart.

And finally, my wife, Stacey. She saw how much this project meant to me yet expected my presence at home anyway. Even so, she covered for me in a thousand invisible ways, which is not surprising given what you'll be reading in these pages. On top of it all, she went through every chapter with a sharp eye toward rooting out anything that might feel pretentious and unreal. Her love and gentleness found its way through me and into these pages.

As I said, we all learn differently and in such subtle ways that we often don't realize it at the time. But you can't do it alone and you've got to be a little lucky. You need to find some good, generous teachers along the way.

—RON TAFFEL

I'd like to thank Liza Dawson for her expert editorial eye and guidance that was always on target; and Jim Levine for his tireless enthusiasm and faith in the book.

I'm especially grateful to Lynn Seligman, not only for her invaluable and inexhaustible advice, support, and levelheadedness, which helped see this project to fruition, but also for always being there—and for being so much more than an agent.

To Ron Taffel, a special thank you. Undertaking this journey together brought many rewards: my understanding of psychology, families, writing, and myself has deepened beyond measure; and what began as a working relationship blossomed into friendship. From first word to last, the collaboration was by turns challenging, demanding, invigorating—but never dull, and always more of a pleasure than I had any right to expect it would be.

Finally, to my husband and partner, David Fleisher, thanks that will take a lifetime to fully express. Becoming parents is an odyssey we're very much in the midst of; there's no one by whose side I'd rather be.

—ROBERTA ISRAELOFF

CONTENTS

WHEN PARENTS DISAGREE
AND WHAT YOU CAN DO ABOUT IT

INTRODUCTION

When Parents Disagree and What You Can Do About It is derived from almost twenty-five years experience, during which time I have run seminars with and treated tens of thousands of families. Parental disagreement is perhaps the most common underlying problem I come up against in my practice and my childrearing workshops. Because I have seen how much family life can be affected by friction on the parenting team, I wrote this book to lessen conflict between mothers and fathers with children of all ages—those who complain of ordinary disagreements over the kids, as well as those who have serious arguments that may be tearing at the very fabric of the relationship

Just yesterday, I was sitting with Anita and Jack. They had come to see me because they'd been arguing a great deal since the birth of their six-month-old son, Danny. I knew this couple from around the neighborhood before Danny was born. And what a wonderfully happy twosome they seemed to be! Jack and Anita emanated an exciting love that everyone around admired and perhaps even envied. But I could quickly see that as a threesome, it was a totally different story. Danny's arrival had created resentments that emerged suddenly, with the fury of a hurricane in late August.

It wasn't just the sleep deprivation—actually, unlike my own two children, Danny slept through the night at three months. And it had nothing to do with whether Danny was a good eater or not—he had been nursing extremely well all along. And it wasn't because he was a little colicky—on a scale from one to ten, Danny's colic rated only a three.

The real reason Jack and Anita were having such a difficult time is that they discovered, like so many other couples (including my wife, Stacey, and me), that the "Battle of the Sexes" begins to get really serious after the kids are born.

Now, it may seem strange that such an old-fashioned term could have such relevance for this modern young couple. After all, Jack and Anita were psychologically sophisticated. They knew all about the trouble men and women have when it comes to dating, communication, and sex. But no one had prepared them for the very different ways in which women and men parent. No one had taught them how to reconcile the often unrealistic expectations men and women have of ourselves and each other about childrearing.

So, as I listened to their familiar complaints, even the angry threats to walk out of the marriage, I *knew* I could help them. And yet it passed through my mind that I wasn't always so sure of how to proceed. Because no one had prepared me either—in my professional training or before we had our children, Leah and Sammy. It was only after I had led hundreds of parenting workshops in schools and community centers around the country that I began to understand the obvious but unspoken impact of gender on parental harmony. In one workshop after another, when mothers and fathers expressed their different views about basic childrearing topics such as participation, discipline, spoiling, communication, and letting go, a once-peaceful auditorium could explode and divide into camps—and the division was *always* between women and men. Fathers who barely knew each other seemed to lock arms in collective, often burning resentment; mothers banded together with knowing expressions and looks that could kill.

Eventually it became impossible to hear parents from every region of the country talk about childrearing without recognizing that, despite all the headlines about "gender-bending," women and men still approach parenting from different perspectives. And because we take this basic fact of life for granted, the inevitable conflict exacts a toll on our children and the stability of our marriages.

I'll never forget the night I decided to write *When Parents Disagree*. I was leading a parent/child workshop and refereeing yet another disagreement between a mother and father. This time it was over how to get their ten-year-old daughter, Jennifer, to do chores around the house. After watching her parents heatedly argue, Jennifer yelled, "Look, I don't care how you do it. But geez, Mom and Dad, just get your act together!"

The entire auditorium became silent. In her blunt, preteen way Jennifer had expressed the unspoken problem of parenting, the hidden force that often makes even the best childrearing techniques useless in everyday life around the house. Slowly, then, with particular attention to the ways gender creates conflict between parents, I began refining techniques that *could* help mothers and fathers "get their act together," so that we can accomplish what all parents really want—to raise good children and have a happy home life while we do it.

WHAT TO EXPECT

That's what this book is about. First you'll see, in a way you'll never forget, how gender warfare intensifies after we have children. Second, I will offer hundreds of concrete techniques to reduce parental conflict. Since we live in a world far, far removed from simpler *Ozzie and Harriet* times, I've included many family configurations—intact marriages, step-families, and couples living together with children. Most of these mothers and fathers report ordinary (but still very frustrating) disagreements over the kids, none more extreme than those of any modern parents trying to bring up children in our often frightening world. Many of the techniques I offer address these common concerns.

But I also counsel thousands of families in trouble. Some of the people you'll read about come to me at their wits' end. Often the central complaint is that differences over the kids are driving them apart, creating a wedge that is beginning to feel irreconcilable. For these families, the idea of a harmonious "parenting team" sounds like a fantasy some childrearing expert cooked up, perhaps from tidy theories, but certainly not from the messy realities of life with kids.

Regardless of which group you identify with—whether you're dealing with everyday disagreements or trying to save a marriage—this book speaks to you. The suggestions you'll be reading about can create astonishing change. Fights should significantly lessen; the general atmosphere of home life will lighten up; even sex may improve (as you'll see, sexual desire is often directly connected to how well the parenting team functions). And, most important, you and your partner may reexperience the love that brought you together in the first place.

WHAT YOU *SHOULDN'T* EXPECT

As dramatic as these changes sound, there are limits to what can be accomplished. First, the techniques offered here won't help if:

- You are in the midst of a bitter divorce settlement.
- There is physical abuse in your home.
- There is a chemical dependency problem—without any family member being in a twelve-step or counseling program.

If even one of these applies, don't bother reading *When Parents Disagree*. Seek professional help instead.

Second, if your goal is to be soothed and nothing more, *When Parents Disagree* isn't for you either. It doesn't sugarcoat reality. Too many genuine disagreements between mothers and fathers arise for childrearing *ever* to be a job without occasional friction. Anyway, fighting doesn't stop simply because you've read an interesting book. You need to try at least a few of the recommendations made—which is easier said than done. Because I work with families every day, I know how artificial it can feel to do anything new that's not part of your established routine. That's why the suggestions are modest and practical. Since they've already been tested out by hundreds of mothers and fathers, I can almost guarantee conflict will lessen *enough* that you'll begin to feel a little more like you're working with, not against, each other.

THIS BOOK IS FOR MOTHERS *AND* FATHERS

Somebody needs to say it: One of the underlying problems in modern childrearing is that "parenting" books are usually read by the parent who happens to be the mom. In fact, over 85 percent of relationship "self-help" books are purchased by women. When it comes to childrearing guides, my experience tells me that this percentage is even higher. Almost everyone accepts this educational imbalance as a given. And yet it creates invisible stress on the parenting team, robbing our children of mothers and fathers who are on the same wavelength.

Realistically, then, chances are that you—Mom—will read *When Parents Disagree* first. At some point, you might try to interest your partner by showing him selected passages, probably those which speak most urgently to you. Be careful, though. The very passages you choose may be the ones to which men can least relate. Remember, fathers are represented in these pages as much as mothers. Therefore, you must be sure to show your husband or partner the sections that describe parenting from *his* vantage point and that ask *you* to change as well. Otherwise, he will dismiss my suggestions as intrusive criticism by another childrearing expert who claims to know it all.

GETTING DOWN TO BUSINESS

When Parents Disagree will describe your family's life in ways that have made every reader so far (including hard-nosed editors who see dozens of childrearing manuscripts a year) rip out pages to show their spouses. I hope you'll react with similar enthusiasm. I also hope you'll keep in mind this basic fact, which I've learned from my two decades working with families: no matter what your situation is, *small* changes in the way you handle parental disagreement can make enormous differences in how effective you can be with your children and how happy you can be with your partner.

So now it's time to begin. Always remember—big changes happen when you think small. To raise healthy and good children, mothers and fathers need all the nourishing, all the support, all the knowledge we can possibly give each other.

PART I

THE
ENDLESS LIST

CHAPTER 1

UNBALANCED PARTICIPATION

The Fundamental Cause of Parental Disagreement

Monday morning. All across America families are scrambling to dress, grab something for breakfast, and get out of the house—just as they have for generations.

But a few significant changes have taken place since "the Beaver" hopped on his bike and set off for school. Mom is most likely dressing for work, too. For a while now, the majority of mothers of pre-school-aged children hold jobs. And Dad is pitching in. In fact, if you were to stand in front of an elementary school or day-care center anywhere in the country, you'd probably notice countless men driving or walking their kids to school, sending them off with a quick kiss and wishes for a good day.

Saturday afternoon. The park is filled to near capacity. Children wait in line for the swings and seesaws. The sandbox is chock-full of toddlers and sand toys, and traffic at the sliding pond is so brisk that kids barrel down nearly on top of one another. Even the benches are full. Moms and dads are everywhere, pushing kids on swings, standing guard at the monkey bars, mediating fights, and dispensing juice cartons.

There's no getting around it. Thirty years of social change have significantly affected the American family. But—despite the profound impact of the men's and women's movements, the taken-for-granted preserve of women in the workforce, and the ordinariness of divorce—one fact of family life has remained constant. Men and women are still trying, though in new and varying configurations, to raise children *together*.

Though headlines trumpet the prevalence of divorce, the divorce rate has in fact leveled off: today, one out of two children can expect to spend childhood with the same parents. Even among divorced couples 80 percent of divorced fathers find a new partner and eventually remarry. And nearly half of all cohabiting couples have children in the household.

There's one other reality of family life that hasn't changed. You can still count on the fact that parents will *disagree* about how to raise their kids. In fact, parental disagreement is so normal it's like the weather—something everyone complains about but feels powerless to change. Though we're continually reminded that an essential part of raising kids is presenting a "united front," for most of us this fabled unanimity remains just that—a fairy-tale standard that certainly doesn't match the untidy disagreements of everyday life.

Don't look to the "experts" for answers, either. During all my training as a child and family therapist disputes over childrearing were never taken at face value, but almost always interpreted as a symptom of "marital difficulties." We rarely thought to turn it around—to consider the ways in which having children leads to inevitable disagreements, placing stress upon even the best relationships.

Only recently have we begun to address the ways in which childrearing affects marriages, and, of course, the difficulties of coparenting after divorce. Yes, we now acknowledge, becoming parents is hard on a relationship. Raising good kids is hard on a relationship. Developmental phases like the "terrible twos" and adolescence are hard on a relationship. Divorce certainly makes it hard to maintain a good parenting relationship. And according to the statistics, getting remarried is harder yet.

But over the years I've found these explanations of parental conflict both distracting and insufficient to explain the problems I've seen so many families encounter. After sifting through the give-and-take of thousands of families, I'm convinced that parenting issues are inescapably affected by gender, a fact that has remained largely unexplored. When we take for granted the natural differences between men and women, it's an easy next step to take parental conflict for granted as well.

LISTENING TO AMERICA

I discovered how much the battle of the sexes extends to childrearing about ten years ago, when I began giving parenting workshops across the country. Mothers and fathers of all types came to talk about tantrums, defiance, sleep problems, eating difficulties, communication, "The Room," rebellious teenagers–all the various troubles they were having with their children.

After leading about two hundred of these workshops, I began to notice a pattern. No sooner did the subject of parental disagreement come up than all havoc would break loose. The same men and women who had sat calmly side by side suddenly jumped to their feet waving their fists as if touched by a live wire. A moment before they'd been allies against their "difficult" children; now they were sworn enemies, facing each other across an enormous battlefield.

Here's what many of the mothers had to say:

"I want him to cooperate and participate more, but his ways are so *different* from mine, it's not worth the trouble."

"At least *your* husband gets involved. Mine doesn't contribute at all. It's like living with *another child* "

"We fight about what we should do and the kids get *forgotten*. They just slip through the cracks."

"It was almost easier when men had *nothing* to do with the kids. At least then things were done *right.*"

The men didn't take this sitting down. They also had plenty on their minds:

"Nothing I do is *right*. It's got to be done her way. She always *criticizes* my approach."

"She wants me to do fifty percent of the work but she wants *one hundred percent* of the *decision-making power.*"

"I think she's too *easy* on the kids. They need to learn that the world isn't as softhearted as their mom."

"She listens more to her friends, her mother, and the magazines than she does to me."

One man spoke with unforgettable poignancy about his frustration:

I spent last Saturday with my kids—alone—and we had a wonderful time. I did things at my own pace and used my own judgment. We got along great. Then my wife came home. It was like a tornado struck. She was everywhere, instantly, and I felt my confidence and spirits deflate like a balloon. There was no way I could match her energy. In a second the kids forgot about me and were back in her orbit. It seemed as if they didn't even remember the day we spent together.

At first, the intensity of these comments shocked me. As I said, nothing in my training or in the parenting literature had prepared me for this blatant gender warfare. But whenever the subject of parental conflict came up, marital loyalty flew out the window. Women who had never before met each other linked arms in solidarity; men who were perfect strangers looked to each other as comrades.

MEN AND WOMEN PARENT DIFFERENTLY

Obviously, this kind of friction isn't new. Struggles between men and women have been raging forever over the issues of sex, money, and power. But the intensity of the gender division over *parenting* issues was a little surprising. I suddenly understood that childrearing advice has always been dispensed as if women and men look at parenting through the same lens—or with the basic assumption that only mothers would be listening anyway. This latter reality, that "parenting" advice is really a euphemism for "mothering" advice, helped me understand some of the anger I was hearing in my workshops.

It wasn't simply that men and women looked at childrearing concerns like discipline, communication, and letting go differently. They were arguing over a more fundamental issue—*job description*. As Arlie Hochschild reported in *The Second Shift*, the basic paradigm of family life has remained stubbornly resistant to change. And according to the thousands of parents I spent time with,

Women are still *primarily responsible* for the kids' daily welfare, and men, though far more involved than their fathers, are still providers who *"help Mom out."*

These are strong words—in fact, you may be asking how I could be making such a "retrograde" statement. As I described, evidence of change is *everywhere*—in the park on Saturday afternoon, in front of schools during the week. National magazines herald the "New Age Man" on their covers, shown with a briefcase in one hand and a baby in the other.

Even surveys, such as one in *Child* magazine (March 1993), appear to indicate that when it comes to the division of labor in families, we seem to be heading in the right direction. According to this survey, today's dads are clearly more involved in childcare than their own fathers were. In fact, only one in ten fathers considered himself (or was considered by his wife) to be a "backseat dad." In addition, 25 percent of today's dads (in comparison to 2 percent of our own fathers) participate in hands-on care for their children—bathing, diapering, dressing, putting to bed—as part of daily life. That's the good news.

But forget the media hype for a moment. Listen instead to the mothers and fathers I meet every day. Turn these numbers upside down and you may begin to both understand their anger and share my skepticism. A full 75 percent of dads are *still* not actively involved in daily hands-on care. Fifty percent of fathers define themselves as "well rounded," but by this they mean that they help with childcare *"as their schedules permit."* In other words, despite all the changes we've been through, three out of four fathers are still not consistently involved in the *daily hands-on care* of children.

The 1993 "National Study of the Changing Workforce" conducted by the Families and Work Institute revealed similar findings. Of 3,400 randomly selected employed men and women, women were:

- 2 times more likely to pay household bills than men;
- 4½ times more likely to cook for the family;
- 7 times more likely to do the family shopping;
- 10 times more likely to do the household cleaning.

These findings suggest that despite the fact that a majority of women are now in the workplace, their responsibility to perform those domestic tasks that are directly related to the care of children has not changed much over time. "This is true," the survey concludes, "even in families where women contribute half or more of the family income, and where workers are young."

Since these studies were done almost a decade ago, it made sense to update them by going to the source. Ellen Galinsky is the president of the Families and Work Institute and one of the primary architects of the 1993 workforce study cited above. I asked her to comment on these significant role differences. Dr. Galinsky says, "Although the gap between men's and women's particpation in household tasks—childcare and chores—has narrowed considerably over the past 20 years, mothers still spend more time than fathers. We are looking forward to the results of our 2002 national study. While we may see that fathers continue to increase the time they spend with children and in doing household chores, we think that mothers will remain 'in charge' of many tasks."

From my work with families around the country, it is clear to me that this question—who feels "responsible" for tasks around the house getting done—is one of the central and most difficult to change realities of daily life. No one is to blame here. Obviously, today's fathers are participating more in family life than their fathers ever dreamed of. But the demands on men and women are increasing at a very rapid pace. Despite everyone's good intentions, if you peel away the facade of the "New Age" family, you'll discover unquestioned beliefs that are startlingly traditional—and cause tremendous problems for the parenting team.

INSIDE THE KNAPSACK

How does this translate into real life? Let's go back to our Monday morning scene. If you were to ask those children going to school with their dads to open their knapsacks, here's what you would probably find: a lunch prepared and packed—by Mom; dessert money or a meal ticket provided—by Mom; books either purchased or covered—by Mom; a permission slip allowing the child to be picked up after school written—by Mom; homework more than likely checked—by Mom; a form volunteering to help out at the school crafts fair signed—by Mom; a can of soup for the food drive included at the last minute—by Mom; and a newsletter listing upcoming school events published by the "newsletter committee" run—by Mom.

To a school crossing guard or a newspaper reporter observing from a distance, yes, family relations have radically changed. But a closer look inside the knapsack, into the private workings of family life, reveals something quite different, just as peering into a microscope at a drop of water reveals a world not visible to the naked eye.

I have spent my professional life looking inside the family at the web of relationships not visible to most people. At work, I do nothing else but talk to parents and children. During the past two decades I have personally worked with over three thousand families and couples—often staying in touch with these families until the kids grow up, leave for college, and have children themselves. I have supervised approximately one hundred therapists and counselors on several thousand other family cases. I've met with tens of thousands of parents around the country discussing the issues of ordinary life. When you hear as many nitty-gritty details as I do, you realize that the participation equation in most families is still astonishingly out of kilter—so much so that we can't get on the same wavelength about the kids. This imbalance polarizes men and women, *magnifying* the already very different views we have about childrearing (all of which will be explored in detail in upcoming chapters—how to discipline, communicate, let go, and network) into an often impossible struggle, powerful enough to knock many otherwise successful marriages off course.

I believe that the explosive combination of gender differences over childrearing and the "Mom is responsible—Dad helps out" paradigm is the *central factor underlying ordinary parental disagreement.* It transforms potential complementarity between men and women into anger and alienation. It leaves a profound imprint on children's minds about what mothers' and fathers' roles should be, which will be handed down to the next generation—to your children and grandchildren. And it practically guarantees that the mythical "united front" of the good parenting team will remain just that—a fairy-tale ending we all strive for but rarely achieve.

MY GOALS

This is serious business. It's no wonder parents disagree and at the same time feel so powerless to do anything about it. Yet I believe that by addressing both the participation equation and taken-for-granted gender differences, we can reduce conflict on the parenting team.

That's what this book is about. Every chapter will deal with a different hot spot of parental disagreement. First, I will address each of these from the perspective of how men and women approach childrearing issues in different ways. Second, I will offer practical solutions to reduce conflict between parents. Third, you'll find quick-read guidelines on how to increase cooperation in particularly troublesome teamwork areas.

My suggestions may at first appear modest—especially in comparison to the depth and magnitude of the issues I raise. But after spending twenty-five years with families, I am nothing if not a realist. Change begins with tiny steps, one small move at a time. You don't have to be optimistic about the outcome. You only have to try.

As you will see, even the smallest change in family routine and expectations can have profound consequences—both on the parenting team and on the health of our kids.

Let's begin right now. Here's my first question: Who's responsible for making sure that things go right for your kids in their daily lives?

Try taking the following quiz.

THE "WHO FEELS RESPONSIBLE FOR THE KIDS?" QUIZ

1. Who first notices the signs that one of your kids is getting sick?
2. Who informs the school that your child won't be coming to school due to illness?
3. Who attended the last parenting workshop in your school, church, or community center? If both of you attended, whose idea was it to go?
4. Who first heard about and actually bought the last book on any aspect of childrearing?
5. If you've ever consulted a mental health professional about your kids, who initiated the contact?
6. Who searched for and interviewed prospective pediatricians? Babysitters? Who found out which doctors and babysitters other parents in your neighborhood use?
7. Who bought the last small "thinking of you" present when your child seemed to be blue?

8. Who thought to call the parents of the friend with whom your child had a bad rift? Who actually made the call?
9. Who thought to call the parents of your daughter's playmates after she came down with the chicken pox or some other communicable illness?
10. Whose mood is most affected when your child has trouble with friends at school?
11. Who calls your son's classmate when he's ill to make sure he gets the homework assignment?
12. Who usually tries to talk to your child when she's feeling sad?
13. Who plans and organizes birthday parties and other special events for the kids?
14. Who first researches nursery schools, camps, and after-school activities?
15. Who usually makes weekend plans for the family?
16. Who coordinates carpooling for ferrying kids between activities?
17. Who remembers to bring juice, wipes, and other essentials to the playground, on a day trip, or a vacation?
18. Who first notices that your supply of "kid foods"—Cheerios, mini-waffles, macaroni and cheese—is running low?
19. Who first notices that shoes are too tight, pants are too short, and sweaters too frayed?
20. Whose datebook contains the dates of the school concert, Little League sign-up, and other kids' birthday parties?

Remember, I'm not questioning who *cares* more about the kids. Nor am I asking (yet) who actually *does* these tasks. What I'm asking you to think about is who feels ultimately responsible for the *daily welfare* of the children.

If your answers are similar to those of the thousands of families I've worked with, then come with me—not into the neutered, theoretical world of "modern parenting," but into the real world of men and women trying to raise children together, disagree less, and love each other more.

CHAPTER 2

SIX STEPS TOWARD SHORTENING MOM'S ENDLESS LIST

Surveying the headlines and magazine covers during 1992's "Year of the Woman," you would think that the fight for equal participation in family life had been fought and won. Yet mothers still complain regularly to me about their spouses' lack of cooperation in the details of everyday life. The same women who wield "man-sized" power during the workday come home at night to find themselves overwhelmed and taken for granted. Hundreds of such high-powered women have sat in my office at wit's end, worrying less about their professional responsibilities than about how they are going to cope with their kids and accomplish all the tasks on their Endless Lists.

Surprisingly, many otherwise sophisticated mothers still don't realize just how imbalanced things really are around the house—or how this imbalance creates serious disagreements on the parenting team. "They just don't get it," a phrase usually applied to men about relationship issues, also applies to many mothers when it comes to the division of childcare responsibilities. Yes, men need to participate more in family life (I'll talk about this in Chapter 3). But I'm continually struck by how much difficulty *women* have in breaking the "Mom is responsible and Dad helps out" paradigm.

To illustrate what I mean, let me introduce you to Kathy and Evan. I've chosen them because in many ways they are an exemplary twenty-first century couple. Both work—he's a full-time business manager and she's a graphic designer who puts in thirty hours a week. Each has been previously married and divorced with no children from either marriage. Now they have two children, six-year-old Eric and nine-year-old Chloe. They came to counseling because both of them complained of fighting over how to discipline the kids. In addition, Kathy felt as if all her efforts around the house were being taken for granted.

At first I couldn't understand the problem. Evan seemed a thoroughly "modern" father and, according to *both*, household tasks were "fairly" divided, with Kathy shouldering perhaps 60 percent of the childcare responsibilities to Evan's 40 percent—by no means a traditional 1950s "Mom does it all" arrangement.

Or so I thought. At one session I asked them to compose a list of what each was responsible for vis-à-vis the kids during the course of a typical afternoon and evening. At first they both resisted. Even though Kathy felt as if her work around the house often went unnoticed, she didn't think that composing a list of chores would reveal anything she didn't already know.

A week later, a rather shaken Kathy and Evan reported back, having done their assignment. Here are their lists:

EVAN'S LIST—WEDNESDAY 5:00 P.M.–11:00 P.M.

1. Call to see if I should pick up anything on the way home.
2. Come home, see everyone. Tell kids to pick up their things.
3. Check dinner plans—are we eating at home?
4. Turn on CNN to see what's happening.
5. Eat dinner.
6. Talk during dinner, ask everyone how was their day, how was school—unless everyone is angry.
7. Put dishes in dishwasher.
8. Put clean laundry away.
9. Watch news, sports, movie; read.
10. Discuss homework with kids.
11. Say good-night to kids.
12. Organize myself for making everyone's breakfast next morning.

As you read this, remember that Evan is quite involved—in homework, preparing breakfast, cleaning up. What happens to the kids matters a great deal to him. With this in mind, let's turn to:

KATHY'S LIST—WEDNESDAY 4:00 P.M.–11:00 P.M.

1. Evan calls me at work from his office four times before I leave to pick up the kids. Buy Christmas present for babysitter on the way to kids' school.
2. I pick up the kids from school. Chloe wants to go to the ice cream store; I want to go straight home. We negotiate.
3. At home, I try to take a short bath but can't because the kids are fighting.
4. Make ham salad for tomorrow's lunch.
5. Eric wants to play Play Station; I tell him he has to wait until 8:00 P.M.
6. Break up fight between Chloe and Eric; he's singing along too loud with his Walkman.
7. Make biscuits.
8. Make about twenty phone calls as class mother to plan the fourth-grade square dance.
9. Heat soup for kids' dinner but they don't want to eat yet.
10. Try to take a bath again.
11. Go to my room but kids are there watching TV. They keep changing channels and playing with the volume, so I hide the clickers and tell them no TV until 8:00 P.M.
12. Put in a load of wash.
13. Wrap babysitter's Christmas gift.
14. Chloe hits Eric for singing too loud with his Walkman.
15. I try to lie down because I feel the flu coming on. Everyone keeps firing questions at me. I WANT EVERYONE TO LEAVE ME ALONE SO I CAN REST. But Eric asks if he can play Play Station. I tell him not until eight.
16. I check Eric's first-grade project.
17. Evan comes home at 6:00 P.M., says he won't eat with the kids or go near them until they calm down: I say, "Dinner's in the oven." He says, "Call me when it's ready." "It's ready now," I say. He turns on the TV.
18. Evan's mother calls. He talks to her for a minute and then hands me the phone. I talk for fifteen minutes while making salad dressing and

trying to deal with Eric, who is bored with no TV or Play Station. "Entertaining you is not my job" I tell him.

19. Eric wants to vacuum but Evan doesn't want him to, afraid Eric will break the Dirt Devil. Eric helps set table and takes out garbage.

20. Call kids to table. Put out forks, glasses.

21. Chloe comes into kitchen, puts a cat brush on the counter next to the food, and walks out. We get into an argument over hygiene. We eat dinner.

22. Evan puts his plate into dishwasher. I clean up rest of the kitchen.

23. Tell Chloe three times that I don't have enough money to give her an advance on her allowance; Evan won't back me up and I get mad at him.

24. Start cutting ham to make stock for Sunday dinner.

25. Make seven or eight phone calls to arrange the kids' sleep-over on Saturday night.

26. Find out Sunday guests don't eat ham; revise menu.

27. Evan and Chloe work together on computer—a few minutes of peace.

28. Check Chloe's homework again.

29. Remind Eric to pack his bag for sleep-over.

30. At 8:00 P.M., Eric begins playing Play Station; Chloe demands equal time and they get into a fight. I negotiate a playing schedule.

31. A contractor comes to discuss redesigning the kitchen. We don't have enough money for the project—should I be the one to say so?

32. Chloe starts screaming because Eric threw two bananas at her during the Play Station fight.

33. Evan complains about the commotion.

34. I try to lie down to read for a little.

35. Chloe comes in and asks me to curl her hair.

36. Chloe begins playing Game Boy; Eric hangs over her and "sticks his nose on my shoulder," Chloe screams. They fight again.

37. I write out check and complete the permission form so Chloe can attend a class trip.

38. Eric asks if he can have a friend sleep over Friday night. I call parents to make arrangements.

39. I call a neighbor about adopting her kitten, something the children have been agitating for.

40. Make and pack kids' lunches for tomorrow.
41. Feed cat; remind kids to clean kitty litter.
42. Go over Chloe's latest report card with Evan. He feels it's not good enough and wants to discipline her; I feel this will be ineffective in inspiring her to work harder.
43. Evan checks me to make sure I checked Chloe's homework.
44. I want to go to bed but can't find my skin moisturizer. It's in Chloe's room.
45. I finally go to bed earlier than usual because I'm not really feeling well.
46. Chloe comes in anyway and asks me if I will buy her platform shoes in time for her friend's party.

It *is* Endless, isn't it? And it represents just a *part of one day*. Multiply what we see here over an entire lifetime, and you begin to see just how much resentment can build up on any parenting team. But resentment is only part of the picture. When things are out of balance, the "Mom's responsible, Dad helps out" paradigm stays completely intact. And this paradigm ensures that:

1. Mothers feel central, yet terribly overburdened.
2. Fathers feel in a one-down position, or slightly defensive.
3. Children look to Mom and depend on her as the real "hands-on" parenting expert.
4. Men feel slightly peripheral, but can't quite figure out why since they're doing so much more than their own fathers did.
5. Mothers and fathers are in danger of living parallel lives.
6. Children pass along the paradigm to *their* children.

Unfortunately, the inevitable fights over childrearing issues such as discipline, communication, and letting go are often interpreted as "relationship" problems. "Liberated" though we may be, we don't see how the participation imbalance creates such different parenting experiences for mothers and fathers that when these "hot spot" topics come up—as they do every day—we're talking at each other in different languages. Conflict is unavoidable when these differences go unquestioned, and resolution seems a tall order indeed.

Both Kathy and Evan, for example, were shocked by how unevenly responsibilities were divided, and what a sham the sixty/forty split really was. When Kathy finished reading her list (which took almost twenty minutes), Evan said sheepishly, "No wonder we fight. Look, I'm not going to promise I'll actually do anything about this, but even I think it's a little unfair."

And then Kathy said something that I'll never forget: "I'm stunned. Everything that happens in the house gets routed through me. But even I didn't realize it. *How can I change something I'm not aware of?* How can I stop being taken for granted if I take myself for granted, too?"

Do *you* have an Endless List you're only vaguely aware of? Until you recognize all those taken-for-granted "mommy" tasks, there's absolutely no way you can begin to lessen conflict on your parenting team. And achieving a "united front" will remain a complete fantasy.

WHY ROLES ARE SO DIFFICULT TO CHANGE

Redistributing tasks more equitably is easier said than done. It's not just fathers who resist change in role expectations; many mothers have an equally difficult time handing control over to their partners.

Why? Is it because (as many men accuse) women don't want to give up the last word over house and home? Or is it because women still don't have true economic and social equality and are hesitant to give up their power base with the kids?

While there's some truth to both of these explanations, I've found far more ordinary reasons why many women have a hard time handing over childcare responsibilities. See if any of these sound familiar.

Reason #1: Why Create More Trouble for Myself?

For many mothers, maintaining the status quo of unequal participation is a matter of sheer pragmatism. Their reasons look like these:

1. "We're in a hurry and it's *faster* if I do it."

2. "He might get it *wrong* so in the end it will be less work if I do it myself."
3. "He's already in a *bad mood;* why create more trouble for myself?"
4. "I need him to be with the kids tonight, so I don't want to *press* him now."
5. "He's got a *deadline* this week at work."
6. "He's a wonderful father and already does a lot more than many men—so *why push?*"

With concerns as pragmatic as these, it's no wonder that many of today's high-tech mothers find themselves in an old-fashioned double bind—feeling burdened yet unable to comfortably relinquish the Endless List duties that swallow up their time.

Reason #2: Mothers-in-Training

Another reason mothers find it difficult to let go of the Endless List is because of the deeply ingrained assumption that women are the *real* caretakers and therefore primarily responsible for the welfare of the children. Whether this caretaking role results from biological or cultural factors, or a mixture of both, there's no question that men and women caretake differently, and that these differences show up astonishingly early—even in infancy.

For example, researchers have found that girl babies respond to other babies who are crying more than boys do. Girl babies are more likely to start crying when other children are upset. And girls at very early ages try to help other children in distress. In other words, if two six-month-olds were playing house you'd probably hear "Daddy" complaining, "You mothers are all alike. Why are you spoiling the kid? Just let her cry a little"—only to have "Mommy" reply, "What do you want from her? She's just a baby!"

Carol Gilligan (*In a Different Voice,* 1982) and Nancy Chodorow (*The Reproduction of Mothering,* 1978), among many other researchers, have found that gender differences become even more apparent as children get older. Girls don't operate from absolute notions of right and wrong as do boys, but view morality in the context of relationships, motivation, and feelings. Boys, on the other hand, often put "the rules" ahead of relationship considerations. Eavesdropping, then, on a couple of eleven-year-olds playing house, you'd probably hear Johnny say, "You're too soft on the kids. A rule is a rule." To which Jane might reply, "How can you be so strict? She had a *reason* to do what she did."

Anecdotal evidence—the stories we tell our friends and hear from others—supports these researchers. For example, a friend of mine recently told me about the Thanksgiving book her son brought home from kindergarten in which each child answered the question, "How does your family prepare for Thanksgiving?" According to sixteen out of eighteen children, Mommy bought, stuffed, seasoned, and roasted the turkey. Most of the kids lived with two parents (in either first or second marriages), and most of their mothers had jobs outside the home. Yet in all but a couple of stories, Dad might as well have been living out of state.

Another friend, who lives in the suburbs, recounts the time she took her five-year-old son and his friend for ice cream. "Dennis, a neighbor, was changing his six-month-old son's diaper on a picnic bench while his wife ate her ice cream cone. After they left, my son's friend piped up, 'That man's doing a lady's job.' When I asked him if daddies didn't take care of their children just like mommies, he shrugged and said, 'I never saw a daddy doing a diaper when a mommy's around.' "

Reason #3: The Blame Game

Finally—and I believe most important—our culture still holds mothers almost exclusively responsible when things go wrong with the kids. Sensing this ultimate accountability, women are understandably reluctant to give up control or veto power. If the finger of blame was eventually going to point in your direction, wouldn't you be?

Thirty years ago mothers were pressured to raise children who were "good eaters"; today they are accused of raising a generation of girls plagued by eating disorders. Thirty years ago mothers were told to stay at home and be available to the kids; today they are derided for having been hovering and oppressively overinvolved. Thirty years ago mothers began entering the workforce; today we are still debating whether working women are responsible for society's "lost kids."

As I wrote in *Parenting by Heart* and *McCall's* magazine, a comprehensive survey of ten major psychological journals found that mothers were held responsible for children's problems over *80 percent* of the time, while fathers were mentioned only *40 percent* of the time. There's more. Mothers were held responsible for *seventy-two* different kinds of childhood problems. The study also reports that in no single article was a mother–child relationship described as simply healthy. And surprisingly, both male and female health professionals blamed mothers equally.

This research mirrors my own experience. After reading hundreds of psychological reports and listening to thousands of case studies, I have *never* seen a mother who is not explicitly blamed for her child's psychological problems.

In one unforgettable case, two daughters had been regularly beaten and sexually abused by their father (who began ejaculating on them when they were three years old). I supervised the therapist handling the case and was shocked when the entire discussion that followed my supervisee's presentation focused on the *mother's* responsibility for not knowing about or not stopping his actions—this from a profession that is supposedly gender-sensitive.

How does all this translate into everyday life and the Endless List? Simply put, women are reluctant to give up control over childcare responsibilities when in the end society holds them accountable for how kids turn out.

CHANGING THE PARADIGM

These three reasons are astonishingly ingrained and resistant to change. Yet they must be challenged if mothers and fathers are to decrease tension on the parenting team. Here are six steps I've developed that help couples divide the Endless List more equitably.

1. The Endless List Exercise

For several days, or even one weekday, keep a list of who does what with and for the kids. Don't show each other your versions as you're compiling them. Be brief; use short phrases—don't worry about eloquence.

Then put aside some time and read your lists to each other. Be *prepared to feel a temporary surge of anger or guilt*. Evan and Kathy's reaction ("Oh my God, are we that bad?") is not at all unusual, especially for today's couples who have repeatedly been told how "modern" they are. As unsettling as the experience may be, it is the necessary first step. Before we can make any changes, we need to be aware of what we still take for granted.

2. Learn the Mantra: "I'm Not Completely Responsible"

If greater awareness alone could produce changes, every self-help author would be a miracle worker. But for most people, insight is only a beginning. What you need next is new information to counteract the generations-old belief that "Mom alone is responsible" for how the kids turn out. Familiarize yourself with the following research. It can be an antidote to the idea that your child is a lump of clay whom only *you*—Mom—can form and deform.

IT'S NOT ALL YOUR FAULT BECAUSE:

- Each child is born with a very different temperament, and this temperament *shapes parents* almost as much as parents shape children.
- Very few individual mistakes can ever have as much impact on child development as the *ongoing fabric* of the parent–child relationship, and no single mistake is irrevocably traumatic.
- Children's personalities are not completely formed by the age of five. You always have the chance to redo errors.
- It's more than just you! No psychological research has been able

to reliably predict from the mother–child relationship how children will turn out as adults.

- *Your* feelings count too! Children have a much greater capacity to empathize than we previously understood. Because of this, they are unhappy when their mothers are unhappy.
- Working won't ruin your kids. Children are less affected by their mothers' absence or presence—even when moms work full time—than by the family's willingness to redistribute responsibilities without conflict.

At those critical moments when you're trying to decide whether to hand over to your spouse the thirty-seventh Endless List item, remember these simple but powerful ideas. I encourage mothers to write down or memorize shortened versions of these findings, which they can refer to when they feel unable to let go of the Endless List.

For example, Louis, a computer programmer, and Monica, a bookkeeper, weren't seeing eye-to-eye about how to discipline five-year-old Christopher. Knowing what a psychologically harsh environment Louis had grown up in, Monica worried that Louis was too harsh. Though he'd never hit Chris, she didn't like his sharp tone of voice. And she'd seen him erupt many times—often during their fights over discipline.

But during one family train trip, as Chris jumped from seat to seat, Monica decided to let Louis handle it. To hold herself back from intervening or reprimanding Louis, Monica repeated the following mantra to herself: "I'm not totally responsible for every moment of Chris's life. One event isn't going to ruin him forever. I am not responsible for Louis's actions. He would never actually hurt Chris."

Calming herself down like this averted the explosive argument she and Louis usually had over discipline. It also allowed something new and totally unexpected to happen. When Louis took care of things in his own way (indeed, a little more "harshly" than Monica would have liked), Chris not only calmed down but contentedly sat next to his dad and eventually fell asleep on his lap for the rest of the trip. This successful experience gave Monica the courage to rethink a few other items on her Endless List. As for Louis, he said, "Not only did Monica and I not fight. But for the first time, when Chris fell asleep on my lap, I felt like I was actually his dad, not a part-time employee. It sounds sappy, but I felt special."

3. Ask for Help

The next step toward cutting down Endless List responsibilities as well as challenging the "Mom's responsible" paradigm is the one most mothers still don't take—asking. As Aaron, a psychologist friend of mine (and one of the fairest, most "liberated" men I've ever met), admitted to me privately, "If my wife would just ask me to do more things with the kids I certainly would. But for some reason she doesn't. We seem to go along without thinking about it. We're on automatic pilot. It amazes me that she still does about eighty percent of the everyday, hands-on stuff. But I'm not going to call attention to this. I'm tired enough as it is. Anyway, I forget. Packing lunches or wrapping birthday presents—these sorts of things are simply not on my mind."

However, after absorbing the shock of the Endless List exercise and then memorizing the "I'm not totally responsible" mantra, many mothers can be encouraged to ask for help—in ways that are less guilt-ridden and therefore less strident.

For example, Marcia and Frank, parents of four-year-old Maggie and two-and-a-half-year-old Michael, fought every time they left the house on a day trip. The script never varied: Frank would go out to pack the car while Marcia readied the "little things" for the kids. As any parent knows, those "little things" could support an army on maneuvers. Of course, she'd be late and he'd start yelling, "I'm waiting! What's taking you so long?" By the time they got in the car everyone was mad at each other, the kids were screaming, and the trip was off to its usual chaotic start.

When I suggested that Marcia ask Frank to take charge of some of the "getting ready" details in the house rather than just packing the car, *Marcia* immediately resisted the idea. She was afraid that he'd forget important items. "If the kids are thirsty, cold, or hungry, it's going to be *my* responsibility, anyway. And who do you think they'll scream at? In the end, it will only mean more work for me."

But I answered her this way: "Suppose Frank *does* forget to bring drinks, or extra diapers or the pacifier. Let *him* deal with it. Some principles are more important than how the day goes. If the kids are hungry or thirsty, it's not going to damage them irreparably. If things go wrong, it's not your responsibility more than Frank's—no matter what each of you thinks."

This didn't go down easily for Marcia. After intense discussion, Frank broke the stalemate. He agreed to take on some of the details if Marcia agreed not to comment on or criticize his performance.

What do you think happened? With so little previous experience in the "getting kids ready for a day trip" department, Frank predictably forgot to include juice cartons. And just as Marcia feared, the kids blamed her for being thirsty and wanted her to take care of it. But as we agreed, Frank dealt with the consequences of his oversight. Improvising, he took his daughter Maggie to a deli that sold juice, and the rest of the day went relatively smoothly.

Did Frank and Marcia forever switch responsibilities for organizing day trips? No. Only occasionally did they reverse roles. However, Marcia saw that she could ask Frank to take on some of the everyday tasks she automatically assumed were her responsibility. For his part, Frank better understood how many tiny details were involved in just getting out of the house. Because of this he didn't become quite so aggravated at Marcia for being "slow." Interestingly, Frank never forgot to bring drinks again.

Here's another example of how simply *asking* challenges the Endless List phenomenon. In the Remsen house, every morning began at 5:45 A.M., when four-year-old Eric would go over to his mother Alison's side of the bed, wake her up, and say, "Make me some cereal, Mommy."

As exhausting as this was, Alison never thought of asking Eric to go over to his father's side of the bed. And as Mark so clearly put it, "Look, if she isn't going to ask me, I'm sure as hell not going to be the one to get up at five-forty-five every morning. True, it's not particularly fair. But I'm not going to change if she doesn't ask me to."

After doing the Endless List exercise, however, Alison saw just how out of balance things really were and began to understand why she always felt so drained. She then decided to ask Mark to fix the cereal three times a week.

It's impossible to overestimate how important it was to this couple that Alison asked Mark to share the morning honors. As Alison said a month later, "I can't believe I never even *thought* to send Eric to Mark's side of the bed. I guess I figured he needed his mommy first thing in the morning or he'd feel abandoned in some way. As if I was totally indispensable or something."

Taking herself for granted, holding herself completely accountable for Eric's emotional welfare, never thinking to ask her partner for help: Alison's assumptions are shared by so many women.

4. Don't Criticize

Without a doubt, the single biggest complaint fathers have about mothers (I think I've heard this *thousands* of times by now) is that when he takes over an Endless List task, she'll find fault. I've tried many ways to help alter this familiar scenario, and have settled on the following four questions you should ask yourself when tempted to comment:

- "Is my child in actual physical or irrevocable psychological danger?"
- "Will this harm my child for life?"
- "Do I want to be in charge of everything forever?"

and especially

- "Is it genuinely important to get 'it' *exactly right,* or would it be better to give Dad a chance to establish a *stronger relationship* with the kids?"

If the answers are basically "No," then do whatever you have to do to keep quiet.

Remember, you're not trying to protect your man's "fragile" ego. Rather, you're trying to dismantle the "Mom's responsible" paradigm. If you supervise and comment on Dad's efforts, then he is still "pitching in" instead of becoming engaged for himself and for the kids. So try not to say a single word. Unless he asks for specific feedback, say nothing. If you can't help yourself, then leave the room.

For example, after being stunned by the results of the Endless List exercise, Angie (a teacher) asked her husband Dave (a journalist) to prepare Sunday morning breakfast for their two children—two-year-old

THE HAND THAT ROCKS THE CRADLE

Who routinely puts the children to bed in your house? This simple, daily ritual is more important than most of us realize. The parent who tucks a child in each night is the beneficiary of a tremendous gift of trust. There's something special, almost magical, about these moments of letting go, when a child drifts from wakefulness into sleep. And the trust that grows during these moments generalizes to other times. Predictably, a child will very likely turn to the parent who puts her to sleep for comfort when she's distressed, sick, or hurt.

Not surprisingly, in many families Mom is still the one who more often puts the kids to bed. She then becomes susceptible to feeling enslaved by the routine—not only because it can take so long, but also because it establishes a self-perpetuating cycle: Since kids turn to Mom for comfort in their most vulnerable moments, she's the one they scream out for in the middle of the night, or ask for during an illness, or look for to bandage everyday scrapes and bruises. With Dad out of the comforting loop, Mom alone has to take care of many situations that should be shared.

That's why one of the most crucial changes you can make in the participation equation is to trade off nights that you put the kids to bed. A child who sees Dad's face as much as Mom's before she falls asleep will more likely call for him when she feels vulnerable. This way neither parent will end up feeling overburdened, but rather each will feel special and trusted. And being trusted by their child to comfort her is one of the most precious gifts mothers and fathers can receive.

Max and four-year-old Marcy—so she could take some time for herself. At first, even though it was her request, Angie could hardly keep herself from rushing into the kitchen to make sure the kids were "eating right" and to prevent the inevitable mess. Every fiber in her wanted to yell: "How many frying pans are you going to use? What are you going to feed them? Do you know where the maple syrup is?"

Her fears weren't groundless. In the end the kitchen just barely survived. Pancake mix was splattered on the walls and the grease-caked pots were almost beyond repair. But Angie bit her lip and didn't say a word except to ask everyone to pitch in to clean the kitchen. The experience was very educational for the entire family. As Angie later reported: "Dave and the kids share something special between just them. But most important, I look forward to that one hour I actually get to spend alone every week. Sunday mornings are a minivacation for me." And the kitchen takes less of a beating each week.

5. Forget Your Manners

Ironically, one behavior that keeps the "Mom's responsible" paradigm intact is *thanking* your spouse for what he's done. This is an extremely hard habit to break—much harder than you would think. Women are socialized to be appreciative, especially of a man's consideration. Men, for their part, expect to be praised and often feel resentful if credit is not forthcoming.

But this behavior will only maintain the status quo, once you ask your husband to diaper the baby or clean up after dinner, don't thank him for it. If you do, you're paradoxically reinforcing the "Mom's responsible" paradigm.

Instead, *change* the paradigm. When your spouse takes on an Endless List chore, thank *yourself* for encouraging him to develop his own relationship with the children. If you're a terminally polite person who has to express appreciation, then tell him, "I know the kids appreciate what you're doing."

6. Hit the Road

The most powerful opportunity for breaking the "Mom's responsible" paradigm (as well as exposing the Endless List) arises when you're offered the opportunity to travel. Whether it's for business, for pleasure, or because of extended family responsibilities, this is something more mothers are and should be considering.

When? Many mothers make the mistake of waiting too long, thinking that the younger their child, the more damaging their absence will prove. In most cases, just the opposite is true. As soon as you're free from nursing, a short trip can be scheduled.

Of course, one of the reasons you might convince yourself not to go is all the extra work it takes just to prepare for leaving. You'll probably worry about the thousand and one things that might go wrong. You may want to set aside food (believe it or not, some mothers *still* prepackage and label meals), changes of clothes, instructions about who to call for help, lists of tasks that need to be done, *ad infinitum*. But this is the wrong way to leave. It underlines an almost mythically potent message: Mom's still responsible even when she's not around.

Instead, leave everything in your spouse's hands—as much as your anxiety (or your spouse's) will allow. Except in "special needs" cases—a sick child, for example—husband and kids should fend for themselves.

Talk about a bloodcurdling initiation rite. No high-impact workout or intense work deadline pressure could be more grueling than when you first go away for even a day or two. Despite—or because of—this trial by fire, your temporary absence affords your partner the opportunity both to empathize with the Endless List experience *and* to develop his own way of doing things.

For example, Nancy went on a "relaxation retreat"—only to come back to a house so chaotic that it looked as if a horde of college students on spring break had moved in for the weekend. Despite the chaos, Nancy swallowed her comments and tried not to feel too guilty about the girls' grousing. "Even though the trip was several years ago," Nancy reports, "my girls *still* remind me of the first time I 'abandoned' them. Arnie routinely leaves for business trips at least half a dozen times a year, but that first time I went away they were ready to call Child Welfare in on me."

Nancy now takes several short trips a year. During this time, I've watched Arnie's relationship with the girls grow as he develops his own ways of being with them. He's incorporated the rituals and confidence gained by his hands-on childrearing experience into daily living. At the same time, as Nancy gains confidence in Arnie's parenting, she's able to relinquish more and more items on the Endless List. Relieved of responsibilities she once didn't even realize she had, her chronic fatigue, resentment, and anger have also greatly diminished. Both Nancy and Arnie date the sea change in their approach to the Endless List from her first solo trip.

THE BOTTOM LINE

Suppose I follow these six steps, you may be thinking. What can I realistically hope for? Will all this make a real difference in my life? If so, how?

I'll let two women I've worked with answer these questions.

Christine's Story: Sex and the Endless List

Several years ago. I had a counseling session I've never forgotten. Christine, a very successful advertising agency executive, had been complaining in therapy about the lack of zest in her sex life since the birth, three years earlier, of her youngest daughter, Deirdre.

Suddenly she remembered something that made her sit up in her chair. "You know," she said, turning to Lance, her husband, "the last time we had good sex was during the summer, about a year ago."

To me, she explained that she'd been put in charge of a large account and had to have a complicated presentation ready in a month's time. Knowing she needed to devote herself to her work almost exclusively, she and Lance, a college professor who took summers off, made a plan for him to pick up the slack with kids and household. "All our preparations worked," she said. "Lance assumed practically every responsibility which usually fell to me. And, you know what? I didn't expect this, but I felt incredibly attracted to him. Remember?" she asked Lance.

He did, indeed. "It was the hottest sex we've had in years," Lance agreed.

"In fact," she continued dreamily. "I felt more of a spark between us than I had since Deirdre was born."

As I listened and felt their warmer, more sexual side begin to emerge (I even considered leaving the room for a while just to let them enjoy the moment alone), I realized that I had heard the exact same story countless times before from women in many different kinds of relationships. The connection between sexual desire and the Endless List became clear to me: when fathers assume some of the taken-for-granted tasks that usually fall to mothers, many women feel more sexual.

It's not hard to understand why. On one level, women don't feel as physically overburdened or exhausted. They have to expend less mental energy worrying. And freed from alienating resentment, they begin to experience their husbands differently.

"I saw you in a whole new light," Christine explained. "You took care of things. You were tender toward the girls, and I felt taken care of, too. That made me feel incredible desire toward you."

In other words, change the "Mom's in charge" paradigm and suddenly your headache may disappear and your exhaustion may not feel so overwhelming. Balancing the Endless List doesn't sound like an aphrodisiac, but many times that's exactly what it is.

Kathy's Story: "I Didn't Believe It Until I Saw It in Black and White"

A few weeks after Kathy and Evan drew up their Endless Lists, Kathy came to see me looking and sounding like a woman in the midst of a revelation. "I never realized how much I was 'command central' for my family. Even when things happened that had nothing to do with me, I was dragged into the middle. If I was sick in bed, I was still barraged with questions. That's not how I wanted it to be. Why did everything in the house have to involve me? Doing the Endless List exercise forced me to pay attention to what I do, and to value what I do. It helped me realize that I needed to make real changes in what I expected of myself to understand I wasn't indispensable.

"For example, I no longer schedule my clients around my kids' daily schedule, and I don't pick them up from school every day. If I have a late meeting, I stay at my studio and do some work instead of going right home in between. And you know what happened? With this extra time, I actually wrote the children's book that was kicking around in my head for two years.

"I also do a lot less cooking since I realized how much time I spent in the kitchen. I used to spend an awful lot of time planning and then cooking a well-balanced meal each night, only to see that the kids didn't eat what I served anyway. And they certainly don't seem to be suffering with this new arrangement.

"Most amazing to me is Evan's greater willingness to do things. Last night I went to the theater; without a word of objection he fixed dinner himself. Also, I had a meeting after church last Sunday, and he said, 'Fine, go ahead. I'll take care of everything.' He used to say, 'What should I do when you're gone? What should I make for lunch? Do we have enough bread?' And I'd have to run him through the plans. Now he doesn't need me to talk him through it anymore. Now he and the kids do it on their own. When he says, 'What's for lunch?' he's not saying, 'What are *you* making?' He's saying, 'Let's talk about it together.'

"In the old days, he would get mad about having to spend extra money if I didn't get items on sale. Now he takes care of it himself.

"Just last night, Chloe called from church. She was at a meeting and it was raining hard and she needed a ride home. For a second everyone looked to me as if to say, 'How come *you* didn't take care of this beforehand?' But then Evan just went out himself and picked her up.

"Here's the bottom line," continued Kathy. "There's less of a sense of what's my job and what's his job. We both feel as if we're doing this together—that's all I really wanted in the first place."

And Evan? "I guess we were on automatic pilot. All these things were not such a big deal to change, anyway. Kathy and I are fighting a lot less, so I guess it's working."

As I said earlier, don't expect miracles, but small changes *can* have a powerful impact on a family's daily life. Start reducing your Endless List and changing the "Mom's responsible" paradigm today.

But then it's Dad's turn. After all, increasing men's participation on the parenting team shouldn't just be a woman's responsibility.

CHAPTER 3

INCREASING DAD'S PARTICIPATION ON THE PARENTING TEAM

"If you had told me five years ago that Jeff would turn out to be *this* kind of father," complained Louise at a recent counseling session, "I wouldn't have believed you. I was so sure he'd be a model dad. But here I am, exactly where I swore I'd never be. Though we both work full-time, most of the childcare responsibilities are left to me. He rarely changes Jenny's diaper or bathes her. He *never* keeps track of when we're low on baby shampoo, Wipe-ees, or formula.

"This is the twenty-first century. I thought things were supposed to be different. And what's worse, I'm sounding like my mother—I never stop complaining. But let's face it," she continued, swiveling to face her husband. "You're a baby, Jeff. *You men are all babies!*"

I winced a little, for her indirect accusation seemed hurled in my direction as well. But even though I have a better track record than Jeff, I couldn't remember the last time I checked the Wipe-ees level in our house, either.

"What can I say?" he replied, with a half-irritated, half-amused smile. "There she goes again. *IT'S TOO MUCH TROUBLE . . . THAT'S WHY!*"

Whenever I think of men's involvement in family life, I'm reminded of the *Honeymooners* episode in which a suave new dance teacher moves into the Kramdens' building and asks Ralph why he doesn't help Alice out more often.

"You want to know why?" Ralph bellows. "You *really* want *to* know why? Well, I'll tell you why . . . because it's *TOO MUCH TROUBLE*, that's why!"

Although the world has changed greatly since 1955, when the Kramdens resided in "Brooklyn, USA," the participation issue still sits like an old wood stove in the middle of a modern microwave kitchen. Despite the fact that men do more at home these days, men and women continue to believe that childcare is primarily *women's* work— even if women put in a full week outside the home, as a majority now do. Although I spend time with thousands of families day after day, I find myself continually surprised and even startled by the sheer stubbornness of this reality.

Dennis and Stella, for example, came to see me about their four-year-old son Lee. They seemed a thoroughly modern family: Dennis is a college instructor; Stella works full-time as a mid-level corporate manager. When I asked what was troubling them, Dennis began the discussion. ("See," I thought to myself, "men *have* changed. This never would have happened twenty years ago.") He said that he and Stella were concerned because Lee was very babyish, and had been having many tantrums. He wasn't making too many friends in school, and had trouble sharing.

I inquired, as I always do, who did what around the house. Dennis was quick to volunteer that he played with Lee often: he took him to the park and playground, put him to bed, and prepared family dinners. ("What a modern, involved father," I thought to myself; in fact, his level of involvement even made me feel a little inadequate.)

Since Dennis had initiated the conversation, I turned to him when it was time to get more specific details: "Tell me what actually happens on play-dates—how does Lee react when he's asked to share one of his toys?"

"I'm not exactly sure," Dennis said.

"*I'd* have a better idea," Stella said, "since I take him to all of his play-dates." (I made a mental note of Stella's comment, but said nothing.) She went on to explain just how Lee had difficulty sharing.

"Tell me what happens during the 'witching' hour," I asked Dennis, "when you're trying to make dinner and Lee throws a tantrum. Would a snack help ?"

"Maybe." Then, looking to Stella, he asked, "Do you give him a snack?"

"Well, on most days I'm home with him alone in the early evening," Stella said, with just the slightest hint of annoyance in her voice. "You know, Dr. Taffel, Dennis has to teach three nights a week."

As the true picture of their day-to-day lives emerged, the imbalance of participation in their home became more evident.

"You *tell* me Lee has trouble with his classmates. What does his teacher say about his behavior?" I asked.

"Well, Stella thinks that his teacher is too strict." "Do *you* think she's strict?" I asked.

"I'm not sure. I was only able to get to one of the parent meetings this year, so I can't really say. What do *you* think?" he asked Stella.

"The teacher believes that Lee has a hard time with those rough boys, Tim and Justin."

"Are those the ones who . . . ?"

"You know, Dennis," said Stella, her irritation now out in the open, "those boys who are always giving Lee a hard time. . . . "

By the end of the session, I was right back at the same place I'd gotten to with a thousand other families. Yes, Dennis was an involved father; yes, he was much more a part of his son's life than his own father had ever been; and yes, this was a twenty-first century family, totally different from generations before. But if I wanted to know the specific ins and outs of Lee's daily life—or the nitty-gritty details about when Lee first walked and talked and how his potty training progressed—I'd *still* have to ask Stella, just as someone would have had to ask *my mother* fifty years ago!

Breaking the "Mom's responsible, Dad helps out" paradigm so that men participate *for themselves and for their children* is the single change essential to creating a more effective and loving parenting team. And rather than waiting for women to change us, we men must assume responsibility for ourselves—the way we think and the things we do. Where do we begin?

STEP ONE: ACKNOWLEDGING THE IMBALANCE

There are five steps men need to take to challenge this paradigm. The first is to acknowledge just how unbalanced your modern household may be—how many of the everyday, moment-to-moment details are *still* left to Mom, even though she probably holds down a job outside the home, just as you do. If you have any doubts about who continues to feel ultimately responsible for the details of everyday life with the kids, just try Step 1, "The Endless List Exercise," which I described in Chapter 2. That's what I asked Stella and Dennis to do.

Stella's and Dennis's lists turned out to be not much different from Kathy's and Evan's. And just like Kathy and Evan, Stella and Dennis were stunned when they saw in black and white just how unbalanced things really were.

STEP TWO: FEARS, BELIEFS . . . OR BOTH?

Becoming more aware is crucial, but it's almost never sufficient for change. The next step is for men to identify the *fears* and *beliefs* that get in the way of changing the old paradigm. Fears and beliefs have to be addressed together, for both prevent men from taking more responsibility in family life.

Most researchers believe that belief systems keep men's and women's participation in childrearing so unbalanced. While this is clearly true, I've also learned, after thirty years of being steeped in family life—my own and thousands of others—that men's reluctance to share childrearing responsibility is far more complex than I first understood. Many men are held hostage by a host of emotional factors that are difficult to articulate. It is not only that men are making excuses—though sometimes they are—but also that men aren't accustomed to voicing certain feelings and fears they harbor—unless they're pressed to.

In fact, from watching mothers' reactions over two decades, I expect that many women reading this chapter will hear men's "reasons" for not participating as *merely* excuses and rationalizations. That's how I used to react, too. But over the years I've found that unless these fears are taken seriously, the status quo never changes. So bear with me.

"Don't Fence Me In"

The most pervasive fear men have about childrearing is blatantly obvious—fear of boredom. This became crystal clear to me one summer day as I was babysitting (now, would a mother ever use the word "babysitting"?) my then three-month-old son, Sammy. As I watched the seconds and minutes tick slowly by, I had to fight every instinct to pull myself away and do something else—write, watch TV, go get the car lubed—*anything.*

Just before my shift with Sammy had begun, I'd been reading Robert Bly's *Iron John* and Sam Keen's *Fire in the Belly.* I felt that despite all their insights, something was missing from both books. That endless summer afternoon, waiting for Stacey to come home and relieve me of the need to entertain our infant son, I "got it"—I suddenly realized what Bly and Keen had left out. Amidst all the mythical images of the men's movement—the initiation rites, the wildman tribal weekends, the corporate samurai warriors—Bly and Keen devoted virtually no attention to the issue of *early childcare!* Perhaps both authors recognized that capturing men's imagination would require grand imagery, not domestic details.

After all, we men seem to need outside stimulation in a big way. If we get unhooked for too long from work, sex, hobbies, sports events, TV, or rewiring the "framersham," we're in danger of feeling bored and trapped. We don't like to think about ourselves. We're not used to exploring our feelings. We don't have "rich internal worlds."

From this perspective, the timelessness of the nursery is not just a bother, but a somewhat fearsome place. Here no job is ever entirely over. Activities are repetitive and yet demand exquisite attention. There's no immediate reward; children just move on to their next demand.

"I don't care how modern I'm supposed to be," confides Dennis in an open moment. "I don't want to have to think too deeply, about myself or anybody else's every need. Give me a job deadline anytime. Keep those 'crucial' sports events coming. Plug me into the Super Bowl. Pencil me in for trips to the amusement park. Or maybe I'll start building a split-level treehouse for the kids in the backyard. But for God's sake, don't leave me *alone* for too long with my demanding kids!"

The details of childrearing, of course, are just as boring for many mothers. But women have fewer options—for one thing, they're *expected* to become childrearing pros; for another, they often feel conscripted into service, in light of their husbands' absence.

So when it comes to breaking the "I'm helping her out" paradigm, I never underestimate the one factor that rarely gets mentioned—boredom, especially during those first few years of childrearing. To feel trapped *and* to have to "put out" without getting paid or seeing a final product is just too much to ask.

Yes, Ralph Kramden was a boor. And yes, he was certainly as unliberated as they come. But what he said almost fifty years ago is still regrettably true: for many men, participating in the nitty-gritty details of family life is simply too boring—and when compared to career demands, "too much trouble."

The Exotic Fears of Ordinary Dads

Trapped-in-the-moment boredom is a pervasive concern, but it's just the tip of the iceberg. Many more dramatic fears lie just below the surface. For example, Gene, a father I know, told me that he'd never given his daughter a bath alone. He was convinced that she'd slip out of his hands and smash her head on the tile.

"Have you been honest with your wife about this worry?" I asked.

"No, of course not. I just avoid it by saying I need some time to relax when I get home." I was ready to dismiss Gene as an incorrigible malingerer—until I remembered my own nervousness (actually, terror) when faced with bathing both Sammy and Leah at the same time. I couldn't imagine getting through this event without calling 911.

Now, most new mothers also harbor these fears. After all, there's no reason anyone should instinctually know how to bathe, hold, or change a baby. But women feel forced to work through their fears. Self-definition requires it, and so does the reality that *someone* has to master the childcare curriculum.

Hal, a thirty-year-old banker with a six-month-old son, had never changed a single diaper. His overworked wife Emily was near the end of her rope, convinced that fatherhood had turned the man she married into just another child. "Why don't you lift a finger and help me out?" she demanded. When I posed the same question, Hal stalled for a long time before giving the usual answers: "I'm too tired after work. She beats me to it. I never do it exactly right by her standards. I didn't have a role model.

You know when Hal began to "lift a finger" on the diaper front? After he finally announced during one session that he was *terrified:* "What if Andy rolls off the changing table and really hurts himself?"

Now, I must admit, I'd heard a lot of excuses from men (and from myself) over the years, and my first reaction was total skepticism ("C'mon, buddy, you can't be serious," I said to myself). But, surprisingly enough, after this admission, Hal's diapering percentage *immediately* rose from once a month to once each weekend day—still nothing to write home about, but a beginning.

Bill, a father I met in a parenting workshop, was also slow on the draw when it came to changing diapers. He confessed to me that he was afraid that his son's dirty diapers would repulse him. Could this be possible, from today's "liberated" man? You bet. Men are often let off the hook when it comes to cleaning up after themselves, and many are particularly queasy about tidying up bodily messes.

I'll never forget overhearing a conversation between a dad and his three-year-old daughter, Liza. "Daddy, come up to wipe me," she yelled enthusiastically from the bathroom. Even I understood what an honor she was bestowing on her father. *This* was a job usually reserved for her mom. But Dad, in his most dismissive and bothered voice, responded, "Nah, I'm reading the newspaper."

"Why didn't you help her?" I asked him later during a private moment.

"I don't know. It just makes me uncomfortable," he said quietly. "Let my wife do it. She's used to these things anyway."

Unless pressed—and a major part of my job for two decades has been to press—men don't openly talk about such squeamishness. Instead, they express disdain or annoyance, or perfect their well-timed disappearing act.

When Shame Gets in the Way

Other fears that prevent men from physically caring for their children are often almost impossible to express. Martin, the twenty-one-year-old father of one-year-old Nicole, so rarely hugged his daughter that his wife Barbara became worried. Here's Martin's explanation: "When Nicole climbs on me," he said softly, as if in a confessional, "I sometimes get a slight erection from the pressure and friction of it all. Is something wrong with me that this happens? Am I one of those fathers you read about in the papers?"

For a year Martin had never mentioned this. Instead, he maintained a not-so-subtle physical distance from his daughter. Barbara, sensing his discomfort, tried unsuccessfully to cajole or demand that he "talk about it," but ended up "covering" for him instead by spending extra time with Nicole.

Some men also have sexual worries about their sons. As a guest on a radio show a few years ago, I received a call from a man who asked, "Is it all right if I hug and kiss my two-and-a-half-year-old son goodnight? I'm afraid it will turn him into a homosexual." I was absolutely stunned at that question, and fumbled my way through a very fragmented answer. But I was naive. Since then I've heard this fear echoed from many fathers throughout the country—especially younger ones who'd like to be different fathers from the ones they had.

Even more prevalent than shame about sexuality are concerns over aggression. Tony, the father of four-month-old twins, began a parents' meeting by announcing that he was scared about his "aggressive impulses." What had happened, he explained, was that after being awakened by the kids one night, he put his daughter back into the crib in a somewhat "rough" manner. "She didn't cry or anything, but I felt as if I was out of control. Am I an abusive father?"

What happened next is crucial. After that incident, Tony withdrew from many childcare responsibilities, quietly nursing his shame. Did he explain to his wife why he was staying away from the kids? Absolutely not. She simply assumed that Tony was "in one of his moods"—a luxury we men are still often accorded.

Tony's reaction is not unusual. I've seen one man after another frightened by the prospect of perpetuating the cycle of physical abuse from which so many have suffered. This is one of the main reasons many men leave discipline to women—they're afraid of their own harshness or potential for violence.

Are these simply excuses to get out of doing childcare? Are they used to prop up old gender roles in a world that is changing faster than many of us can handle? Sometimes. But more often than anyone realizes, men are compelled by unvoiced fears to keep a subtle distance between themselves and the kids. Not only does this have a lifelong impact on the nature of the father–child bond, but it also keeps the paradigm intact: "Mom is the primary parent and Dad helps her out."

As a man, do you harbor fears or concerns that keep you from fully participating in family life?

THE DAD'S PARTICIPATION "FEAR" QUIZ

1. I have worries that something terrible will happen when I'm in charge of the kids.
2. I can't deal with all the different demands they make. I'm afraid I'll explode.
3. They're so noisy, poorly behaved, and wild that I get nervous being with them.
4. The thought of my wife going on a business trip strikes fear in my heart.
5. My wife is just "better" at caretaking than I could ever be. I'm afraid I'll never really master it.
6. I worry about losing control of my anger with the kids; I could hurt them.
7. It makes me uncomfortable to be physically affectionate with the kids.
8. I often feel like a stranger in my own home. I don't know how to bridge the gap.
9. No matter how involved I am, the kids are still more attached to my wife than to me. I don't know how to connect.
10. If I do too many things with the kids, I'm afraid I'll lose my career.

Once men are able to talk directly with their partners about such concerns, behavior *sometimes* changes. Martin, who had been afraid of hugging his daughter lest she arouse him, begin enjoying physical closeness with her after he admitted his fear. Tony, the father of infant twins, stopped feeling like a potential child abuser for his one-time three A.M. "roughness." He even learned to trust his ability to control aggressive feelings enough to participate more decisively in discipline. Bill began to (occasionally) change diapers once he admitted to his fear of being disgusted.

Now, sharing feelings of inadequacy, discouragement, and hurt don't always change the way men act. But sometimes it is a first step toward addressing the "Mom's responsible" paradigm, enabling men to engage more directly with the kids—*for themselves*, not just as Mom's assistant.

"I Want Mommy!"

Boredom and fearfulness are not the only reasons that some men are reluctant to share childcare responsibilities. Men also get *discouraged*. They feel as if they have tried to involve themselves in family life, but their best efforts and intentions go unappreciated. And even though they may rail against their wives for not showing enough gratitude, the main hurt men experience is *feeling rejected by the kids*.

Take my own "chicken soup" experience. One rainy afternoon on a summer vacation when Leah was two and a half, I decided to make soup for dinner. Leah wanted to "help Daddy," so she handed me the spices one by one. She supervised as I sliced, chopped, and poured. She was an eager taster. "What father–daughter bonding," I thought. "This is real quality time."

But I was in for a letdown. When we were all seated around the table, Leah suddenly exclaimed, "Mmmm, this soup is yummy. Thank you for making it, *Mommy!*"

Both Stacey and I were stunned. I felt like throwing in the towel. My years of experience working with families and kids, my familiarity with child development, and my firsthand knowledge of how intense a child's attachment is to her mother didn't make me feel any better. I *still* felt unappreciated and couldn't stop myself from wondering "Why should I even *bother?*"

Worse, I secretly worried that something was the matter with me. Regardless of how much I participated, I sensed Leah's greater closeness to my wife. In my head I knew this was normal. In my heart, though, I felt hurt and wondered what I was doing wrong.

Only after I started asking other men about this hurt—my friends and those I met professionally—did I begin to feel better. And, I have to admit, it wasn't easy to ask. I was ashamed. I felt as if I had failed. But I soon discovered that I was not alone.

In Charlie's house, for instance, childcare was divided in thirds among himself, his wife, and a babysitter. "Do you know what my son's first words were?" Charlie asked, with unmistakable resignation. " 'Bye-

bye, Daddy.' He's one and a half years old. He spends as much time with me as he does with my wife. But he already thinks of me as on my way out the door."

Another man I work with, Jim, spends every evening and weekend at home with his family. He takes a full two-week summer vacation with them. "I'm with my kids almost as much as my wife is, and I consider myself a very involved parent. But if the girls fall off a bike or have a fight on a play-date, they run right past me and make a beeline for their mother. I don't get it. Given all I do, I'd like to see them trust me the way they do her."

Another man, Ed, told me poignantly that his kids' deeper connection to his wife was one of the biggest hurts he'd experienced in his life—no less painful than the end of a relationship or a death. "Don't get me wrong," he continued. "I'm happy they're so attached to their mother. I just wish that things could be more solid between us."

Frank, the father of six-year-old Scott, can't understand why he feels so peripheral in his family. Though his wife does more with Scott than he does, he's still a very active father. Yet recently he mused to me, "For the past three years I keep having the fantasy that Scott would someday whisper to my wife, 'Who is that guy? What is he *doing* here? And do we really *need* him?' "

These men are not so unusual—they're not just "sensitive" souls. Time after time the most hard-bitten man registers, even if for a brief moment, that certain hurt look when his toddler stubs a toe and immediately runs to Mom; the on-the-sidelines "denseness" when he finds out three days later that something happened to his daughter in school; the just plain irrelevance he experiences overhearing the everyday back-and-forth between mother and child:

"Did you call Chuckles the Clown for my birthday? Tommy had him and he was great."

"Yes, dear, but I don't know if the party favors were so good with Chuckles, remember?"

"Oh, yeah, but the cake was chocolate layer, right? I definitely want that cake. . . . "

It's not simply that men are whiny bellyachers. Men's remoteness is almost always accompanied by a deep sense of inadequacy. One man after another—teachers, high-powered lawyers, machinists, corporate executives, salesmen, deal-makers, brain surgeons—all have told me that as the initial glow of fatherhood fades they often experience an overwhelming sense of *incompetence* unlike any they'd experienced in their entire adult lives.

With my prodding, men admit that fueling their insecurity is the attitude: "She's just *better* at this than I am." Actually, there's more than a kernel of truth to this belief. Penelope Leach, the noted early childhood expert, observes that if fathers are just slightly less involved, within two weeks they are already "less good" with babies than mothers are. This may be the beginning of a childhood-long vicious circle. The *better* she gets at it, the more incompetent he *feels;* the less *involved* he is, the more incompetent he actually *becomes;* the more he relates to his partner as if *she's the one in charge,* the more he engages only to *help her out.*

This familiar cycle feeds on and then helps reaffirm beliefs that are generations old, discouraging men from redefining their roles and participating more fully in family life. See if any of these apply to you.

THE FATHER'S PARTICIPATION BELIEF QUIZ

1. No matter how hard I try, she still seems better at childcare than I am.
2. During the first few years of a child's life, a father's role isn't that important. Only when kids get older do fathers need to be more involved.
3. Children mostly need fathers to be disciplinarians—to prepare them for the world.
4. Work is more important to me—even if women work, their lives still revolve around home and family.
5. Women are "naturally" better at basic nurturing than men are.
6. I earn more of the money, so I expect her to do more with the kids.
7. Kids need to be more attached to mothers to grow up healthy.
8. I didn't have a close relationship with my father, and though I'm not happy about it, I turned out okay.
9. My career is the main thing that's important to me and my family. Without it, not only am I unhappy, but we don't eat.
10. My father participated so little in family life that I have no way of knowing how to be an involved father.

A preponderance of "yes" answers is not terribly encouraging. In my experience, beliefs are even harder to change than fears. But even the merest sprinkling of "no" answers leaves the door open to change.

STEP THREE: START DOING IT FOR YOURSELF

Next, answer the following question: "For whose benefit am I participating in the family?"

If you're honest, more times than not you will say, "For my spouse, girlfriend, my child's mother." Men just don't "get" that the reason to become involved is for *ourselves*. Doing more with our children won't simply make women happier or keep them "off our backs," but will create a deeper, more positive connection with the kids.

At first, many men look at me with a vacant stare, as if I'm speaking a foreign language. It simply doesn't compute because their true involvement is in other areas—primarily ambition and career. Unfortunately, these men don't "get" that a positive connection with children might actually make them feel *happier* in their everyday lives. But when men cross this barrier by making a small change in their routine, I'm amazed at how quickly they can discover the purely personal pleasures of greater involvement.

For example, Jules, an insurance salesman, and Rose, a librarian, the parents of two-year-old Max and four-year-old Laurie, came to see me because they were fighting a great deal about typical childcare issues—discipline, sibling rivalry, spoiling. One representative squabble concerned Laurie's upcoming birthday. "When does Rose think I have time to go shopping for party favors?" Jules asked rhetorically. "I work late almost every night."

"Getting the party favors isn't to help Rose," I said to him. "It's for *you* and *Laurie*. Laurie will feel good toward you. She'll remember you during the party. And I guarantee you'll feel closer."

Elementary as this sounds, I could tell that Jules had never thought about it this way before. Most men haven't. They've been through so many fights over dividing childcare responsibilities that it's almost impossible not to confuse what men do for the kids with what men do for their wives. And that's a trap—because most men don't want a second boss, and the last thing most women want or need is another child.

Whenever I begin pressing that point—"Do it for you and your child, not for your partner"—I am taken aback by how much sadness pours out of men. And it's almost always about their own fathers. For example, the third time I said to Jules, "Buy the party favors not to help Rose, but for your daughter," he began to cry. "Sometimes there's a wall around her and the kids," he said. "I feel like I could disappear and no one would notice. So I start criticizing or yelling, but inside I'm worrying that I'm turning into my father—alone and isolated."

Chip, whose thirteen-year-old son Terrence treated him disrespectfully, and whose wife LeAnn criticized him for not backing her up in discipline matters, came to me for counseling. "Spend fifteen minutes hanging out with Terrence," I told him, "not to give LeAnn a break, but to *strengthen the connection with your son.*"

Suddenly Chip's eyes filled with tears. He said he'd *never* done anything "fun" with his dad. "It was like living in a world of robots. All we did was work. I never knew him in any other way because the only time we talked, it was about his business or my homework. I've never learned to do anything with my own son just for the fun of it."

STEP FOUR: TRY TO REMEMBER

Jules and Chip voice a familiar plea: "Since my own father never paid attention, I have no role model to teach me how to be a different kind of father to my son." Men who say this are sincere, and I used to feel absolutely stuck—what can you say in the face of such barren histories? After all, with no authentic experiences of father–son bonding from their own childhoods to draw on, how could they learn to change?

The men's liberation movement has also emphasized the total absence of many fathers. But when I ask men in the presence of their wives or partners (whose memory of interpersonal events is often more reliable than men's) to relate personal histories, a very different picture emerges. The word "never," as in "My father was never there," doesn't quite capture the more complicated reality. Men's relationships with their fathers are neither as black-and-white nor as totally nonexistent as they first seem.

This is an important point to understand, especially in our parent-blaming culture. It has become very chic to remember what we *didn't* get as children. The few moments of connection that *did* exist—and the potential foundation for change they represent—are then lost.

So I now always follow with a second question: "I understand that your father wasn't there most of the time, but I'd like you to remember even one time when you and your father did something together that you liked. Try to remember how you felt toward him *at that moment* because that's how your child will feel toward you.

Sure enough, Jules remembered a weekend when his mother was out of town and his father nursed him through a sudden bout of the flu. "I never realized he could be that gentle," he sighed. And Chip recalled one Saturday when his father didn't go to work and instead treated him to breakfast at the local diner. Thirty years later, he could still describe exactly what they ate.

I have memories, too. After my father and I spent the day working together in the family shoe store, he would sometimes take me deep into the woods of New Jersey, to a "mysterious" clam shack. He'd buy twelve cherrystone clams for him and six for me. I would down those slimy little creatures as if they were the greatest delicacy on earth.

Just about every man has at least some special memory of his father, no matter how brief or insignificant. One man closed his eyes for a moment and said, "Yes, I remember something. Every year we went to church on Christmas Eve, and my father would hold my hand as we walked home from the service. I can still feel how warm and comforting this was." When he opened his eyes, they were filled with tears.

STEP FIVE: CREATE A NEW HISTORY

Each of these memories is meaningful because of the following characteristics:

1. They took place between father and child without mother as initiator or intermediary.
2. They were ordinary, not special, high-excitement times.
3. Father acted on his own terms without later reporting to mother.

4. The child could feel father's enjoyment of the activity.
5. Father and child were alone, usually without siblings present.

Even if such a moment occurred just once, you can draw on it to break the stalemate—to *create a new history with your child*. For example, two weeks after Chip recalled the diner breakfast with his father, he "coincidentally" took his son Terrence to a baseball game—the first leisure activity they'd shared in years. A week or so later, obviously feeling more secure, he managed to involve himself during a disciplinary struggle, fully backing up his wife. And after I asked Jules, "Can you think of any way to caretake your kids the way your father took care of *you* that weekend?" he decided, on his own, to initiate special Saturday lunches with the kids. During this time, Mom was "banished" from the kitchen.

Why Small Changes Can Create Meaningful Differences

In each case, new rituals developed that had seemed unthinkable just weeks before. Why? Because both Chip and Jules began to get positive feedback from their kids. They could feel a different sort of reaction from them—not the "I'm crazy about Daddy" kind of excitement, but the more enduring signs of bonding that we usually associate with mothers.

And *that* is what motivates men to stick with activities that at first seem artificial. Men begin to understand that doing ordinary things with kids may feel forced, but will evolve into something worth doing again—not to help Mom, but for themselves. Chip's son Terrence, who had always been very close-mouthed about his school life, approached his dad two weeks after the ballgame and "out of nowhere" said, "Dad, something bad happened in school today." Laurie broke her usual pattern of relying only on Mom when she was sick and said to Jules, "Daddy, I don't feel well. My tummy hurts."

I used to be stunned (I still am a little surprised) at how quickly kids respond when they sense that their fathers are joining in as *separate people*—not as *mother's helper*. Now, hundreds of experiences later, I can practically guarantee that a couple of weeks after the old "Mom's responsible" paradigm is challenged your son or daughter will do something new with you—confide, share, or approach you in an unexpected way.

After Jules instituted Saturday lunches, for example, his daughter, Laurie, no longer waited for him to complain about her commotion; instead, she actually asked *him* if she was making too much noise on weekend mornings. And after Chip disciplined Terrence for breaking curfew, Terrence spent the rest of the day shadowing his father, asking if he could help with chores around the house.

Chip—this hard, uncaring, peripheral father, a man "married to his work"—came in for our next meeting absolutely rejuvenated.. "I love it!" he said. "Terrence is finally beginning to know I'm here and to accept me as a kind of guardian angel." He then repeated what I've heard from so many different men on so many different occasions:

> "I never knew getting more involved was for my own sake, too. I always though I was doing it to help *her* out, to lighten *her* load."

This technique doesn't *always* work. Some men have such bitter memories of their own fathers, or such a lack of confidence in their capacity to connect, that they can't create something new. But for most men, these steps are a beginning. Not only will there be less friction on the parenting team, but you'll more easily remember that having kids is not just about being a provider, but about giving and receiving love. Ultimately, this is how the next generation of fathers—your children—will learn to be more involved than ever before.

Creating "Quality Time" That Has Clout

Many fathers need help connecting with their kids in ways that have enduring impact. Joining in the following daily rituals—that are tender in nature—creates a more trusting connection with your child than any high-excitement, special activity ever could:

1. Become regularly involved in the bedtime ritual.
2. Bathe children (until the age when *either* child or parent feels uncomfortable).

3. Prepare meals for kids that they will eat when they're away from you, such as school lunches.
4. Go with your child to the doctor, especially when he's sick or due for shots.
5. Instruct your child to come to you in the middle of the night for comfort after a bad dream.
6. Read to children—of all ages.
7. Sing to children.
8. Do school projects and homework together; keep abreast of all school events.
9. Cook together for other family members.
10. Shop for presents for friends and relatives, wrap them, and make cards together.
11. Attend school plays, talent shows, and science fairs.
12. Purchase small "thinking of you" presents for your child.
13. Go clothes shopping together—even with your balky early adolescent.
14. Do good deeds together.

IT'S NEVER TOO EARLY TO BEGIN

When men's liberation writers discuss male initiation rites, they focus on the traditional time for such rituals—adolescence. In my view, adolescence is much too late. By this time, the Endless List and the "Mom's responsible" paradigm are hopelessly ingrained. And whether we want to or not, we've handed down this legacy of imbalance to yet another generation. Mothers and fathers need to start changing these roles *during infancy*. If not, the seeds of an imbalanced connection with the kids and tension on the parenting team are already sown. And we can't even begin to discuss male–female differences in childrearing approaches unless we face this imbalance first.

Nothing is more central to the strength of the family or to raising healthy kids. Dorothy Dinnerstein, in an astonishingly powerful and prescient book, *The Mermaid and the Minotaur* (1976), described the fundamental imbalance between men and women in terms of childcare. According to her a man's hand should rock the cradle, too. So that his children can absorb his presence while they sleep—his spirit, his body, his smells, his touch. So he can feel himself to be an equal with his partner. So that Mom doesn't have to feel entirely responsible—and isn't held entirely responsible by the world.

But change doesn't begin with grand gestures. To challenge the "Mom's responsible" paradigm, we need to start small—to involve the 75 percent of fathers who *still* do not *regularly* participate in daily, hands-on childcare. These five steps will help you do your part, to get things moving, so there's at least a chance that conflict on the parenting team can lessen.

PART II

HOT SPOTS FOR WOMEN AND MEN

CHAPTER 4

DISCIPLINE

The Pragmatist Versus the Idealist

Scratch the surface of just about every disagreement between parents and you'll discover a dispute over discipline. Countless books have been written about how to stay in charge of kids, each with its own unique approach and yet running through all this divergent advice is a single common thread: *You've got to be a consistent parenting team.*

It sounds so simple, doesn't it? Yet most of the parents I meet can't seem to locate this elusive consistency. In fact, by the time they come to see me they're pretty much tied up in knots. They've reversed themselves and contradicted each other so many times that nobody even remembers where the argument began.

Why in the world is it so hard to be consistent when we become parents? The most overlooked reason is also one of the most obvious. Men and women approach the whole subject of discipline from dramatically different perspectives—although not different in the way you might first believe.

THE STEREOTYPES

Let's start with one of the most commonly held stereotypes: Men are strict, hard-nosed realists; women are more empathetic, flexible, and softhearted.

Like many stereotypes, it contains a kernel of truth. As I wrote in Chapter 2, the research on gender and morality shows that women and men look at the world through very different moral frameworks. Men tend to think in terms of "justice" or absolute "right and wrong," while women define morality through the filter of how relationships will be affected. Given these basic differences, why would men and women suddenly agree about disciplining children?

It is astonishing how early childrearing arguments over discipline emerge. In one case, a mother complained to me that her husband was accusing her of "babying" their son—who was a full two months old at the time. Or take Matt and Judy, a couple I saw recently in counseling. They were fighting about the eating habits of their six-month-old son Brian. Matt believed that Brian needed more discipline when it came to food: "He has to learn to eat what's put in front of him; he has to learn who's the boss."

But Judy saw it another way: "Brian's only a baby. How can you turn what a six-month-old eats into a discipline problem?"

When it comes to issues of "who's in charge," couples will heatedly disagree even in front of a group of strangers. For example, Michelle and Howard, a couple I recently met at a workshop, had recently taken their four-year-old daughter Lydia to a Raffi concert. Howard was so aggravated over Lydia's behavior that he actually yelled at Michelle in front of over a hundred people at the workshop, "She couldn't sit still the whole time. She wouldn't keep her voice down. And what about the way she walked up and down the aisles? If we don't start to teach her now, how will she ever learn? How will she behave in school if she runs around like this? You're just too softhearted!"

"What do you want from her?" Michelle yelled back just as unselfconsciously. "She didn't nap. She didn't eat much for lunch. She's only four. At least we managed to stay for the whole concert without her screaming the entire time." Then the audience began yelling at each other, and I almost had another men-versus-women parenting "riot" on my hands.

As kids become preteens and adolescents, every decision about setting limits can turn into a major hassle between parents. Ned and Irene, whose continuous bickering was eroding their feelings toward each other, came to me for help with their thirteen-year-old son Andrew. "We work out an agreement," Ned explained, "for example, over what time Andrew's curfew should be. But then I come home and find Irene has let him stay out later than we agreed. She'll say, 'He had a hard time today,' or 'He's tired because of baseball practice and needed to have some fun'—any excuse to break the rule. A rule is supposed to be a rule," Ned says, "but for 'The Prince' there's always an exception."

BENEATH THE STEREOTYPES: TOUGH DADS AND LENIENT MOMS

In each of these scenarios, the men run true to form, sounding stricter than their wives. They think of themselves as teachers on an important mission: kids have to learn about authority and about the "real world" out there.

These men also live in different time frames from their wives. On the one hand, they feel as if they must protect the *past*—regardless of how absent or harsh their own fathers had been. They are upholders of tradition, even if that tradition had been painful: "My father spanked me when I misbehaved, and I turned out just fine."

At the same time, however, they can't stop thinking about the future. While Mom focuses on the present, Dad often rockets years ahead of the situation at hand: "If he doesn't learn to eat what he's given, he'll never learn. The time to start is *now!* "

Of course, mothers also worry about such long-term character issues, but they seem to be bogged down in one tiny, insignificant detail—*the here and now*. Once again, arguments over parenting may have more to do with the combination of imbalanced participation than ingrained gender differences. Judy, for instance, who felt that food shouldn't be turned into a disciplinary issue, ended one meeting with me by screaming at her husband, "It's fine for you to have these ideas about setting limits on how Brian should eat, but who actually *feeds* him most of the time?!"

Michelle was also more present-oriented than her husband. Her point was that under the circumstances, Lydia had behaved like a normal four-year-old. No, she hadn't been perfect, but she had made it through the concert without one major tantrum and no embarrassing moments. Given what could have happened, she did pretty well.

Irene's complaint, similar to Judy's, was "Of course I worry about Andrew's 'character.' But to me that's something of a luxury. All I want to do is get through the evening. Listen, big-shot, I'm the one who negotiates with Andrew about his curfew—and most everything else. At the same time I'm trying to get dinner on the table, return phone messages, and go through the mail."

Basically, these mothers are saying: "Since I deal with the children more of the time, I'll do *whatever works*, even if it means bending the rules when I have to."

Now who's beginning to sound like the pragmatist?

REVERSING THE STEREOTYPES

After listening to thousands of couples disagree over every childrearing issue imaginable, I began to realize a stunning truth—a truth that flies in the face of the prevailing stereotypes:

> Because mothers generally participate more, they are usually the disciplinary *pragmatists*, while fathers are often the romantic *idealists*.

This fact hasn't changed all that much since Lucy and Ricky had their first battles over setting limits with Ricky Junior.

Just a few months ago, I had the chance to see this point driven home once again. Five families had gathered together for a Christmas Day celebration. There were about a dozen kids, ranging in age from eight months to thirteen years. They were playing and running through the house, creating a festive holiday spirit that bordered on the chaotic. Some of the fathers, including me, were sitting around a dining room table half monitoring the action while discussing the economy.

All of a sudden a fight broke out between two of the girls over who could play with the Slinky. The girls' dads quickly got involved—this is, after all, the new century, and the fight was happening in the public domain. What was interesting was *how* we tried to resolve the situation. The importance of "sharing," "taking turns," and "doing the right thing" were our main concerns.

Unfortunately, neither girl budged. In fact, these discussions about what each "should" do only intensified the fighting; meanwhile, the three-and-a-half-year-old was moving over the edge toward major tantrum territory.

Her screams brought Mom in from the living room. She entered quickly, surveyed the situation, and said to the host, "Is there a second Slinky around anywhere?"

Within moments both Slinkys were lying on the floor, forgotten along with the tantrums, and the girls had moved on to play with their *Beauty and the Beast* figures.

What simplicity. All of us high-minded dads looked taken aback. I know I felt just a little befuddled. "Is this right?" I thought. "Isn't learning to share the point?" But secretly I was relieved that everything had calmed down so quickly and we could resume our discussion about the economy and the upcoming college bowl games.

Once again, we fathers idealistically tried to "teach" while the mothers took a different route, pragmatically solving the problem ("Do we really need this headache now?") while dissolving hostilities along the way.

THE ROOTS OF PRAGMATISM

In part, we men were right—theoretically, kids *should* learn to share. And, of course, mothers want their children to learn to share just as strongly as fathers do. But since the person more involved on a nitty-gritty, daily basis has many opportunities to teach standards, not every difficult situation needs to be turned into a lesson; some, especially those in public, can be pragmatically "finessed" with as little aggravation as possible. In this light, many arguments over discipline arise from the same lopsided participation equation I discussed in Chapters 2 and 3.

Take, for example, Stan and Gale, who often fight over their five-year-old's eating habits. Stan claims that Gale lets Gretchen snack on a hefty sourdough pretzel in the late afternoon, which ruins her dinner *and* teaches bad eating habits. "We discuss this all the time. I think we've reached an agreement," Stan says, "but then I find out that she gave Gretchen another snack. First of all, I don't like the broken agreement. But more important, how will this kid ever eat the right things?"

"You can preach all you want to about your ideals," Gale replies, "but since I get home from work an hour before you do, I'm the one who has to survive the 'witching hour.' If she doesn't have something to eat she starts climbing the walls and driving me crazy."

Gale speaks for many women: "When it comes to staying in charge, *I'll do whatever works.*" This male–female difference about discipline—whatever works versus theoretical standards—is so pronounced that it's amazing how little it has been discussed in childrearing circles.

Actually, it's not so surprising. As long as we underestimate the importance of the participation equation—who assumes responsibility for the bulk of hands-on childcare—we miss its profound implications for every aspect of childrearing. And when discipline is concerned, the parent who has to make it to the end of an eighteen-hour day—who works at a job and *then* takes on a second shift with the kids every night—is much more likely to adopt the survivor's motto: "If it works, I'll use it." From this perspective, dads who are even slightly less involved and emphasize firm limits or character-building might as well be talking a foreign language. They just don't get it.

THE MARTYR SYNDROME

But this doesn't mean that men's concerns should be dismissed or discounted. What "tough-minded" fathers often react to is a common family phenomenon—whichever parent hangs around the kids for any length of time is very likely to assume the mantle of martyrdom. Mothers are particularly susceptible to this syndrome, not only because they usually spend more time with children but also because of their socialization to be caretakers.

Here's an example. Liz has been amusing her four-year-old daughter Amanda all afternoon. After a snack in the kitchen, Amanda decides to knock all the magnets off the refrigerator. Liz asks her to pick them up. "No," Amanda says. Liz suggests picking them up together; Amanda declines. Liz begins negotiating with her daughter: "If you don't pick them up, you won't be able to watch Hey Arnold tomorrow morning." Amanda is still defiant. Then she refuses to go to her room for a time-out. Finally, after fifteen minutes of infinite patience, Liz blows her stack and yells. Amanda runs out of the kitchen in tears. Not five minutes later, Liz, feeling guilty, is cradling Amanda, asking her if she wants another cookie.

Gerry, Liz's husband, can't believe his eyes. His wife's inconsistency dumbfounds him. He's also angry—both at Liz for allowing herself to be treated like a doormat, and at Amanda for being so difficult. He has a valid point. Liz's swings between "Earth Mother" and the "Wicked Witch of the West" don't make anybody feel good. Endlessly patient, she has reserves of flexibility that can make her seem hopelessly inconsistent.

Before you know it, one of two things happens. Either Liz and Gerry become embroiled in a furious argument over Liz's inconsistency, or Gerry throws up his hands in the face of it all and withdraws from his wife and child, causing Liz to feel overwhelmed and once again susceptible to the martyr syndrome.

Meanwhile, the real problem remains unaddressed. Neither Liz nor Gerry can discuss the participation imbalance in their family which caused their once workable differences to become toxic—so much so that by the time they came to see me, each felt that the marriage itself was in danger. And without addressing this imbalance, they'll never figure out a way to be more consistent either with Amanda or with each other, or to rebuild the core of lost trust between them.

LENIENT DADS AND TOUGH MOMS

The fallout from this basic imbalance of participation in family life also affects those couples in which Dad seems more lenient than Mom. Over the years I've worked with many families where Mom is the one who says, "I'm constantly screaming and have to be on top of everything. He never sets any limits." And then Dad complains, "She's much too strict. Why does she have to make a federal case out of everything with the kids?"

In these couples Dad is "Mr. Nice Guy" and Mom is the more rigid of the two. Does this contradict the idea of Mom as the pragmatist and Dad as the idealist? Absolutely not. In most situations Mr. Nice Guy is able to maintain his good nature precisely because he is slightly (or significantly) less involved with the Endless List of childrearing.

For example, an even-tempered father, Jim, complained about all the screaming around the house in the morning. "You should hear what happens between Sally and the kids [ages five and eight]. I can't believe this is the way the day has to start. Why can't she just lay off them?"

"He's right," Sally said. "I'm impossible. I can't stand myself either."

I then asked, "Well, tell me how it works. Who does what with the kids?"

Sally began to describe the morning chaos: brushing teeth, getting washed, finding the right clothes, fixing lunch, dealing with unexpected tantrums, and so on. Many of these tasks were pretty evenly divided between Jim and Sally—except for one small detail that both mentioned without even realizing its significance: somehow, Jim was allowed twenty extra minutes in bed and then had the bathroom *to himself* to prepare himself mentally for the workday. (By the way, Sally has a full-time job as well. She's the president of a large clothing business.) Yet during these precious morning moments, it was up to Sally to get the ball rolling, a fact *both* of them took entirely for granted.

This imbalance set the tone for the rest of the day. Behind her tension and nagging, Sally was a hard-boiled pragmatist (who every once in a while "lost it" anyway) trying to make a dent in the Endless List. "Things have to get done by a certain time; otherwise, the school bus will leave without Rebecca, or the lunches won't be packed, or . . . , or . . . "

ROLE REVERSAL: IN THE TRENCHES EVERYONE'S A PRAGMATIST

I encouraged Sally and Jim to change their roles for just one or two mornings, allowing Sally an extra twenty minutes alone while Jim launched the kids on the morning routine.

At first, Sally refused. "This is ridiculous. The kids will bother me anyway—what's the big deal? Let's leave things the way they are." But I reminded her of the "Mom's not always responsible" mantra. "Let Jim handle their 'Where's Mommy?' reactions," I encouraged her. "One mistake isn't going to ruin them forever. If it doesn't work, we can *always* go back to the old way." Finally, she agreed.

Sally chose to ride her exercise bike for twenty minutes while Jim began working on the Endless List. After one morning, Jim—previously Mr. Nice Guy, the sweetest guy on earth—turned out to be not such a saint either: "I screamed, I threatened, I yelled. I did anything I could to get it all done in time." After just two mornings of walking in each other's moccasins, Jim and Sally's differing theories of discipline gave way to the same reality. Instead of fighting each other, they were now moving toward the same pragmatic wavelength.

Phil and Janice, another example of a lenient dad and strict mom combination, came to see me to discuss the underachievement problems their twelve-year-old son Theo was having at school. Phil complained that Janice was too demanding and constantly on Theo's back about homework, his room, and too much Play Station. Janice complained that Phil never set limits. "He's such a pushover that it's no wonder Theo doesn't work hard enough at his studies."

Since homework was always a contentious issue on this parenting team, I asked them to trade jobs for three nights, putting Phil completely in charge and Janice on the sidelines. After the second evening, "mild-mannered" Phil had already taken away Theo's phone privileges and his video game time, and was threatening to ground him for a "month of weekends." He came into the next few sessions as much of a hassled nervous wreck as his wife had first appeared.

Balanced participation is the great equalizer, transforming even the nicest, most lenient and patient father into an inconsistent, "I'll do whatever it takes" pragmatist.

LESSONS FROM THE PLAYGROUND

Mothers' pragmatism doesn't arise solely because of the Endless List, however. There are several other reasons why women are usually more pragmatic when it comes to discipline. For example, since mothers are more likely to take children to their activities—the playground, ballet or karate class, birthday parties—they get a chance to *see other children in action*. This gives them plenty of real-life opportunities to see how their own kids compare with their peers. All you have to do is sit in the playground for half an hour and you can't help but notice the wide range of children's behavior. Fathers usually don't spend as much time with other people's kids; because of this, they have a narrower view of what constitutes "normal" behavior, and therefore what should or shouldn't require parental discipline.

I didn't fully understand this myself until Glenn, an English teacher and the father of a four-year-old girl, wrote me the following beautiful summary of a childrearing lesson he'd learned. "I took Rachel to her friend's four-year-old birthday party. Getting Rachel ready for this event was like swimming in a sea of whining: her dress was 'too long,' her hair was 'too straight,' and the bows on her shoes were not 'exactly right.'

"After an hour of this I was ready to throw in the towel. Trying to talk Rachel out of her fussiness, I also complained to my wife, 'What's going on here? Do you always allow this kind of whining without doing anything about it?' I was thinking to myself, 'How will Rachel ever grow up if we let her get away with this kind of behavior' My father would never have stood for this sort of shrieking—plus, she's driving me crazy!

"To her credit, my wife kept trying to deal with Rachel. True, she got extremely exasperated and screamed a few times. But she also reasoned, distracted, gave Rachel choices, and went through several outfits with her. In the face of my accusations she simply said, 'Kids this age just whine a lot. It's no big deal.'

"That's exactly what these mothers say, I thought to myself. I didn't believe her.

"Then we went to the birthday party and I saw what my wife meant. I spent the entire time observing closely. I noticed that after all the kids devoured enough birthday cake, the eight boys started bouncing off the walls, alternating between whining and 'killing' each other as they fought over an action figure named 'Metal Head.' In contrast, the eight girls remained at the table. But while they didn't move around a lot, they weren't exactly quiet: 'I want the *pink* hat, not the blue one!' 'You *promised* me a red flower on the birthday cake, not this yellow one, yech!' 'I want to sit next to *Amy*, not Justine!'

"Compared to the whiners at this party, my Rachel was an amateur."

Glenn *was* lucky. After just one afternoon of paying attention, he came to see how "normal" his daughter was. But think how many opportunities his wife, and most other mothers, have to familiarize themselves with the wide range of normal children's behavior. How many play-dates, shopping trips, hours in doctors' waiting rooms, school plays, and school trips had Glenn's wife sat through over the course of

Rachel's life? No wonder women often have more practical expectations about how kids *really* behave.

THE HUMILIATION FACTOR

There's still another reason why women are pragmatic disciplinarians while men are more likely to be idealistic. Whichever parent deals with the kids' everyday lives (usually Mom) is more open to *humiliation*—in front of other mothers, extended family members, teachers, and even strangers on the street. In fact, many mothers feel as if society never stops monitoring what sort of job they're doing.

Humiliation begins early, and can strike at any time. Alice, a mother at a parenting workshop, described her intense embarrassment over a seemingly trivial event at her daughter Jeri's Gymboree class. When the instructor asked the children to form a "parachute circle," Jeri didn't feel like going along with the idea. "She refused to budge, and then proceeded to lie down on the floor and throw an enormous tantrum." Alice said she felt as if the rest of civilization had gone off, leaving the two of them behind.

Most mothers adapt and try to avoid these situations by doing "whatever works"—whether it's giving a child a stick of gum to head off a supermarket tantrum or ignoring the fact that you were just called "butthead" in an elevator crowded with disapproving strangers.

Fathers, on the other hand, are usually less vulnerable to humiliation. For one thing, they are unlikely to have ongoing relationships with the other parents in a group the way mothers are—"So what do I care what they think?" Also, fathers are still given as much leeway by mothers as wizened veterans on any sports team give to enthusiastic rookies. After all, any father who's involved enough to show up at Gymboree with his child gets credit "just for being there." Expectations for effectiveness are reserved for mothers—the *true* professionals!

TURNING THE TABLES

Unbalanced participation often magnifies gender differences over discipline to the point where men and women become stuck in polarized positions.

But when men become more involved, they turn out to be just as incon-sistently pragmatic as their partners. In other words, when participation is equalized and both parents put in equal amounts of time with the kids, there is no such thing as total consistency or absolute standards.

Remember Gale, whose husband Stan was furious about their daughter's four o'clock pretzel? In the midst of an argument about set-ting limits, Gale snapped, "What really makes me furious about this is that *you're* the one who got Gretchen hooked on pretzels in the first place." She then explained that one afternoon when Stan was home with Gretchen, he gave her a pretzel because she kept bugging him every five minutes for something to eat—and it was "driving him crazy." Grudgingly, Stan admitted that this was true.

Another dad, Kurt, learned the meaning of pragmatism the after-noon he was "home alone" supervising his six-year-old daughter's play-date. By the time his wife Beatrice returned, she found both girls "playing Cinderella"—scrubbing the kitchen floor on their hands and knees soaked to the bone and wearing only underpants.

"How could this have happened?" Beatrice screamed. "You're always accusing me that I don't set enough limits. Just what do you think Erica's mother is going to say when she comes home sopping wet?" All Kurt, the so-called family disciplinarian, could mutter in his own de-fense was "Well, at least it's keeping them happy and quiet."

Obviously, the most powerful way to create a more consistent team is to redistribute childcare arrangements. Make the Endless List every-body's problem, not just Mom's. More equal participation almost guar-antees that both Mom and Dad will share a more pragmatic approach and not waste their time shouting at each other in different languages.

However, if nothing else after twenty-five years of practice, I have also become a pragmatist. I understand how difficult it is to significantly change the participation equation in any family—and how much time this will take. In the meantime, as we work on change, we need a consis-tent discipline framework, one that includes the following three goals:

THE THREE GOALS OF A CONSISTENT DISCIPLINE FRAMEWORK

1. It must bridge the gender-based differences about discipline men and women often bring to childrearing.

2. It must narrow the gap between the strict and the lenient member of the parenting team—whoever they may be.
3. It must help parents sort out the most effective disciplinary techniques from the confusing array of methods childrearing experts suggest.

GETTING LOST IN A SEA OF TECHNIQUES

So many discipline fads have come and gone in the past thirty years that I completely sympathize with parents who feel utterly confused. But if you were to look at each fad individually, you'd notice something interesting: each one is either stereotypically "male" or "female" in its approach to discipline. In fact, the two giants of the childrearing world, Benjamin Spock (who leans toward a harder line) and Penelope Leach (who espouses a more nurturing stance), embody the stereotypical male–female split.

Listen to how they differ on just one fundamental issue: what to do about the "unsettled infant." Spock believes that parents of infants six months and older need to begin setting limits and not pick up their babies each time they cry so as to avoid "spoiling." Leach, however, believes that infants cry for a reason and that they ought to be picked up and attended to pretty much whenever they're upset; spoiling is not a primary concern for her.

In other words, the split between pragmatists and idealists also exists among the experts. This leaves parents with diametrically opposed solutions to the exact same discipline problem. On one side of the shelf in your neighborhood bookstore you'll find the "stricter," limit-setting approaches: "Tough Love," "Time Out for Tots," "Contracts," and "Ferbering." On the other side, you'll find the child-centered books emphasizing Praise and Acceptance, the Star System, P.E.T., Creative Discipline, the Family Bed, How to Build Self-Esteem, How to Encourage Cooperation by Listening Correctly, etc.

These approaches *all* have merit and have helped many parents stay in charge of kids. The problem is that neither extreme *alone* has withstood the test of time. Democratic and child-centered techniques leave many fathers (and some mothers) grumbling about "too much psychology and not enough limits."

In a way, this isn't so surprising. The three greatest child psychologists of this century—Anna Freud, Margaret Mahler, and D. W. Winnicott, whose influence on today's child-centered experts is incalculable—had no *children of their own*. While unquestionably brilliant, these clinicians simply did not have to deal with children during the "witching hour," or at three in the morning, or on a backed-up supermarket checkout line. No wonder that the child-centered approaches to discipline, originally derived from their theories, strike so many parents as therapeutic and far too permissive.

However, rigidly applied techniques that stress limit-setting and "tough love" seem arbitrary to many parents, especially mothers—or impractical given the messy give-and-take of daily life.

And yet, if you study each of these techniques closely, you'll find a common theme that will appeal to both the pragmatist and the idealist in your family. What they all share is the conviction that children learn when their actions lead to *practical consequences*.

PRACTICAL CONSEQUENCES

I have carefully chosen the phrase "practical consequences" because it creates a bridge between the pragmatic and idealistic approaches to discipline. Being "practical" is essential—parents who are in the trenches with their kids need techniques that really work! But "consequences" are also essential—because kids need to learn that their behavior affects others, resulting in reactions they may not always like. After all, the world does not have endless patience for those who don't follow the rules.

How do you create practical consequences that put both the pragmatist and the idealist in your family on the same wavelength? Follow these criteria:

1. *Consequences should express your feelings about what your child did, and this is almost always more than simply anger.* After watching thousands of mothers and fathers struggling to come up with consequences, it's clear that the reason most punishments aren't practical is that they arise from one primary emotion—anger. "You're

grounded forever!" is an example of what often comes to either the pragmatist's or the idealist's mind when we feel pushed to the limit and blinded by anger—hardly a practical consequence.

Remember, consequences that arise from anger alone:

- *Polarize* the pragmatist and the idealist. The pragmatist says, "How can you possibly enforce that punishment? I'm not monitoring him—will you?" The idealist replies, "If you don't stand up for your beliefs now, where will things end ?" Before you know it, parents are fighting each other while the kids slip through the cracks, forgotten.
- Are *predictable*. By age six, just about every child can accurately tell me which punishment will be threatened during parents' angry outbursts. Because of this, kids discount and dismiss angry threats, and don't take their parents seriously no matter how severe the punishment.
- Feel *inauthentic* to kids. This is because anger is only the tip of the iceberg. Kids trigger all kinds of other feelings, such as panic (eleven-year-old Warren is late from school); hurt (nine-year-old Sasha forgets your birthday); fear (four-year-old Erica hangs upside down from the top of the monkey bars); guilt (six-year-old Steven is left alone with his grandparents while you and your spouse take an overnight trip together); resentment (during the holiday season your children act like bottomless pits—all greed and no gratitude); jealousy (five-year-old Sarah is going through a "Daddy" phase—and seems to have forgotten Mom exists except when she's sick and needs her).

These other feelings children evoke in us are difficult to express for both men and women. Most people agree that men have trouble showing hurt, jealousy, and fear—but even mothers, whose wider emotional range is often taken for granted, also seem more comfortable with anger than these other "unparentlike" feelings. This is probably because several generations of mothers have now been twelve-step-programmed and pop-psychologized enough to believe that expressing hurt, fear, anxiety, or dependence will create pathological guilt in their kids ("I'll never do to my kids what my mother did to me"). In the end, both mothers and fathers inhabit the same emotional straitjacket in which anger often masks other feelings we're unaware of or afraid to explore.

Unfortunately, when the consequences we come up with aren't rooted in authentic feelings, they don't make any sense to our kids. For example, because nine-year-old Brian had been relentlessly badgering his mother Vivian to buy him a new baseball glove, she sent him to his room, saying, "No computer games for a month." Vivian later admitted to me that underneath her anger, she also felt hurt that Brian hadn't been more considerate toward *her*.

However, Vivian hadn't let Brian know that she needed his help to feel better. She thought to herself, "Parents aren't supposed to ask children for help, right? It's unparentlike." So instead of creating a consequence that flowed from her authentic feelings—"I'm really upset tonight; I need your help. Please don't come in here until you can be nice to me"—Vivian created a consequence that made no sense and was unenforceable to boot.

2. *Consequences should fit the crime.* Parents often complain that they can't come up with original consequences, and so find themselves recycling the same ones over and over. One of the benefits of asking yourself "What do I feel besides anger?" is that it opens up your thinking. Suddenly many consequences that would never have come to mind are now quite imaginable.

For example, suppose your seven- and eleven-year-olds are acting up at the dinner table. You're drowning in a sea of preteen insults and put-downs. Nobody's eating much of anything. "I don't like chicken with sauce," your daughter complains—though she'd requested chicken in the first place. Your son can't stop squirming in his seat, which is driving your husband up the wall. Suddenly he shouts at you, "*Do* something already!" His words are the final straw.

"No more videos for the next six months," you scream.

Now does this consequence have any connection whatsoever to acting up at the dinner table? Because it doesn't, the kids will probably greet your threat with that knowing (and maddening) smirk. Failing to see any connection between crime and punishment, and recognizing that the threat will prove difficult to enforce once your anger passes, they couldn't care less about your ranting. And if you think things were tense between you and your spouse before, wait until you try to enforce the "no videos for six months" proclamation.

However, if you were to focus on what you're experiencing besides anger—that you feel taken for granted, like a dishrag—you might come up with a practical consequence that both fits the crime *and* teaches kids that their behavior has an impact on others. Perhaps you don't have to cook most nights of the week; or maybe on some nights the kids should eat alone and you and your spouse will eat later; or perhaps you could buy microwavable food for the kids to fix for themselves. These are practical consequences that flow from feelings and are logically connected to what was going wrong in the first place.

3. *Consequences need to be age-appropriate so your child can learn from them.* One of the biggest stumbling blocks parents encounter as they try to agree on discipline is that neither the pragmatist nor the idealist considers children's developmental level—what they're capable of learning at any given age. The pragmatist on the team often feels so overwhelmed, bouncing between martyrdom and oversolicitousness, that she desperately uses whatever works without taking the developmental abilities of her child into account. The idealist, who is not involved in the child's everyday life, doesn't always notice subtle changes in the child's development; instead, he superimposes what was expected of *him* (or at least what he remembers) as being developmentally appropriate for his child.

The battle between Howard and Michelle over four-year-old Lydia's behavior at the Raffi concert, which I referred to earlier in this chapter, is a perfect example. "I had to sit still in my seat as a kid—or else I had to go to bed without any supper. There's nothing wrong with setting limits like that. I turned out okay," Howard tells his wife. But Michelle, trying to be a patient, understanding mother *and* to counteract her "harsh" husband, allows Lydia to be a free spirit. Ultimately, however, even her patience is exhausted, and she explodes.

Both Howard and Michelle would have benefited from a true understanding of Lydia's developmental capabilities. Children learn best when we tailor consequences to suit their ages (see Chapter 7,

"Practical Consequences by Age"). All team sports need referees, and these guidelines might help you settle some disagreements with your partner.

4. *Consequences should not cause you more hardship than they do your child.* Who really suffers when you ground your child for the next three months or ban movie videos forever? Much of the burden will fall on you, having to deal with a cranky kid who needs *extra* supervision. This is bound to increase the burden on whichever parent is responsible for everyday details around the house—and to lead to enormous battles between parents over following through.

Meanwhile, children slip through the cracks. Or they endlessly badger and negotiate with you to change your mind. They know that at some point at least one of you will feel too worn down to continue arguing. This scenario also prolongs an event—like "bad behavior at dinner"—far past the time it deserves. Instead of settling on a quick, practical consequence and moving on, you're left dealing with the fallout of the situation far longer than is necessary. Does either of you need this extra burden?

5. *Reserve the right to change your mind.* Unfortunately, many parents mistake consistency for rigidity. We're afraid to change our minds. "It's inconsistent. You'll confuse the kids," we're told. This parenting bugaboo practically obligates us to cling to whatever anger-based consequence we first came up with—illogical, unenforceable, and developmentally inappropriate as it may be. Suppose, for example, your twelve-year-old son arrives home from a bike ride through the neighborhood a half-hour later than he was supposed to for the second time in a week. "That's it," you yell, "you're grounded for a month!" You soon realize that this consequence, arising out of anger, is disproportionately severe. So don't feel obliged to stick with it. Children respect parents who reconsider consequences that don't make sense and *try* to come up with a better solution. Explain to your child, "I was angry before. Now that I've given it some thought, I've decided to ground you for two days, since you were late twice this week. Then you'll have the chance to earn my trust back." In the end, children learn from parents who reflect on their actions and aren't afraid to admit that they were wrong.

A SUMMING UP

I've chosen these guidelines because they contain the six principles common to *all* effective disciplinary techniques. More important, they bring women and men together rather than dividing them.

Mothers—or whoever is responsible for the greater portion of hands-on childrearing tasks—appreciate the pragmatic, "I'll do what works" approach. Women also need permission to express "unparent-like" emotions so they don't end up feeling taken for granted. The age-appropriate aspect of practical consequences appeals to mothers who are trying to empathize with the "here and now" of their child's psychological development. Finally, women feel good about an approach to discipline that allows them to change their minds, to make mistakes, to stop worrying about being a "perfect" parent.

Fathers relate to these principles because they promise consequences and limits to behaviors. This feels like "good preparation for living in the real world, where no one's going to baby you or grant special consideration." Because these guidelines allow men to express feelings other than anger, they're freer to be more open with their kids. This makes them less likely to withdraw or feel isolated from the family's everyday life. Finally, most men need to learn more about what is developmentally appropriate—a task that should not just be "woman's work."

In the next chapter, you'll see these principles in action. As two families adjust their approaches toward discipline, entrenched positions begin to shift: The "I'll do anything" pragmatist gets better at creating consistent consequences; the rigid idealist becomes more practical and involved. Parents who had been needlessly haggling find themselves on common ground, operating on a similar wavelength.

Sound too good to be true? Read on.

CHAPTER 5

FATHER KNOWS BEST?

A Strict Dad and Lenient Mom

To illustrate how "practical consequences" can lessen conflict between parents, meet a "strict dad–lenient mom" combination—Faith and Carl Stewart. When they came to me, they were hopelessly stuck, reeling from daily arguments and almost at the point of giving up on the relationship. Carl, an electrical engineer, couldn't stop criticizing Faith for being "too easy" on the kids. Faith resented this, saying, "Sure, it's easy for *you* to talk about your theories, but *I'm* the one who's with the kids more of the time and has to carry everything out."

Here are some of Carl's gripes about twelve-year-old Jeff and eight-year-old Susan: during dinner they fought so intensely that mealtimes were a nightmare; their rooms were complete disaster zones; they left common areas in the house littered with debris; they treated Faith disrespectfully, answering back and often bullying her into giving in; and they talked only to Faith, leaving him out in the cold.

Faith agreed that the kids were too disrespectful. She added that she felt like the household maid much of the time, always picking up after them. But what she hated most was Carl's open criticism of her. And she was concerned that the constant battles over discipline were sapping her energy and interfering with her career as a graphic artist.

Carl was also exhausted by the bickering that resulted when they tried to take charge of their kids: "We spend so much time arguing over discipline that our marriage is definitely being affected." The last straw, however, was a call Faith had received from Jeff's teacher: Jeff had been getting into fights at school and was in danger of being suspended.

First I reassured them that despite their obvious differences, we could find common ground. Next I introduced them to the concept of practical consequences, and said, "Okay, pick an issue for us to start with. What leads to the most conflict between the two of you?"

1. Mealtime Madness

Without hesitation Faith and Carl said they hated mealtime most of all. "After a hard day at work, I want a peaceful, civilized dinner," Carl demanded. Instead, he found himself sitting down to bickering, bratty kids who traded insults nasty enough to make him lose his appetite.

Then Faith spoke up: "The kids whine and complain nonstop. If I make chicken they say they want fish. If I make fish the next night they say they want chicken."

"Tell me, what happens when the scene at the table has reached that certain pitch of screeching pandemonium?" I asked.

"After a few minutes," Faith answered, "Carl gets so angry that he explodes. He screams, 'That's it! No television for a week! Go to your rooms, you're grounded!' Or he tells them that they eat like animals, something like that. I get upset when he yells, and try to get him to be more reasonable."

"What happens next?" I asked.

"The kids smirk. They realize that we don't see eye-to-eye on any of these threats. Then the two of *us* start arguing and the kids get even wilder."

This was the perfect time to introduce the notion of practical consequences. "Besides being angry," I asked, "how else does mealtime make you feel?"

Faith immediately answered, "Like a slave."

"I feel resentful," said Carl." All I want is a quiet meal. I can't live like this."

"What would be an enforceable solution that would leave you, Carl, feeling less resentful and you, Faith, feeling less like a slave? I'm not talking about your anger now, but what's underneath it. *Create a consequence from these other feelings.*"

All of a sudden Faith said, "Wait a minute. Why am I cooking every night?" (Her chronic anger at Carl, herself, and the kids had prevented her from asking this astonishingly simple question before.)

Over the next week, Faith decided that she would prepare family meals only twice a week. One evening Carl would be in charge of dinner—a task he'd never done regularly before. On the other days, the kids would have microwavable foods they could prepare themselves, leaving Mom and Dad free to have a couple of meals alone each week. Given the kids' ages, these solutions were entirely appropriate.

Carl and Faith presented the new plan at a family meeting., Predict, ably, Jeff and Susie were outraged. They accused their parents of "child neglect" and other assorted buzzwords designed to bring back the old, familiar order. Out of sheer defiance, they left the kitchen a chaotic mess for several days.

However, Carl and Faith held firm, and within two weeks something dramatic happened. Faith realized how much extra time she had on her hands now that she didn't have to prepare meals every day. She felt markedly less pressured both at work and at home. And two "civilized" adult meals a week put Carl in a better mood. He found himself inclined to spend more time with the kids after dinner—at least on those evenings.

After a month of this new routine, no one could remember doing it any other way. A small change—challenging the belief that "Mom *has* to make dinner" markedly decreased mealtime madness and the amount of time Carl and Faith spent fighting each night.

But this was just a beginning.

2. Laundry Lunacy

One of Faith's biggest gripes concerned laundry. Both kids habitually left used towels strewn on the bathroom floor. This meant that they would go through an entire linen closet of towels in a week. Despite her work responsibilities, Faith would get lost in the laundry room for evenings at a time. Was she angry about this? Absolutely!

But anger wasn't all Faith was experiencing. A typical martyr, she alternated between resentment over her extra work, angry explosions, and the inevitable guilt that followed. Then she'd attempt to make up for her loss of control by giving in to the kids when the next issue arose.

This vacillation inevitably prompted Carl to exclaim, "You see! Look how inconsistent you're being!"

So I asked Faith, "Besides being furious, how do you feel when your kids treat you this way? How do you feel when Carl puts in his two cents but doesn't offer to help out with the laundry?"

"Like they *all* take me for granted. Sometimes I even question whether anyone in this house actually loves me. Why should they? I just provide services for them." By admitting how *hurt* she really felt under her anger, Faith's head immediately cleared and within minutes she came up with an enforceable, practical consequence—one so simple that she was again shocked at not having thought of it before.

"You're each going to be issued one towel a week, that's it!" Faith told Jeff and Susie. They couldn't believe their ears.

"How do you expect us to use these disgusting wet towels?" they snapped, thoroughly indignant.

"I guess you need to figure out how to take better care of them," Faith replied.

"We'll walk around smelly!" Jeff threatened. "How would that make *you* feel?" Susie jibed. "All I'm saying is I'm a little tired of being taken for granted," Faith said. She persisted—no anger, no screaming, just practical consequences.

Predictably, the kids tested her by each continuing to leave their one towel on the bathroom floor. But since Faith's position wasn't based on a temporary flash of anger but flowed naturally from a more basic sense of being taken for granted, she persisted. No freshly laundered towels were supplied regardless of how soggy and smelly they became. Soon, to everyone's amazement (including, I must admit, my own), Jeff and Susie began hanging up their towels on hooks!—as if they were prized possessions. After a week, Faith's laundry problem was history. The kids were beginning to learn that their behavior had consequences, and Faith and Carl found themselves with one less reason to argue.

3. Problems at School

As Carl and Faith felt more confident, they decided to tackle Jeff's school difficulties. Faith was unhappy about her role as intermediary. Because she was home from work early enough to receive calls from

Jeff's teacher, she felt that she was on the front line when it came to dealing with the school. Then, she had to relay this information to Carl who, true to gender stereotype, assumed the role of "The Enforcer."

The trouble was that Jeff wouldn't listen or take responsibility for his school problems. Instead he would whine defensively or lie: "I left my books at school; they didn't give homework this week; the ditto was stolen from my locker." In the face of Jeff's stonewalling, Carl took away so many privileges that Jeff eventually said, "I don't care." Other times, Carl would lecture relentlessly enough that Jeff would practically slide from his chair in a comatose daze. Then Carl would turn on Faith, angrily blaming her: "You have so much trouble setting limits at home, it's no wonder he has trouble at school."

"Besides being furious at Faith *and* Jeff, how do you feel about all this?" I asked Carl.

He thought for a moment and then said, "Out of it. Like I have no real impact in this situation except to come in and be a paper tiger."

I asked him to come up with a practical consequence, based not on anger alone, but on feeling disconnected. Carl was quiet for some time. Faith, in her Earth Mother role, kept trying to bail him out. Each time she came up with her own suggestions, I asked her to let Carl think for himself. To Faith's amazement, he finally said, "I ought to go to school this week and see for myself what they have to say about Jeff. Maybe I shouldn't always rely on Faith for information." Now it was Faith's turn to fall off her chair.

The following week Carl went for a private conference with Jeff's teacher. He found out that Jeff was having trouble remembering instructions concerning homework. Armed with this new information, Carl approached Jeff not as a distant or angry disciplinarian, but as an involved parent.

"I went to school and Ms. Ford told me you're having trouble remembering instructions. Do you have any idea how we could handle this better?" he asked Jeff.

"I don't like being in my room alone. It's hard for me to get started," Jeff explained. "Maybe it would be better if I stayed in the den with you and then I could ask you for help when I get confused." Of course Carl agreed. After just a few weeks of hanging out together, Carl got a hands-on look at Jeff's work habits. No longer the removed, armchair quarterback, he was able to help his son in a few concrete ways.

Now, Jeff's grades did not dramatically improve. But the fighting in the family over homework indisputably decreased. And with Carl more involved, Faith was able to cross yet another item off her Endless List.

4. Privacy

The big TV was in Carl and Faith's bedroom, and because of this they had a major privacy problem: Jeff and Susie were constantly hanging around, leaving crumbs in the bed, discarded juice and soda cans on the floor, and candy wrappers under the pillow. Carl, in his typical way, took an I-have-to-build-your-character-for-the-future position: "No boss would ever stand for this kind of behavior!" he bellowed, and was, of course, promptly ignored. He would then turn on Faith, blaming her for the kids' lack of character. Faith, once again caught in the middle, tried everything she could with Jeff and Susie—wheedling, coaxing, nagging them to clean up after themselves. And, as usual, it got her nowhere.

Again, I asked, "Besides being just angry when you wake up and find a soda can under your pillow, how do you feel?"

"Violated!" they said almost in unison, the first time Faith and Carl spoke like a united front since I'd met them.

"Well, what's a practical consequence when someone feel violated? What can you do?"

The answer—a lock on the bedroom door—was so stunnigly simple that once again they both looked shocked.

Instead of an authoritarian consequence based on anger or with an eye toward "building character," this consequence came straight from the heart. Because the kids were both in grade school, I encouraged their decision. (This is not appropriate for children under five years old, or at any age if there is a medical or psychological condition that warrants special concern.)

Initially, Faith had a little trouble accepting this solution. Intellectually she was all for it, but she worried that it would "hurt the kids' feelings." Yet her sense of violation was significant enough that she just needed some reassurances before proceeding. Carl and she agreed that the lock wouldn't be used routinely every night, but only when they wanted to be alone.

That week, they explained to the kids exactly why they were installing a lock—to *stop feeling intruded upon*. How did the kids react? At first they were totally puzzled. Demonstrating a bit of classic preteen logic, Susie screamed, "Why in the world do *you* need a lock on your door? Kids' rooms are supposed to be off-limits to their parents, not the other way around." And Jeff remarked, "You mean you were *serious* about the messy bedroom?"—a comment that helped Carl and Faith realize how totally the kids had dismissed their previous attempts at discipline.

"Yes, we're serious," Mom and Dad replied. "You don't clean up after yourselves when you use our room, so this is our way of telling you we need our own space kept the way we like it."

As it developed, simply installing the lock got the message across— Jeff and Susie were in no way going to jeopardize their access to the bigger TV. The bed remained crumb-free. In fact, Faith and Carl never actually had to lock the door, except when they wanted privacy. Again, Faith's Endless List shrank by one item, and the couple had more occasions for intimacy.

5. The Martyr Syndrome

If Carl fit the "strict but somewhat distant" father stereotype, Faith found herself vacillating between the archetypical roles of Earth Mother and Wicked Witch of the West. She was caught in the familiar martyr cycle: patience, resentment, explosion, and guilt—and then back to patience again.

Faith's unhappiness with this state of affairs was apparent as she described how often she put her needs on the back burner to tend to the kids: "I drive them everywhere. I cancel appointments with clients to be home when they need me. I squeeze job deadlines between school conferences and trips to the doctor. . . . " The Endless List went on and on. "Yet it seems if I ever need a favor from Susie or Jeff, all they do is bitch and complain." Although Carl didn't offer to help out a lot, he did use these moments to remind her, "You're too easygoing, and you're spoiling them."

Like most of us, Faith needed a dramatic event to precipitate a change. One day after I'd been working with them for a couple of months, she related the following incident: "I told Jeff that I'd have to stop at the Xerox store for a moment before taking him to the movies. He made such an incredible fuss about it that I was ready to wring his neck. One lousy minute of his time was all I needed and he couldn't stop complaining."

Faith was so angry that she literally *dragged* Jeff into the store with her. Immediately she experienced that familiar guilt that follows "losing it." "But Jeff didn't even notice how upset he'd made me," Faith continued. "We'd barely gotten back in the car before he asked if I would get him ice cream on the way to the movies. And I'm ashamed to admit this—I actually *got* it for him!"

"It's clear you were angry. But when the kids treat you this way do you feel anything else?" I asked.

"I don't feel like being nice toward them, or in fact, doing *anything* for them."

I asked her to take the next week and think about a practical consequence consistent with her unkind feelings, which resulted from being treated unkindly.

Three days later a similar incident occurred. Faith asked the kids for another small favor and they put up the usual fuss. Later that evening Susie approached her about getting "that red shirt we saw in the mall last week." Faith surprised herself by answering, "No. I don't feel like doing you a favor. You haven't been considerate of me. This afternoon I asked you to help me out and you refused. So I don't even want to discuss that shirt with you now. In fact, get out of here and leave me alone." Susie, normally "Ms. Smart-ass," ran out of the room as if she'd seen a ghost.

At our next session, Faith said, "That afternoon was revolutionary. I don't want to sound overly dramatic, but it was the first time since they were born I felt *entitled* to act like a human being, not just like a 'mother.' For once I could say, 'You're not being nice to me, and I don't have to go out of my way for you.' It was that simple. Susie got the message loud and clear."

6. Make Room for Daddy

As Faith's firmness with the kids grew, it became apparent how isolated Carl felt. Though Susie fought with Faith, at least they had some sort of relationship. Susie talked to, shopped with, and occasionally confided in her mom.

Like so many men who basically feel left out, Carl tried to make conversation with his daughter, but unfortunately ended up lecturing. He criticized her clothes, slovenly habits, and superficial values. Carl realized he was shooting himself in the foot each time he tried to promote "good values," but he didn't know what else to do. Typical of many affection-starved dads, he was only comfortable in the role of "standard bearer." I also suspected that being the "critic-at-large" was a way of not having to get involved with the nitty-gritty details of everyday life around the house.

As always, I believed Carl's anger toward Susie was just the tip of the iceberg; I was sure he felt much more hurt than he let on. But because he considered "hurt" to be "unfatherlike" (the way Faith believed expecting to be treated fairly was "unmotherlike"), these feelings stayed suppressed. He was then unable to come up with any practical consequences that seemed authentic to Susie. As a result, she simply wrote him off as "that guy who yells at us all the time."

So one day I pressed him. "Come on, Carl. I don't believe that all you experience toward Susie is anger and disappointment. What else is going on with you?"

Faith answered for him. "I think he feels pushed away and rejected by her. I see him sulking when Susie acts as if he's not really there."

Carl responded, "I try to tell myself it will change one day, but in the meantime I'm like a stranger to my own daughter. I can't understand it. Until a few years ago we were buddies."

I then asked Carl to think of a practical consequence to feeling like a stranger to one's own daughter. Carl was stuck. He couldn't come up with anything. Finally, I suggested that he bring home a "thinking of you" present—one of my favorite strategies for disconnected, hurt fathers.

At first Carl balked. "She doesn't deserve it! She's such a lazy goof-off!"

I replied, "Look, Carl. What you just said stems from your anger. But there's this painful distance between the two of you. Does it seem so illogical to make a small peace offering?"

After about half an hour of wrangling with me, Carl agreed, though he protested that he had no idea what to get her. Faith, true to form, offered, "I'll buy the presents for you and then *you* can give them to her." I suggested that she not volunteer any new items for her already Endless List.

Sure enough, one day during lunch hour Carl saw a street vendor selling bracelets. They were junky and cheap, but he thought Susie might like one of them. He gave it to her just as I instructed him to, no explanations or speeches, just "Here. I thought you might like this." Susie was taken aback. "She didn't say 'thank you,' " he reported, "but for a split second I could see she softened."

That moment marked the beginning of a thawing out between them. A few weeks later, Carl had to run an errand and asked Susie to go to the mall with him. "Since she didn't immediately retch and act as if she'd be humiliated to be seen with me, I said, 'C'mon. We'll be back real quick.' " They said practically nothing to each other in the car, but they didn't argue, either. A week after this, Susie walked into the living room and asked Carl to help her with a homework assignment. Two days after that Carl found himself—to everyone's amazement—defending Susie in a family argument.

Bit by bit Carl was becoming more involved in the details of Susie's life and less involved in his role as the family disciplinarian. He started to appreciate why she made certain decisions about clothes and boys, and the pressure she felt not to look like a "dweeb." The more he learned firsthand about Susie, the easier it was to come up with practical consequences for her behavior.

And just last week, Susie—who not too long ago was distant, aloof, and maddeningly arrogant—"out of nowhere" plopped down on the couch and snuggled against her father while he was watching TV.

SUMMING UP

Of course, not everything in the Stewart family is perfect. They still argue quite a bit over cleanliness. The kids are still sometimes disrespectful toward Faith, and Carl can't entirely give up his occasional tirades and lectures about values. But there is no question that the more Carl and Faith give up their entrenched positions as "The Disciplinarian" and "The Martyr," the less they fight.

And here's the bottom line when it comes to parental disagreements: as parents become more fluent in creating practical consequences for their children's behavior, they find that *their approaches to discipline aren't all that irreconcilable.* Faith trusts that Carl will treat the kids more fairly; Carl trusts that Faith will stand up to the kids.

Thanks to this shared perspective, Carl's and Faith's roles have shifted.. Faith has actually become a presence to be reckoned with in the family. At the same time, Carl has become more accessible to the kids.

Think about how these simple changes created a more effective parenting team:

1. Carl's involvement means that Faith's Endless List is significantly shorter. Now that she's aware that "everyone expects me to do everything," Faith can say no to tasks that had always been taken for granted as hers.
2. Faith and Carl no longer fight every day, but only a couple of times a week.
3. Faith doesn't cook most nights, or do laundry several times a week, and she isn't "nice" when she doesn't feel like it. Because of this, she feels much more kindly toward Carl.
4. Carl and Faith look forward to one civilized, "adult" meal every week together.
5. They have a regular Saturday night date during which they don't have to worry about returning to a bedroom trashed by their kids.
6. They can lock the door and "be private" without being interrupted or intruded upon.
7. Jeff's grades improved a little (though not dramatically), but he takes more pride in his work and argues less about starting his homework now that he studies with Carl.
8. Most important, Carl and Faith have stopped blaming each other. They are learning to work together. Not coincidentally, the kids, following Mom and Dad's lead, are not fighting with each other quite so viciously.

Remember, small changes often bridge the gap between even the most polarized couples. From such seemingly irreconcilable approaches, Carl and Faith were actually beginning to develop a shared vision, and to implement it in everyday life.

So can you.

CHAPTER 6

ONE WOMAN
AND THREE BABIES

A Strict Mom
and Lenient Dad

Carol and Terry Allen, parents of six-year-old Scott and nine-year-old Lewis came to me at the urging of their sons' school psychologist. The boys were getting into fights with classmates and not following teachers' directions. Both parents had jobs outside the home—Dad worked in swimming pool sales; Mom worked full-time as a medical office manager.

"We disagree a lot about how to handle them," Terry began. "I think she's much too strict. She's constantly correcting the boys, or yelling at them about something. When I get involved, she always interferes. My confidence as a parent is at a low ebb. I'm spending more and more time at work because, I figure, what difference does it make if I'm home."

I then asked Carol what she thought. "Our relationship is definitely being affected. He isn't home enough, and when he is, he never stands up to the boys. That's why they're in so much trouble. He's much too lenient with them. What kind of role model does he create? As soon as I get things running somewhat smoothly, he comes home and creates more chaos. It's like having another child."

Next, I asked what they thought about the problems the kids were having in school. "I think she's exaggerating things," Terry said, "and because of her worrying, the school has labeled them troublemakers. I keep telling her they're just *boys*. Stop expecting them to be so perfect!"

"You know, I hate this," Carol interrupted. "Why am I always the heavy? I'll tell you why. The school always calls me. I'm the one who goes in and has to listen to the teachers complain. He's just sticking his head in the sand. You know, Terry—they're *your* sons, too!"

Not ten minutes into our first meeting, the Allens were launched into the argument they've had hundreds of times, blaming and upbraiding each other as if I weren't there. Hoping to prevent a full-scale battle from erupting, I asked, "Which of these problems do you want to work on first?"

BEDTIME NIGHTMARE

Carol wasted no time. "We've got to take care of one thing first; otherwise, this will be useless. Terry comes home late a lot. By the time he arrives, the boys have eaten dinner, Lewis is doing his homework, and I'm getting Scott ready for bed. In walks Terry. He starts fooling around, wrestling and tickling them. He gets them excited and all my hard work settling them down goes out the window. It's impossible to calm them down again. So, instead of being finished by nine, the whole bedtime routine gets stretched out to nine-thirty or ten. Now, maybe that doesn't sound late to *you*. But the boys are exhausted the next day, and I get no time to take care of anything I need to do for me."

Thinking to myself, *Carol doesn't mince words, does she?* I pushed on. "What do the boys do when they stay up longer?"

"Scott calls me in and says, 'Scratch my back. Get me water.' Lewis won't turn his tape deck off . . . I don't really know. I'm so tired by then I'm not paying much attention. I just want it to be over."

"So, Terry, maybe *you* can fill me in."

"Not really," he responded. "Usually, the boys call for Carol. That's one of the reasons I want to play with them before bed. It's my only time to see them all evening. But after I kiss them goodnight for the second time, I flip on the TV and relax."

Like most parents, Carol and Terry weren't aware of the repetitive, predictable patterns that exist around trouble spots. Clearly they had an Endless List imbalance that led to different attitudes toward discipline and created enormous resentment. Yet neither of them could see how unbalanced things really were.

So I said, "I'm going to ask you to do something that will make you temporarily angry but, in the long run, will help. I want you to pick one evening this week and write down everything each one of you does *just around the bedtime ritual.* That way we'll see how things need to change."

Carol snapped, "Don't I have enough to do already? Now I have to make a list, too?"

"Good point. But just do it once. And use simple phrases, like 'Water. Tape deck.' Don't waste extra time on long descriptions."

When they arrived for their session the following week, we compared their lists. They were even more lopsided than I had expected. Carol would get the boys bathed, supervise their toothbrushing, and read bedtime stories to them. Terry helped with some of these tasks as well. Then, just as he had described, he began playing with the kids.

Carol also played—drill sergeant—trying to keep things moving along until the boys finally got into bed. But after this was accomplished, Carol's list continued—like the battery that "just keeps on going": "Ma, I'm thirsty . . . Mommy, I want some water . . . Ma, the room's too hot . . . Mommy, it's too cold . . . Scott's making those stupid noises again . . . Ma, do I have to bring in something for science tomorrow? . . . Mom, do I have a play-date tomorrow after school with Ben? . . . Ma, did you feed the fish? . . . Mommy, Lewis is getting into my things . . . Ma, Scott's 'sliming' my models."

There were only three words in the Allen household when lights were out—Ma, Mommy, and Mom. Sometimes Carol would say, "Call your father." Here's what her sons said in response:

"No, I want *you* to scratch my back . . . No, I want *you* to lie down next to me . . . and so on.

Seeing this imbalance in black and white made a big impression on all of us. I turned to Terry and asked, "Does this seem fair?"

"No," he gently replied. "Even if she didn't work at all and was just home with the kids, it still wouldn't seem totally right. But in my own defense, what can I do? They scream for *her*. And if I go in and give it my best, she corrects me. You know, I do feel guilty—but not so guilty that I want her to become my second boss!"

"Then here's what I suggest, Terry," I said. "On those nights when you come home close to bedtime, *you* be the one who's responsible for getting the kids settled. When they yell for Mom, say, 'I haven't seen you guys all day, so I'll do the bedtime stories tonight.' Carol, your part is to do everything you can to ignore their screams and then not comment on Terry's style.

"The first night you try this, it will be murder on both of you. The kids will put up a big fuss and, I expect, get to bed even later than usual. But, Carol, when you're tempted to intervene, remember your *fatigue,* not just your anger. Tell them, 'I'm tired and I have to take care of myself.' And then disappear. They'll probably follow you at first, so go into your room and if necessary lock the door."

"Am I that bad?" Carol half-joked.

"Not really," I said. "Many people have trouble giving up control."

Carol and Terry agreed to try this experiment. That night, they explained to the boys what would happen and why these changes were taking place. Preparing for the kids' counterreaction proved necessary indeed. When Scott started screaming, "Mommy, come in right now. I'm scared about that bad dream I had last night!" Carol was ready.

"Daddy and I are going to take turns helping you guys go to sleep. Tonight I need rest and Dad wants to spend time with you, too, so talk to your father." She then retreated to the bedroom and turned on the TV loud enough to block out Scott's scream.

After one frenzied night, Terry had firsthand experience of how much "after hours" activity the boys generated. For the first time, he realized how much work he undid each time he came home and got the boys into a wrestling frenzy.

For her part, Carol began to acknowledge that it was difficult to give up being in charge. When she came into the boys' bedrooms after they'd fallen asleep and saw them in the "wrong" pajamas, or sleeping "backwards" in their beds, or found their rooms messier than she would have liked, it took all her resolve not to comment on Terry's lax parenting. But she also soon realized that having an extra hour to herself at night meant more to her than wrinkled clothes or an untidy room.

A few weeks after this new routine had been established, Scott woke up from a nightmare, and for the first time ever approached *Terry's* side of the bed. "Can I sleep next to you for a little, Daddy? I'm frightened. I just had a bad dream."

At the following session, Terry told me, "Who wants to be woken up at three in the morning? But I have to say that I felt closer to him at that moment than I can ever remember. I felt like he actually *needed* me." This show of appreciation and connectedness gave Terry real motivation to continue taking on his share of the Endless List. What had started out as an artificial exercise to "help Carol" and go along with me developed into something meaningful between him and the boys.

THE WITCHING HOUR

Now that bedtime in the Allen household was decidedly less tense, Carol and Terry continued discussing their different discipline styles. "Carol's always moving the boys from one activity to another," complained Terry, "as if they were two of her office workers. I try to lighten things up in the house, but she's always making things more tense."

Surprisingly, Carol agreed. "Sometimes, I can't stand myself—the way I'm all over the kids. I *do* have a controlling personality. But still, Terry has no idea what goes on around here at dinnertime." Building up a head of steam, she turned to him to say, "That extra hour when I'm alone with them is the hardest part of the day. You can't imagine how much I have to get done."

Terry replied, "I work more than full-time. Plus, I have an hour's commute. You're always complaining about the 'witching hour,' but where am I—on vacation somewhere?"

"Don't give me that shit," Carol screamed. "All I'm asking for is cooperation when you get home. I see the way you look at the boys and roll your eyes if I ask you for something."

"Okay, so you're both angry," I interrupted. "Terry, when you roll your eyes at the boys, what are you feeling besides anger?"

"Like I have no right to object. I *am* around the house less than she is, and she *does* have to handle dinnertime alone. But I still think she's too tough."

"Is there any way you could leave work earlier a couple of nights a week?" I asked. "I think you'd have more rights if you were occasionally home during the witching hour."

Carol interrupted, "I'm not sure I want him home—he'd just create more problems."

"Well," I continued, "would you be willing to try an experiment and see what happens?"

After considerable discussion, I suggested that Terry ask his boss whether he could work through lunch and get out a little earlier on Tuesdays and Thursdays. Terry agreed; as a result, he was able to come home forty-five minutes earlier than usual twice a week.

Now, an extra hour and a half a week might not seem like a lot, but remember: in families, tiny changes in the participation equation can make a huge difference.

It took just two nights for Terry to see that Carol wasn't "making mountains out of molehills," and that the school counselor hadn't unfairly labeled his sons. In the hour preceding dinner, Terry found himself mediating the five or six fights between Scott and Lewis, continually limiting TV and Play Station time, curtailing predinner snacking, urging the boys to start their homework, handling their procrastination, and fielding half a dozen phone calls from grandparents, the boys' friends, and parents of the boys' friends—all while dinner was being prepared.

Terry soon dreaded the grind, which was exactly the way Carol often felt. Now, however, at least they were in it together. Instead of going at it from opposite positions, they felt like comrades-in-arms, still sniping at each other, but at least speaking the same language.

HIGH NOON

Most of the disagreements Terry and Carol experienced over discipline arose from the fact that they were locked into antithetical positions: Carol the pragmatist and Terry the idealist. That's why I decided to first address the participation equation with them. As I said earlier, greater participation turns everyone into a pragmatist.

True to form, the more Terry became involved, the more he began to accept that Scott and Lewis needed hands-on, practical limits. Terry also realized that he wasn't particularly good at setting them. One day, he and Scott had a dramatic showdown. Scott was playing with an action figure he had just received as a present when suddenly it broke in half. He went ballistic. "Daddy, go out and get me another one right now!" he screamed.

Terry, always Mr. Nice Guy, patiently explained, "These things happen. I'll try to fix it later. Or I'll get another one tomorrow." The more patient he was, the more furious Scott became. Eventually, Terry, already exhausted from his workday, buckled under Scott's unrelenting pressure tactics. "All right, all right. I'll go out and get another one," he muttered to himself. Then he looked out the window at the snow falling and the thermometer, which read 18 degrees.

Even martyrs reach their boiling points. When Scott whined, "Come on, Dad," Terry became enraged and felt like slapping Scott across the face. At that moment, Terry remembered the question I'd asked him: "Besides anger, what else do you feel?"

His answer? "Like a sucker! For some reason, an old Rolling Stones song started going through my mind." He turned to Scott and said, "Sometimes toys break. You can't always get what you want. I'm not going out, no matter what you do."

Needless to say, Scott's counterreaction was fierce. ("Hey, what's going on here? *Mom's* supposed to be the strict one," you could almost imagine him thinking.) His tantrum intensified to outlandish proportions. Carol, following my suggestion, steered clear, barricading herself in the bedroom so she wouldn't be tempted to intervene. When Scott began throwing toys around, Terry held him tight and said, "No matter how hard you scream, I won't let you do this." Finally Scott calmed down enough so that Terry could let him go without worrying. Still crying, the boy ran into his room and slammed the door.

Terry's first thought was "Serves him right!" This was soon followed by self-doubt: "What have I done? He'll *hate* me forever." (Interestingly, this is often a lenient dad's real worry—the loss of the bond to his child. On the other hand, mothers who have trouble setting limits worry that "I've damaged him emotionally forever.")

Meanwhile, back in the bedroom, Carol's reaction was mixed: "Now Terry's finally getting to see what it's like. I knew he couldn't handle it. That Taffel is an idiot." But instead of getting involved, she called a friend to complain about me.

And Terry hung in. He didn't chase Scott and "make nice." After fifteen torturous minutes, Scott came out of his room. He had drawn a "thank you" picture for his aunt who had given him the toy. Snuggling on Terry's lap he said, "Could you mail this for me, Daddy?"

I've seen this outcome a thousand times. If parents stand firm and hold on through the counterreaction, kids calm down, as if they're relieved. It's not hard to imagine what an impact this experience had on both Carol and Terry.

CHORE WARS

Despite this success, Terry and Carol still argued about how to handle the grinding responsibility of everyday chores. Both boys, but especially Lewis, balked at doing all the usual stuff that needs to be taken care of around any house. They promised—and then forgot—to clean rooms, brush teeth, hang up jackets, pick up after themselves, put away dishes, and so on. Carol was constantly reminding them while Terry made excuses for the boys and got down on Carol for being "compulsive."

When I asked them how they felt (besides being just angry), they both replied, "Helpless. We negotiate and make agreements, but we're almost always disappointed because the promises are broken."

"Why don't you set up situations where the boys can't disappoint *you*, but rather themselves," I suggested. "Make them live with the results of their own actions.

"For example, rather than negotiate endlessly with Lewis about brushing his teeth, say, 'The longer it takes to brush now, the less time we'll have to read together later; which do *you* want?' or 'If you're dressed for school by seven-thirty, then you'll be able to watch a few minutes of *SpongeBob*; it's up to you' or 'If we don't hassle now about cleaning your clothes up from the bathroom floor, I'll have more energy to play with you later. I've got just so much energy, so *you* decide.' "

Carol spoke up. "Doesn't this put too much control in *their* hands? It sounds like we're bribing them."

"No," I answered. "What they'll learn is that there are personal and logical consequences to actions. Think about it—when you have to hassle with them over their clothes, you *are* too tired to play later; if they dawdle endlessly in the morning, there *isn't* time to watch TV and still get out on time. The kids will begin to hear your requests as reasonable, not as arbitrary demands. And they'll stop thinking of you as unfair, angry parents, and starting thinking of you as human beings who have limits, who can't be endlessly pushed around.

"Are you willing to try?"

The yelling and unenforceable punishments had gotten them no-where. Terry and Carol shrugged. "Why not?"

At first, Lewis didn't see the "wisdom" of his parents' new ap-proach, and kept up his usual preteen sputtering: "Get off my back! I'll do it later, I promise!" But one morning, he finally started to "get it." That particular day he dawdled and procrastinated more than usual getting ready for school. Instead of lashing out in ineffective rage, Carol "got under" her anger and said to him, "Look, if you miss the bus and I have to take you to school myself, I'll be an hour late for my job. Not only will this leave me feeling rotten all morning, but tonight I'll have to catch up on my work and I won't be able to play with you."

A battle-scarred veteran, Lewis was used to his mother's angry threats; he also knew that these punishments tended to be forgotten as soon as her anger faded. Without even flinching, he met Carol's state-ment with his usual nonchalance, and continued his slow-motion prepa-rations for school. Needless to say, Carol was an hour late to work.

That night, though, Lewis was in for a surprise. When he asked his mother to play, Carol said that she was tired and that she had an hour's worth of work to make up due to her lateness. In other words, she stood by the consequence she'd decided on that morning—because it was created out of feelings deeper than just anger.

As you'd expect, Lewis counterreacted. He used all of his preteen negotiating and arguing skills to get Carol to relent and pay attention. Even angry attention would have made him happy. But Carol stuck to her position, continuing to do her own paperwork just as she said she would—and he was at a loss. Carol kept repeating, "I meant what I said. By dawdling, you created this situation." No yelling, no nagging, no lecturing. Now *Lewis* was disappointed—not his parents—and saw for the first time that his actions had very clear consequences.

The next night, seemingly out of nowhere, Lewis said, "You want to talk about how *you* feel? Well, let me tell you how *I* feel." He pulled out a piece of paper onto which he'd scribbled some notes. It turned out that some of the boys at school had been scapegoating him—a topic he'd never brought up to his parents before.

For the next hour, he and Carol sat together in a dark closet. Hiding how stunned she felt about this development, Carol first listened in-tently and then began to talk. Lewis actually seemed interested in her advice about how to handle being ostracized from the group. It was one of the closest moments they'd had in years.

When parents dig beneath their anger and come up with personal and logical consequences, kids "get it." If consequences are perceived as personal, practical, and enforceable rather than as angry pronouncements from above, children understand and are touched. Communication feels genuine—not just between "parent and child," but between two human beings.

Carol came in the following week saying, "That conversation with Lewis blew my mind. I saw him as a person with real feelings, not just as a lazy, rebellious kid who needs a drill sergeant. Things are far from perfect, but I'm not spending all my time nagging. And there's no question that the boys are taking their chores more seriously. The other night, for instance, Lewis left dishes all over the kitchen table. In the past, this would have led to a fight between Terry and me. But instead, I said, 'Lewis, you can clean up your dishes now and have time for Play Station later, or you won't—it's up to you.' Maybe because I'm not sounding so harsh these days, Terry backed me up completely.

"Lewis did his usual routine and 'forgot' to clean up the dishes. He made up some excuse like 'Oh, I thought you meant *tomorrow* night. But we simply said, 'I guess you don't want your Play Station time,' and went about our business. The next night, without our saying a word, the dishes disappeared from the table. This business about figuring out consequences that are not only connected with my anger is working. And I like Terry and myself better."

CAROL'S TURN

With these few changes, Carol's Endless List was slowly shrinking and Terry was gaining confidence in himself as a stronger parent. More specifically, Carol and Terry spent less time fighting with each other over discipline; Carol wasn't haggling as much with the kids over every little chore; and Terry was participating more in the tedious evening ritual. Now that some of her caretaking chores were lifted—even a little—Carol was ready to start focusing on the one person she'd been ignoring—herself!

For example, she'd almost never allowed herself the luxury of staying out any weekday evening for a non-"caretaking others" event. PTA meetings, community action groups were okay—as long as they benefited *others*. But if an out-of-town friend was in town and wanted to meet her for dinner, or she wanted to take a class at the community center, Carol was still hesitant to leave the kids alone with Terry. She worried about two things: that she'd return home to find the house in a shambles, creating so much more work for herself that it wasn't worth the few minutes of personal pleasure; and that Terry would resent her for the imposition—even if he didn't say anything right away.

And though Terry downplayed her concerns, he really *wasn't* too thrilled with the prospect of Carol's evening out. Regardless of how much more involved he felt, being left alone with the kids after working all day was not exactly his idea of relaxation. Terry admitted the unfairness of his position. After all, his job required some travel and a once-a-year, three-day sales retreat. But fair or not, twenty-first century or not, Terry's attitude and Carol's worries made her hesitant to leave the house to pursue any interests that centered exclusively on *her*.

"Besides feeling resentful and angry, how does this make you feel?" I asked.

"Like a hostage in my own home," she replied.

"Look Carol, instead of staying trapped in resentment, start freeing yourself in small ways. First, leave for just a few minutes—as long as you can tolerate—and slowly increase the interval that you stay away. Say to the boys: 'I need to take care of myself. I'm going out for a bit of fresh air.' Build up from there.

"Instead of experiencing you as just angry, the family will slowly learn to recognize that you have needs and feelings, that you're not just a mother."

By this time, Terry had enough confidence to say (not without a little tension), "Just do it! I'll handle things. But I have one condition. Promise not to comment on my style with the boys or criticize me when you get back."

A couple of days later, Terry and the boys were roughhousing. Instead of exploding about everyone's "lack of cooperation," Carol simply said, "I can't handle this right now. I'm taking a five-minute walk outside to calm down."

Scott and Lewis were so taken aback that they stopped rolling around on the living room floor. They ran to the front door, yelling, "Mom, are you okay?"

"Yeah. I just don't want to get into a fight with you guys. I'll see you in a couple of minutes."

As I've said, in family life, small changes make a huge difference. Instead of getting bogged down in another power struggle with the "men of the house," Carol clearly informed them by her actions, "I'm taking care of myself. I don't want to get upset. I'm worth it." She was also saying, "Everything around here isn't going to collapse if I leave for a few minutes. I'm not ultimately responsible for everything."

When Carol returned, she made no "supervisory" comments of any sort. In fact, she was surprised at the state of relative peace in the house.

Soon afterward, Carol was invited to go out for dinner with some friends on a Wednesday night. She accepted—for the first time in the nine years since Lewis was born (no wonder mothers carry around so much resentment). When she returned home at 9:30, she found both boys still up—but in bed, waiting for her. Scott said, "Oh, Mommy, I'm glad you're home. I couldn't sleep until you got here." All they needed from her was a hug.

Small changes do make a big difference. Carol no longer felt like a hostage. A few months after her first dinner out, she formed the monthly reading group she'd been thinking about for years. "I can't tell you how much I look forward to our meetings," she told me. "It's interesting, at the beginning of each meeting, all we talk about are the home situations we left behind. Only after we're done rehashing this do we get down to business." Obviously, she found comfort in the fact that she wasn't the only mom struggling to get out from under her Endless List.

SUMMING UP

After three months, the school psychologist reported that Scott and Lewis both were more organized and cooperative at school. Lewis's grades had improved. Scott seemed less demanding and immature. This good report didn't surprise me. Think how many changes the family had recently undergone.

First, Terry was coming home earlier twice a week. Because of this, he experienced what Carol was up against and immediately let up on his criticism of her for being "too strict."

Second, Carol relinquished her role as "household prosecutor," and Terry was no longer the bleeding-heart "public defender." Their once extreme positions on discipline were moderating.

Third, as Terry contributed more, Carol relaxed a little. She started to actually have some *fun* with the boys—playing Play Station, watching videos, and occasional junk movies—rather than spending virtually all her time nagging and reminding.

Fourth, Terry's role as the "third child" had all but evaporated. He was now involved with the boys for his *own* sake, not just to "help Carol out." And he was tougher. Lewis reported to me (with obvious pride), "Yeah, Dad doesn't let us get away with murder so much anymore."

"Doesn't that bother you?" I asked, already knowing the answer. "Nah. There's less fighting now and more games."

Finally, Carol felt better. Her Endless List was somewhat shorter. She was sharing, not shouldering, responsibilities for her sons. And her burgeoning outside interests helped her feel more vital and alive.

With these changes under their belts, Carol and Terry stopped their counseling sessions. I can't say that things were perfect. I helped them cut down on fighting—especially over discipline. However, they still weren't going out on regular dates. They didn't spend enough time together. But before making judgments about other people's relationships, you must remember that everyone has different goals. Carol and Terry, though still somewhat distant, were becoming better friends. And learning to be better friends is a necessary first step for so many married couples with children.

Regardless of how well things turned out for the two families you've just met in Chapters 5 and 6, disciplining remains an extremely complicated matter. There are times when you may have trouble translating feelings other than anger into practical consequences. Because of this, the parenting team needs to have as many options as possible in its repertoire. The following chapter contains a wealth of age-appropriate disciplinary techniques to choose from, increasing your flexibility and capacity to work together.

CHAPTER 7

EVERYTHING YOU NEED TO KNOW ABOUT DISCIPLINE

Practical Consequences by Age

As I've said in the previous chapters, relying only on anger to get your message across simply doesn't work. In the same way, relying on any one disciplinary approach—time-out, negotiation, tough love, the star system—puts the parenting team at risk. Why? Because children adapt to any method very quickly; today's effective technique becomes tomorrow's worn-out dance.

Since the parenting team is constantly under pressure to come up with new ways of staying in charge, the more options mothers and fathers have at their fingertips, the more flexible they can be. And flexibility is the best antidote to disagreements over discipline. Let's face it, most heated arguments arise when parents find themselves locked into "either/or" positions. (Dad threatens, "You've tried the star system already. That psychological nonsense doesn't work. What he needs is a good spanking." "Don't you dare go near him," shoots back Mom.)

To help "cut down" on parental arguments over discipline, here are over twenty-five time-tested, age-appropriate practical consequences that thousands of parents have found most effective.

AGES TWO TO FIVE: "TAMING MONSTERS"

1. Distraction is the bread-and-butter approach at this age, especially for the parent who puts in more time on the front lines. It is particularly effective with children who are younger than three or four.

   Unfortunately, distraction often causes dissension on the parenting team. Most mothers use this technique willingly, thinking to themselves, "Why create an unnecessary fight when we've got hours ahead of us?" Meanwhile, Dad often interprets her actions as "giving in" or as a form of bribery. He would be more comfortable if Mom could set clearer limits.

The truth is that with our youngest kids, *everything* has the potential to become an all-out battle. Particularly with preschoolers, the best strategy is to learn to use distraction more effectively, not to get rid of it.

Distraction works best before your child's tantrum begins escalating and he becomes unreachable. Young children can be sidetracked pretty easily, with a different toy or other desirable object. But as kids get older, usually after age three, you need to become more creative by focusing on something *entirely* different from whatever the fight is about.

For example, suppose your child is fixated on getting another stick of gum. You say "No," and offer several different kinds of fruit. Your child becomes increasingly angry. Instead of offering something else to go in his mouth, change direction immediately—start playing with a yo-yo, or show him a magic trick. At that moment, any food substitution will simply remind him of the gum he's not getting.

This abrupt change of direction can jar your child out of his tunnel vision. It also helps to spice up your new offering with a bit of silliness, an appeal to curiosity, or, at this age, gross humor. As one mom reported, "My four-year-old Jeremy and I were locked in a struggle—he wanted to pick up a piece of delicate pottery in a gift shop and I said he couldn't. His tantrum was moving along full-tilt until suddenly I said, 'Hey, is that a piece of bird poop on the window?' Jeremy's angry trance was immediately broken. 'Where?' he demanded. Within seconds he'd forgotten the fight. Instead, we tried to figure out from the color and size of the poop on the window what kind of bird it was, and what he must have had for dinner that evening. End of tantrum."

Remember, the earlier you intervene and the more original your distraction, the greater your chance of success.

2. Some tantrums simply won't respond to distraction. Of these, you must learn to identify—and then ignore—*manipulative* tantrums. These are fits of anger that occur immediately after you say "No." On the other hand, *temperamental* tantrums should be tended to immediately. These occur when a child is ill, tired, hungry, or over-

stimulated. Recognizing the difference will help parents find themselves on the same page when trying to rein in the hurricane force of a child's fury.

The next point of contention between parents is this: When do you approach a child who's having a nontemperamental tantrum? The answer is simple: Never approach while her rage is escalating. Wait until you see the first sign that the tantrum is leveling off. This reinforces the idea that your child will get what she needs when she's *in*, not out of, control. Then, suggest a kiss or that she sit on your lap.

3. Physically removing your child from a difficult situation can also work. The change of context often releases children and parents from feeling locked in. Who should remove the child? Not the one who "cares" the most about the issue—as is often suggested. (This subtly reinforces the "Mom's in charge" paradigm.) The parent who's more *resilient* at the moment needs to take charge. Prepare yourself: When you change locations, your child will at first become even more upset. If you can hang in through this temporary escalation, both of you will absolutely begin to calm down.

4. Always restrain children from hurting themselves or others. Kids should not be allowed to hit—you or anyone else—even if it doesn't hurt. Sometimes mothers are more patient with young children who hit them than fathers are. Many men have complained to me about the "indignity" their wives suffer allowing themselves to be hit by an upset youngster, and how such tolerance spoils the child. Mothers, on their part, are often afraid to "squelch" a show of spirit.

But in this case, I feel that the dads are usually right, for several reasons. Hitting doesn't end at home, but often generalizes to other places and people as well. Reacting physically is also a difficult habit to break once it takes hold. Furthermore, you don't want your kids to grow up thinking that Mom—women—will tolerate almost anything, even physical assaults.

Here's one extremely effective way to teach your child to keep his hands to himself: try holding him in a big bear hug to prevent him from lashing out. Forcefully say, "I won't let you hit." Again, there's no magic: be prepared. At first he will scream louder and struggle even more violently. That's when you have to hold on especially tight. Slowly, as he begins to feel your conviction—and your power to securely contain him—he will begin to calm down.

5. Use brief time-out periods, but only with children younger than five or six. As children get older, I guarantee they'll begin to defy your command to leave the room.

    Here are some guidelines to keep in mind when you use the time-out technique:

    • Shorter and enforceable periods work better than longer, nonenforceable ones.
    • Send children to a quiet place—no entertainment centers, please—preferably one with a door between you and them.
    • Explain in one brief sentence why you've decided on a time-out: "I can't think straight when you scream and yell like this."
    • Don't add to the power struggle by saying, "Think about what you did wrong."
    • Calm yourself down while they're gone.
    • Don't bring up the subject once they come out—it will likely st:art up the whole argument again.

6. Sequential rewards are those activities built into everyday routine, and are the most natural way of getting things to move along: for example, "If you get dressed more quickly, you can watch five minutes of *SpongeBob* later." This is not bribery, as I have heard during many a parental argument over discipline, but real leverage that doesn't seem arbitrary or artificial to children. Because it's part of the rhythm of life, kids understand better where the "punishment" comes from; it also teaches them that there are consequences to unwanted behaviors.

AGES SIX TO EIGHT: "IT'S NOT FAIR!"

1. Sequential rewards also work well with kids this age. But (and it is a big but) you've got to expect more *negotiating*. For example, when you say, "How about if you put on your socks and shoes now and then watch two minutes of *SpongeBob* later?" don't expect immediate compliance. Your six- to eight-year-old will try to bargain for just socks, and five minutes of *SpongeBob*, instead of simply accepting your terms.

    If you're continually negotiating everything—which often leaves your spouse feeling aggravated (and left out) it's time to put a cap on bargaining. Just lay out the reward plain and simple—"Shoes and socks now or no *SpongeBob* later"—and leave the room. When you return, though, and there's been no movement, you've got to follow through with your warning.

2. To deal with a more sophisticated child, offer her *limited* choices. "You can wash your face first, or brush your teeth. Which do you want to do?" This positive approach makes kids feel as if they have some say-so over their lives, which they begin to need at this age. At the same time, the chore is getting done with you setting the parameters. Limited choice is one of those discipline techniques that both the stricter and more lenient parent in the house appreciate.

3. Leave a situation once it gets too hot. Children this age have perfected pushing buttons by the artful use of favorite phrases like "It's not fair!" Such phrases seem to physiologically provoke many parents, let's say Dad, into screaming, "Well, buster, life's not fair!" This is the perfect moment for Mom, who's feeling frustrated herself, to jump in with an angry defense of her child.

   In truth, there's no point wrangling with child or spouse—when your child's this defiant. It makes more sense to say to both, "I can't think clearly now. When we all calm down, we'll talk about this." Both mothers and fathers may object to this approach, thinking it sounds like giving in (men are especially hesitant). Actually, it teaches your child that:

   • There's a time to talk, and a time when it's useless.
   • There are consequences to his behavior.
   • There are limits to your endless reserve of patience.

   These are all messages both parents can usually agree on.

   But beware: once you walk away, your child will probably follow you. You may have to go into another room, and close (sometimes even lock) the door. After an initial burst of fury, almost every kid I've ever run across (remember, this is for children old enough that there's no concern over their physical danger) gets the message and will slowly calm down.

4. Ask your child for solutions. This technique is especially effective because elementary school-aged kids are hungry to take on more re-

sponsibility. Say, "Look, Harold, you've been taking so much time getting dressed in the mornings we've been late to school every day. Plus, I've haven't been on time for work. We need to do something about this. What do you think is a solution?"

This puts children in positions of responsibility while at the same time it lets them know that you don't always have the answers—a healthy message for latency-aged kids. Often, children are so eager to give their input that they'll practically bubble over with suggestions.

For those of you who are skeptical, I didn't believe this technique would work either. But surprisingly it often does. For example, Harold's idea was to get dressed in his older brother's room instead of having to be alone. This worked without fail for a number of months—an excellent track record for any childrearing technique. So when you're stuck, don't fight with your spouse. Ask your child to contribute a fresh perspective.

5. The old-fashioned star system of rewards works with grade-school kids because they're very rule-oriented and appreciate a systematic approach. Make sure the stars on a chart, for example, are visible and lead to a modest reward.

    Unfortunately, this method has a short shelf life: once demerits start outweighing stars, or the rate of earning rewards slows down, it quickly loses its appeal, gets forgotten, or becomes boring. It's best used with a specific purpose in mind, as when you want your child to perform a certain chore—and then only for a short period of time. A couple of weeks, or perhaps a month, is the most that you can expect.

6. Post schedules and lists of chores on bedroom doors, refrigerators, or in the bathroom. Like the star system, this approach is both highly visible and systematic. Let your child choose the order of tasks to be done, and check off each as it's accomplished.

7. Use hypothetical situations involving another child to problem-solve with yours. For example, say, "Gabriel has a hard time sharing his toys. How do you think his parents can help *him*?" This is an excellent way for mothers and fathers to have nonconfrontational discussions about rules with children. This usually appeals to both the stricter and the more lenient parent in your family. But remember, initiate these talks only between fights and when tempers have cooled.

Also, books, television programs, or movies are excellent spring-boards for problem-solving conversations.

A final word: When you try any of these indirect methods, be sure not to end with a question that brings "reality" into the discussion, such as, "How do you think Gabriel's situation applies to you?" This will immediately undo the good feelings and erase the worthy message you've been attempting to get across.

8. Appeal to your child's sense of empathy; for example, "It doesn't seem fair when you talk to me like that. You wouldn't like it, either." Kids this age are so obsessed by fairness that they can understand your point—if it's presented between confrontations. When grade-schoolers aren't upset, they are childhood's biggest proponents of the Golden (Do unto Others) Rule.

For example, this technique is especially useful when visiting other people, or when you have company—a prime time for parental tension and disagreement. Prepare your child so she knows exactly what you expect of her, as in, "When we get to Aunt Elsie's house, we want to enjoy ourselves, too. So remember, be polite at the table and no baby talk. If you slip into it, we'll give you this signal." The more you're specific and ask for what you need to feel good (as distinct from an arbitrary, impersonal, "because it's right" approach), the more you tap into your child's "do unto others" philosophy.

AGES NINE TO ELEVEN: "THE ART OF THE DEAL"

1. Put a time limit on all negotiations: "We'll give you five minutes to prepare your best case, then we'll make a decision." Otherwise you sign your life away. The capacity for endless negotiation is one of the hallmarks of preadolescence: Everything before was simply a warm-up. Allowing yourself to be sucked into every negotiation they desire puts an enormous strain on the parenting team. For one thing, preteens love the "art of the deal" so much and are willing to devote such energy to this purpose that it will eat away at those few moments when parents can get to see each other. Second, many fathers view Mother's patience and open-ended willingness to negotiate as spoiling. To protect everyone's sanity, put a time cap on all negotiations.

2. Short-term contracts kept in plain sight are helpful with this litigious age group. Since they're masters at reinterpretation, use sim-

ple terms—"If you come home at four P.M. [versus "on time"] from your friend's house Monday through Thursday [versus "every day this week"], you'll be entitled to stay out until five P.M. [versus "an extra hour"] on Friday afternoon." Insist that everyone sign it. And remember, after the signing, don't reopen negotiations: stick to your terms. Like major league baseball players, kids this age think contracts exist to be renegotiated. Try not to fall for it.

3. Your greatest leverage at this age is limiting their access to pop culture and friends, TV, video games, phone privileges. However, be sure to set limits that are *enforceable*. An impulsively said restriction such as "No TV or phone for two weeks" will come back to haunt you. Your child will do anything he can to get you to rescind it. This includes playing one parent off against the other, and enlisting the less angry parent to soften the restriction. It's better for the parenting team—and your child will learn more about consequences—to think modestly and realistically when it comes to creating consequences that have real impact.

   Also, since limiting pop culture is so powerful, make sure that it logically connects to the crime committed and is not just some arbitrary punishment from on high: "Since you didn't clear off the table like you were supposed to, you lose a half-hour off your video privileges for the evening. When you don't do your job, you create extra work for everyone else, so you don't get to relax as much either."

4. As with younger children, ask for solutions. And, of course, given their predisposition to haggle, be prepared for ludicrous first offers (the best I've heard, from an enterprising nine-year-old: "If I make sure my room is clean for a whole month, how about a trip to Hawaii?"). As always, limit the ensuing negotiations; otherwise, you'll be up all night, half of it fighting with your partner. Remember (especially as anger toward your spouse increases) that kids love negotiating more than they care about the privilege or the material object they're negotiating for. This helps you keep matters in perspective, making it more difficult to get lost in a parental argument.

5. Respect your child's moodiness—whether after a confrontation over the rules, or even if it's inexplicable. At this age, he shouldn't be pushed to talk. Unlike six-year-olds, preteens cannot be cajoled out of moods by the promise of ice cream or by your persistence. And,

as I suggested earlier, one parent will rush to a "badgered" child's defense. So instead of pushing, suggest an activity you can do to-gether but that doesn't require direct engagement. Go to the hard-ware store, for instance, or ask his help in preparing a snack. This kind of parallel activity often triggers unexpected conversation.

6. Each parent should write up a "gripe list," compare them, and then begin to work on those areas of agreement first. If you include only the struggles that you believe will physically or psychologically harm your child for life, your list of essential gripes will be short-ened by at least 50 percent. You'll see that the rest simply aren't worth the aggravation, or a parental fight.

   For example, if sibling disagreements bother both of you more than messiness, concentrate on this area and let neatness tempo-rarily slide. With both parents in agreement, your consequences will have bite and will definitely be more enforceable.

   What if you can't agree on *any* essential area? This is one of the few times that I recommend you immediately go to counseling, or seek some form of parental guidance. If you and your spouse can't agree on at least one or two areas of importance, you may be expe-riencing an underlying marital difficulty that needs to be addressed.

7. Try to forget "the room." This topic is genuinely divisive, but in my experience with families I've learned the hard way that you should try to disengage on this one as much as possible. Preteens interpret attempts to interfere with their rooms as encroachments on their bodies. If, however, the mess in the bedroom *threatens* the rest of the house (for example, there's an odor, or the potential for insect infestation), then you must draw the line. Give your child a limited choice: "Okay, Peter, here's your choice. Either (a) you clean it up on your own by tomorrow; (b) we'll do it together; (c) I'll do it alone; or (d) I'll pay your younger brother to help me."

8. As preteens approach adolescence, their quest for greater freedom can create tremendous tension on the parenting team. The most ba-sic and helpful stance for both the parenting relationship and your child is the following: Expanded privileges need to be *earned*; they are not inalienable rights.

   Since children this age are capable of empathy, explain to them during a calm moment that you need to see some indication of increased responsibility and sensitivity to *your* experience before granting more privileges: "Patricia, you can ride into town if you come home by five o'clock. This way we'll learn that you can handle yourself, and I won't worry so much."

AGES TWELVE TO FIFTEEN: "LET ME GO! ... EXCEPT WHEN I WANT YOU"

1. Longer-term contracts (for example, "If you maintain a B average all semester, you can take riding lessons") help to keep you and your adolescent out of each other's hair, and can lessen nightly parenting battles. Since most young adolescents think of any parental demand as a form of persecution, contracts help make the rules seem more abstract and therefore less emotionally charged.

   Kids this age should, of course, be allowed input with the understanding that you, the parenting team, will make the final decision. Some families even stage elaborate signing ceremonies. One of the more inventive and inexpensive I've heard about took place at Pizza Hut over a large pepperoni pizza.

2. Pick your battles wisely, but be willing to "go to the mat" for those issues that are especially meaningful to you. For example, you may decide to concede on the hairstyle but insist on an appropriate curfew. Try to strengthen your team by connecting with other mothers and fathers in a peer group for parents. (I describe these groups in great detail later in this book and in *Parenting by Heart*.) Parent groups help you:

   - Learn about what's going on around the neighborhood. This immediately puts you and your spouse on a similar wavelength;
   - Feel stronger making tough decisions once you know that other families are struggling to set limits just as you are. Remember, in unity there is strength, making it easier to set consistent guidelines for parties and curfew.
   - More effectively counter the "everyone's doing it" argument your teenager will offer up.

   Kids are at first outraged that parents actually talk to each other—peer groups are supposed to be for kids, right? Then they secretly feel relieved that someone's trying to be in charge.

3. Learn as much as you can about your child's world. Listen to some of her music, go see a movie she loves, accompany him to an activity you can't stand. Yes, Mom, a monster-truck marathon is not exactly appealing, but it is a very effective way to build a bridge to your otherwise ornery adolescent. Dad, her music may disgust you, but it will help you to see a little bit more about what makes her tick. These efforts not only give you more to talk about, but also give you greater leverage in negotiations since you know better what matters most to her.

4. Learn the language of relationships to gain cooperation ("How do you think others will feel about what you did?" "I need you to be punctual; otherwise I worry."). Teenagers are extremely social beings and can—if you're straightforward—understand the importance of your feelings and your desire to keep your relationship intact. They may mock you at first, but hang tough and insist that you have needs as well.

   If you cannot ever get your adolescent to understand your needs, even when she's calm, it may be the sign of a problem that should be explored. Again, this is one of the times I recommend that you seek out short-term counseling to discuss what else may be going on in your child's life.

5. With adolescents, *all* consequences should contain three points. These set limits and recognize your inherent lack of control over your child's growing independence:

   • This is exactly what I want. ("I don't want you smoking at the concert.")
   • This is what will happen if I find out you didn't comply. ("I won't trust you and will end up worrying, so no more concerts for three months.")
   • But I can't always be there with you and monitor everything. ("In the end, you'll have to make your own decision, knowing exactly what I think, and what will happen if you don't listen.")

All of these techniques will help teach your child consequences and lessen tension on the parenting team. But *you must remember to vary them*. When a technique loses its effectiveness, don't blame yourself or your partner—just try a new one. The more options both parents have, the less you'll feel locked into untenable situations and susceptible to taking it out on each other. With children of all ages, consistency isn't the hallmark of parents who work together—flexibility is.

CHAPTER 8

HOW WOMEN AND MEN COMMUNICATE DIFFERENTLY WITH KIDS

What We Can Learn from Each Other

There's no way around it—having conversations with children of any age is a difficult art to master. Of course, why should this come as a surprise? Adults rarely have an easy time talking to each other, either. Men and women, in particular, seem to have such trouble communicating that dozens of books about our different communicational styles and emotional needs are published every year. Isn't it interesting, though, that almost no attention has been paid to the impact of these differences on *children*?

After watching thousands of parents and kids try to "get through to each other," it's clear that mothers and fathers do communicate differently with kids and that this has a profound influence on how well the parenting team operates. However, despite our differences and the tensions that arise from them, men and women can learn a great deal from one another about how to talk better with children—and at the same time cut down on needless fights between family members.

KIDS SPEAK AT THE DARNEDEST TIMES

That kids talk more to mothers than fathers about "the things that matter" is one of the most noticeable imbalances in family life. Longitudinal research has shown that even recalcitrant adolescents turn to their moms more than dads to discuss emotional issues. I'll never forget fifteen-year-old John, who said with *pride* in his voice: "My dad and I have a really strong father–son thing. But of course, we never say anything *personal* to each other. I save that stuff for my mom."

This imbalance strikes at the very heart of families. When one partner is more trusted and has access to more information, the whole parenting team is thrown out of kilter.

Why do kids (as always, there are exceptions) open up more easily to their mothers? Do mothers intuitively know the secret words that unlock their children's hearts and loosen their tongues, or is it simply that women are socialized to be better listeners than men? While each of these explanations is partially correct, neither gets to the bottom of the problem.

The fundamental reason for the communication imbalance is so simple and obvious that we completely overlook it:

Children open up when you least expect them to, during the ordinary moments of daily life, to whoever happens to be around— and even in this day and age, who is that most likely to be?

A friend of mine tells a story of driving Max, her eight-year-old, to his basketball game. They were running late. Max was listening to the radio; she was mentally reviewing the next five items on her Endless List, which had to be taken care of before dinner. All of a sudden, while they were stopped at a red light, Max turned to her and said, "Mom, did you ever use drugs when you were a kid?"

"I knew he'd ask something like that one day," my friend said. "I just didn't expect it would be this soon. And I didn't think he'd pick a moment like this to ask. I'd always imagined that he'd see an antidrug ad on TV, and that would spark a discussion. Why he asked me then, in the car, I have no idea."

Most definitely, it was because they were together during a quiet moment. Think of the last meaningful conversation you had with your child: Where did it take place? You were probably rushing to the library to return books before it closed, sorting laundry, setting the table for dinner, or driving to the mall.

That's when kids open up—out of the blue. The art of talking to children rests on one immutable fact: *Conversations, like quality time, can't be penciled in*. To kids, talking is done while you're doing something else, or during downtime. A heart-to-heart isn't something you can plan on, but something that unexpectedly happens when you happen to be together.

The author of the children's book series about Samantha Parkington understands this reality as well as any child psychologist. In *Meet Samantha*, Susan Adler writes that nine-year-old Samantha and her adult friend Hawkins

> had their best talks when Samantha followed him around on his jobs, washing furniture, beating the carpets or washing the windows. . . . Now Hawkins handed Samantha a polishing cloth. He knew how much easier it is to talk when your hands are busy.

LETTING CONVERSATIONS HAPPEN

This fact of life—that kids talk in the midst of doing other activities—almost *guarantees* that children have many more opportunities to communicate with Mom than with Dad. The less Dad is involved, the fewer natural opportunities arise for spontaneous communication.

What about all those special, "up-time" daddy events? Unfortunately, these don't count when it comes to fostering communication. Try making yourself heard at a basketball game, on a Ferris wheel, or over a blaring PA system at the circus. You may get a thrill when "The Wave" surges through your section of the ballpark, but the setting is far from intimate, and it's certainly not the quiet sort of activity that encourages kids to open up. Once again, the basic participation issue—who does more of the daily hands-on caretaking—casts its long shadow.

Burt, a father I work with, knew that his eight-year-old stepson Charlie was having trouble at school but couldn't get Charlie to talk about it. Burt's information was mostly secondhand, from his wife Yvonne. Feeling more than a little peripheral, he'd second-guess and criticize her. Predictably, Yvonne would then feel aggravated with him for being a backseat driver and not showing sufficient interest.

"But I *am* interested," Burt objected to me. "I ask Charlie every day how school went and he doesn't answer me. What am I doing wrong?"

"You're too goal-oriented," I responded. "Just because you ask a question doesn't mean that he'll open up. Do something ordinary with him on a regular basis, and you'll see—he'll naturally talk to you about the things that matter to him."

So Burt began to take Charlie with him every Saturday and Sunday to get the newspaper—a leisurely fifteen-minute stroll into town. After just a few weeks of this tiny change, Charlie "out of the blue" mentioned that he had become the class scapegoat. Burt was shocked *and* encouraged at how open his reticent boy had suddenly become.

This fifteen-minute change of routine—and that's all it often takes—accomplished three things: First, it created a way for father and son to communicate without Mom as intermediary. Second, Burt and Yvonne fought less about who was the real "expert" when it came to Charlie. Finally, it allowed Mom a few treasured minutes alone.

IS THIS ALL THERE IS?

Mothers don't usually have to be reminded to spend ordinary downtime with their kids. However, they often discount the importance of these on-the-run conversations. Many mothers believe that unless they're having heart-to-hearts (like those Supermoms on TV) they're doing something wrong. True, a conversation in the midst of getting the house ready for company or driving to pick up pizza doesn't have the same official stamp of "intimacy" as snuggling on the couch or having a quiet talk at bedtime.

But this is when kids naturally open up. The best you can do is accept that the most important information you'll get will be in the form of a two-minute sound bite dropped in your lap when you least expect it.

WHAT KIDS HATE ABOUT TALKING
TO MOM AND DAD

Spending enough time with your kids to encourage conversation is the first step. Next, you have to understand that certain aspects of *both* women's and men's communicational styles drive kids up the wall. Here are the major gripes kids have about the way their parents approach conversations—and what you can do.

"Earth to Dad"

When I ask kids why they don't talk more to Dad, they usually complain, "Dad is too busy," or "He's in a bad mood," or "He's worrying about other things." What they're intuitively sensing is their fathers' emotional preoccupation or absence.

When Dad is not fully present, kids act up in all kinds of creative ways. Suddenly Billy "accidentally" trips on the stairs. Out of nowhere, Julie and Amy start fighting over a toy neither of them really cares about. Francis won't get out of the way of his father's favorite TV show. From my perspective, incidents like these are often attempts to make Dad sit up and take notice, to rouse him from his worried slumber.

Unfortunately, "pay attention to me" gestures can escalate into battles—not just between parent and child, but also between Mom and Dad. After all, when children complain about Dad's inexpressiveness, mothers are put in a difficult position: If you defend your husband by saying, "Daddy's really listening to you," it may sound inauthentic since ten minutes earlier you lodged the same complaint yourself. On the other hand, if you agree with your kids too often, you enter into a troublesome alliance against Dad.

When Bad Things Happen . . . Dad Opens Up

This "Earth to Dad" phenomenon frustrates children. But what confuses them even more is that their fathers do occasionally open up. After years of watching the ups and downs of family life, I've observed that fathers most often open up *during a crisis*. When there's a death in the family, a business failure, or a divorce, the wall around Dad may crumble. This is when kids learn facts about their fathers' lives they'd never previously known.

For example, seventeen-year-old Julian told me that the best conversation he'd *ever* had with his father, Ed, took place when he was twelve, after his dad had suffered a mild heart attack. During Ed's recuperation, Julian mustered the courage to ask, "Dad, do you get heart attacks because I do things that upset you?"

Ed, feeling more vulnerable at this moment, said, "Of course not. I worry about a lot of things. I worry about work. I worry about the stock market. Sure, we sometimes argue with each other, but the last thing that could ever cause me to get sick is you! Actually, I used to feel guilty about the way I acted toward *my* parents, too. Did I ever tell you that . . . ?"

Frank, a man I see in counseling, complained that the only time his father truly complimented him was after his grandmother died: "Son, I guess I shouldn't wait for times like these, but I want you to know that I really admire what a good person you've become. I'm very proud of you." Frank couldn't stop crying when he related this memory.

The idea that men often open up to kids during some kind of emotional trauma resonates with women's resentment about the men in their lives. As Rhonda told me after her father-in-law died, "It's very hard to admit this, but I've *enjoyed* the last few weeks since Eric's father died. He's been more open. We've been going through something together and we're sharing it. And because he's more vulnerable, he's been telling me things that are usually very hard for him to talk about. I'm sure that as life gets back to normal, he'll go back to being his typical closed self. Do I have to wait for something bad to happen before we really communicate again?"

What to Do

As a result of this wall of silence, women and kids complain, and mothers and fathers fight. What can you do?

Divide the chores on the Endless List more evenly. Nothing works as well to open up the lines of communication in every direction. Participation in ordinary, down-time activities leads to free-flowing communication. Take your child along on that fifteen-minute stroll to get the newspaper; make pancakes with the kids on Sunday morning; alternate putting the kids to bed each night (bedtime is far and away the favorite time for kids of all ages to open up); take turns arranging play-dates.

When both parents participate in the hands-on fabric of everyday life, we simply have more to talk about. We stop living parallel lives and having to bridge the gap between us with resentful accusations. Dividing up the Endless List won't necessarily bring romance back into your relationship (although many mothers report that their anger subsides enough so that they do feel more sexual)—but it's the right place to start.

"Be More Specific, Dad"

Unfortunately, when well-intentioned, loving fathers do engage in conversation, they often ask questions that are too vague and not specific enough for kids' tastes. Speaking for many of us, Jerry, a dad in a parenting workshop, poignantly said to his nine-year-old son Josh, "I'm tired of hearing everything from your mother. It really aggravates me. Why don't you give me a straight answer when I ask you about school?"

"Because you don't ask specific questions," Josh articulately replied. "When you say, 'How was school today?' I don't know what you mean. If you were more specific, I'd remember better and I'd also believe that you *really* wanted to know what was going on."

Josh's words plunged one hundred parents and children into total silence. You could feel sadness spread throughout the entire room. This classic misunderstanding between father and son is both tragic and incredibly familiar. Jerry *does* care—you should have seen the pained look on his face. But his inability to ask precise, detailed questions causes Josh to question his sincerity. Like too many fathers, Jerry then ends up feeling rejected. The cycle of imbalance is perpetrated—he subtly withdraws, relying on, yet increasingly resenting, his wife's position as family switchboard, and she feels central, but increasingly overwhelmed.

Of course, kids don't always answer their mothers' questions about school either, but for different reasons, which I'll discuss shortly. In this specific situation, Jerry and Josh's predicament says something to all fathers: Dad, if you really want to know what happened in school, then you've got to know exactly who's in the class, who rides the bus, what project they're working on in science, and how your child felt that morning. Was she tired or hungry? Did all her homework get done? Was she looking forward to music, or was she anxious about the spelling test?

Without these facts at your fingertips, all you can really think to say is "So how was school today?" And you've got to be prepared for the inevitable answer—"Fine. Got any gum?"—which will probably leave you wishing that you'd never asked.

Dad, Don't Be So Polite

Kids of *all* ages give off "don't bug me" vibes that are impossible to miss. They avoid important questions by changing the subject, by answering a question you didn't ask, or by saying nothing at all. Unfortunately, many fathers interpret these maddening responses to mean "I don't *ever* want to talk about it."

When you combine men's reluctance to appear intrusive with their ignorance of specific details, you end up with a recipe for a conversation that will go nowhere:

DAD: So how was school?

DAUGHTER: Fine.

DAD: What did you learn?

DAUGHTER: I can't remember.

DAD: Did you have a good day?

DAUGHTER: Mom, can I have macaroni and cheese tonight?

Facing a roadblock like this, many fathers feel subtly rejected and then angry at their partners. In response, they withdraw, creating more of an imbalance and greater tension on the parenting team. Eventually, as the years of imbalanced communication accumulate, Dad can end up feeling irrelevant and like a guest in his own home, This is a surefire recipe for anger and resentment between parents, especially when decisions have to be made and one partner holds all the relevant information.

What to Do

Now, look what happens to the same conversation if at this point you're armed with specific details and aren't afraid of being slightly intrusive:

DAD: Was Emily in math today?

DAUGHTER: Yeah.

DAD: Did she still have that cough from when she was sick last week?

DAUGHTER: No. Just a little. . . . But you know what? There was a fight between her and Suzie. All the kids got in trouble. Mrs. Haber was very mad, so Emily had to get a time-out, and then . . .

Of course, it doesn't always happen this way. Sometimes all the specific information in the world won't tempt your child into conversation. But instead of giving up (which many fathers and some therapy-minded "give them space" mothers do), remind yourselves that a conversational impasse doesn't always mean "No" or "Don't ask." "No" may also mean:

1. "I'm involved in something else right now."
2. "I don't remember back that far."
3. "You're not asking the right question—try another."
4. "Tell me about your day first."
5. "Try again later."

"Lower Your Voice, Dad"

Whenever I begin to work with a family to improve communication, I always ask the child this question: "If you had three wishes, what changes would you make in your family?"

What do you think the most popular response is? "I wish my father wouldn't yell so much."

It isn't that mothers don't yell at their kids. In fact, in many families mothers yell a great deal more than their spouses. But children perceive Dad's anger as more threatening and disruptive. This fact creates tension on the team, since mothers often protect their kids or feel forced to take sides.

Why is Dad's yelling harder to take than Mom's?

1. Men are used to sitting on their feelings, letting them out only when they become overpowering. The resulting explosion often frightens children precisely because it is so different from the usual flow of things around the house.
2. If the balance of participation is even slightly unequal, Mom talks to the kids more than Dad. When she gets upset and her voice rises a few decibels, it's not that unusual, and it doesn't threaten her

connection with the kids. But a raised voice from an even slightly removed father is likely to be heard as a rupture.

3. Fathers are more likely than mothers to withdraw after they get angry, partly out of guilt, and partly because the basic "Mom's responsible" paradigm gives them the space to withdraw at least momentarily. But parental withdrawal truly frightens children, even adolescents.

4. Kids often equate Dad's yelling with disappearing. This is partly because fathers are often the ones who leave the house in the event of a separation. These days even preschool-aged children are aware of divorce and have reasons to fear that if Dad gets angry enough he just may leave and not come back.

5. Often Dad explodes over something that happened outside of the home—usually having to do with work. Because the source of the anger isn't explained, Dad's yelling mystifies kids.

But Dad's yelling is *less* upsetting when he:

- Is involved with everyday, hands-on care.
- Explains what he was upset about.
- Doesn't sulk and withdraw afterward.
- Takes responsibility and apologizes for "losing it."

"Dad, No More Lectures, Please!"

Another conversation-stopper fathers specialize in is the temptation to look upon conversation with kids as an opportunity to *teach*. Men often find this professorial role comfortable because it's one of the main ways to be nurturing. Being the mentor, the one who instructs children in the ways of the "real world," seems the perfect complement to Mother, who (even though she's out in the world as well) may be more identified with emotional needs.

For the most part, teaching *is* a natural and valuable way for men to nurture. I remember when I was four years old and my own father taught me how to catch and throw a ball. His advice is indelibly etched in my memory: "Ronnie, make sure you hold your hands together like *this*. Then the ball can't slip through." I have the same vivid memory of a trick he called "thumbs around," a way of hooking your thumbs around the monkey bars. "You'll see, Ronnie, it's practically impossible to fall off when you do it this way." What pleasure I took in teaching my own son and daughter the same skills, feeling I was involved in a ritual that was generations old.

Mothers also teach—about *everything*. They too pass on skills, values, and ethics from one generation to the next. But for mothers, teaching is counterbalanced by Endless List hands-on care. Because men don't usually provide as much of the everyday nurturing, they rely too heavily on connecting with kids by teaching. And that's when trouble begins. A five-year-old automatically changes the subject as soon as there's a hint of yet another "lesson" on the way. "Daddy's lecturing again," huffs an impatient grade-schooler. "He's always telling me stories about when *he* was a kid," smirks an eleven-year-old.

This same overreliance on teaching also gets Dad into trouble with Mom. For example, thirteen-year-old Mitchell is having trouble in school. His parents, Dan and Alice, regularly argue over how to handle his underachievement. Practically every time Dan gets home from the office and discovers Mitchell glued to the telephone or staring at the television screen, Dan launches into his "value of hard work" lecture: "If you don't work harder now, how are you going to get into a good school? Your other friends seem more serious, and remember, they're the ones you're competing with. It isn't easy to get ahead. If I had taken your attitude as a kid, I wouldn't have gotten anywhere. . . ."

Unfortunately, Dan doesn't have much of an audience. Without special effects, few thirteen-year-olds can stay focused longer than it takes to say "Arnold Schwarzenegger." Mitchell mutters something along the lines of "Stop bothering me. Don't be such a dork."

Drawn in by the confrontation, Alice replies, "You *are* boring, Dan! No wonder he can't listen to you. And why are you coming home so late, anyway?" Dan and Alice then start arguing, at which point Mitchell throws them out of his room, invoking his "inalienable right to privacy."

Dan's problem is that he's not around enough to earn the right to teach or—even worse to a thirteen-year-old—to be *boring*. A workaholic, Dan spends virtually no time hanging out, joking around, or watching TV with Mitchell.

If, like Dan, teaching is the primary way you connect with your kids, you're in danger of becoming a peripheral, almost comical figure in your house. You're dismissed, much the way grade-school kids dismiss substitute teachers. And why not? Substitute teachers and professorial dads often haven't put in enough ordinary time. They haven't earned the right to demand respectful students or to teach much of anything.

When I suggested that Dan stop lecturing and start becoming involved—by checking homework assignments every other night, going to school meetings, or occasionally joining Mitchell to watch "dumb" videos—he started to gain some credibility. Mitchell didn't turn into the class brain, but he and his father had fewer fights. And Alice, heartened by Dan's increased presence, stopped automatically taking Mitchell's side against Dan.

Try a Little Tenderness

Most kids naturally look to Mom for tenderness, which creates a significant imbalance on the team. Many fathers, feeling left out, try to break into the communication loop. They offer exciting activities like trips to the circus; they roughhouse and toss kids into the air; they yell, criticize, or pout; they do *anything* to be heard. Many of these jarring techniques create tension on the parenting team.

One approach that works for both the team and children is tenderness. Here are some suggestions:

1. Approach your child slowly and respectfully. Get a sense of his mood and rhythm. Instead of gathering him up in a mighty bear hug, place your hand on his head, touch his shoulder, or give him a peck on the cheek.
2. Besides joining your child's mood, join her activities. Too often dads come home, create excitement, and don't get directly involved with the activity that had been in progress.
3. Show affection when you're most disappointed. Kids never forget the time that Dad greeted a poorer than usual report card with understanding rather than a lecture or a cold shoulder. Tender clichés, like "I love you no matter what" or "Next time you'll do better," help kids through difficult moments.
4. Share stories of your own childhood with your kids—but keep them brief. It's especially important to recall times when you were vulnerable, when you had hurt feelings, were disappointed, or cried.
5. Remember to say, "I love you." Don't fall for your preadolescent's

pseudoindependent act; she needs to hear it as much as she did when she was a toddler. If you're not the affectionate type, leave an "I love you" note on her bed, stuff it in her lunch box, or deliver the message over the phone.

6. Expect nothing in the way of gratitude or a show of affection from your kids. Similarly, don't expect that one moment of closeness will make the next one any easier. Children may seem unaffected by your tenderness. They listen with one ear, take it in stride, and are off to the next activity. But they store up these moments like pearls.

HOW GETTING HOME FIRST AFFECTS CONVERSATION

One of the most vexing difficulties parents have talking to their kids is trying to find out what happened in school. As most parents know, the answer to this simple question is almost invariably "'Nothing" or "It was fine."

Of course, kids *do* open up, *eventually*. Over a snack, they'll divulge who got the highest score on the math test, or who was punished during recess—but they only want to talk about it once. Kids hate to repeat themselves; I've heard this complaint literally hundreds of times: What this means is that whoever gets home first—and in my experience, this is usually Mom—gets the inside information firsthand.

Even mothers who work full-time often organize their day to arrive home first, preceding their partners by anywhere from ten minutes to several hours. That's why they tend to hear all the details about school, and why dads are so often left in the dark.

If Dad arrived home first a few times a week, he too would receive the few crumbs of information kids feel comfortable dispensing. The details and logistics may be difficult for men to arrange, but it means the difference between knowing what's going on in school—which, after all, takes up the bulk of a child's day—and getting secondhand information through Mom. This tiny change, alternating who gets home first over the course of a week, makes an enormous difference. It's as simple as that.

MISTAKES MOMS MAKE

Mothers Who Pounce

If kids complain that fathers don't talk enough or ask vague questions, they complain just as vehemently that mothers have the opposite problem. Moms *pounce* at the first sign that kids might want to open up.

This is understandable. For several decades the importance of "good" communication between parent and child (read: *mother* and child) has been stressed so thoroughly that today's mothers can't help but think of themselves as personal failures if kids don't open up to them. Whenever I do parenting workshops and a mother proclaims, "My child tells me everything!" the other women look at her with the same mixture of admiration, envy, and disbelief as forty years ago a group of mothers would have greeted the announcement, "All my children are perfect eaters!"

Of course, mothers have reason to be concerned about keeping the lines of communication open. These days, who gets to see each other? Everyone needs a datebook to keep up. Between your full-time job and the kids' hockey practice, gymnastics, art class, and a homework tutor, it's harder scheduling an appointment with a ten-year-old than with the CEO of a *Fortune* 500 corporation.

Unfortunately, our "Hello, I must be going" lifestyle unfolds against the backdrop of frightening concerns. Several generations ago a make-out party or a lit cigarette behind the barn would have driven parents up the wall with worry. How innocent these childhood rites of passage seem compared to drugs, AIDS, casual sex, street crime, kidnapping, and violence in the schools. Given the realities of modern life, who can blame mothers (or some fathers) for pouncing on their children at the first hint of a conversation?

However, Mom's pouncing often causes problems on the parenting team. Many fathers become extremely irritated when they hear Mom trying to extract information from a reticent child. Mom's relentless questioning, her furtive diary reading, and her secret room searching remind Dad of how *he's* supposed to open up more. Very often, he'll jump to his child's defense, accusing Mom of being overprotective or intrusive—and that sparks their next fight.

When there are important decisions to make—such as whether ten-year-old Freddy should be allowed to bicycle into town; whether five-year-old Nicole can go on the school bus by herself; or whether to grant fourteen-year-old Dimitri permission to attend a party without parents—Mom's vigilant need to know every detail may encourage Dad to take an overly permissive stance: "I just can't stomach the way she doesn't give them any space," he'll complain. Even though parents have a responsibility to know what's going on, Dad is partially right. Mom's eagerness for open communication won't work any better with the kids than it does with him. As soon as children sense that opening up means more to us than to them, they automatically clam up.

What to Do

How can you handle this quandary, finding out what you need to know about your kids' lives without turning them off?

First, if probing bothers your partner more than it does your children—and you *have* to probe because of safety concerns—then conduct your questioning when Dad isn't around. Why inflame the situation by subjecting an unwilling spouse to your third degree?

Next, don't drop everything immediately and pounce on your child just because it looks like she might want to talk. In fact, try putting your child off for a moment or two. She may become temporarily angry—"How *dare* you not listen when I've got something to say!"—but she may also become increasingly determined to speak her mind.

Third, trust that ordinary time together will create opportunities for you and your child to bring up mutual concerns.

Fourth, the quickest way to find out about what's happening in your kid's life is to talk about *your* day. Children of all ages take the cue to talk from their parents' conversation.

Finally, remember that worry is what often fuels a mother's pouncing. Learning to identify the "red flags" of emotional distress helps many mothers ease up on their need to be constantly vigilant. If you suspect that something's troubling your child, *stop forcing conversation.* It's unnecessary. Even the most uncommunicative children leave all kinds of signs and signals that they're in trouble. Keep these guidelines in mind, and you might not feel so driven to pounce.

THE RED FLAG CHECKLIST

You need to consider professional help if you notice:

1. A change of mood—a loss of interest in usual activities and friends, or inexplicable up and down periods.
2. Changes in biological rhythms, such as appetite, sleep patterns, and activity levels.
3. Change of attitude toward you—if your child seems uncharacteristically withdrawn, very defensive, and coldly hostile.
4. Declining school performance and attitude toward school.
5. Changes in the "crowd" he hangs out with—especially if the new crowd is one of the fringe groups at school.
6. Your child's diary left in *public places* on more than one occasion. This is usually her way of inviting you to read it and find out something she can't say face-to-face.
7. Your, child making comments about running away, or saying things like "You'd be better off without me." These need to be taken seriously, even if they turn out to be manipulations.

"Mom, Don't Use That Funny Tone of Voice"

Children have other problems communicating with mothers. When modern mothers rely too heavily on child-centered, "therapeutic" approaches, they tend to drive kids away with their forced sincerity. By "child-centered," I mean those communicational techniques that ask you to *always*: respect your child's space; speak in modulated tones so as not to overpower or oppress children; make direct and intimate eye contact; not respond with your own emotions; and name and validate feelings. ("Oh, Suzie, you must feel really happy about winning the race!" or "Oh, Joey, you must have been angry when that little boy hit you.")

This parent-as-therapist stance works very well some of the time, especially with younger children. But after a while, it drives even the young ones a little buggy. Preteens and adolescents often tell me, "Whenever my mom starts talking in that funny voice, it makes me want to puke!" The mother of seven-year-old Ilene reported that after one week of trying a child-centered communicational approach her daughter screamed, "Don't ever talk to me in that funny voice again!"

These techniques, applied too religiously, create trouble on the parenting team as well. Fathers, who usually haven't read the latest how-to book, often interpret this mode of communication as "babying" a child. Part of this reaction is fueled by Dad's *envy*. As Bill, the father of two children, said: "Her tenderness seems reserved for the kids. All *I* get is the anger and criticism."

To offset this "precious" handling, many dads feel compelled to balance matters with "good, old-fashioned" bluntness: "Enough of this psychology!" they demand. Mothers then recoil at Dad's approach. It sounds unnecessarily harsh, especially after reading dozens of magazine articles by child experts who warn about the danger of harming children's self-esteem. Before you know it, a full-scale parenting battle ensues.

What to Do

To lessen the chance of "overtherapizing" your child, hurting your spouse's feelings, and starting a parental fight, USE CHILD-CENTERED TECHNIQUES ONLY:

1. When children are *under* five years of age.
2. If children of any age are very *scared* or *sick*.
3. If your child has been *humiliated* or suffered a loss.
4. During *tender, vulnerable* moments, such as bedtime, or when he's sharing something with you for the first time.

DON'T USE THE TECHNIQUES:

1. When your child is *angry* or frustrated—she'll only become more upset.
2. With feisty *preteens* or *adolescents—they* need to "mix it up" with you.
3. *In front of other kids*—it's humiliating.
4. *All* the time. Your kids will tune you out before you can catch your breath.

"Mom, That's Not What I Mean!"

Another problem mothers have is *assuming* they know what's on a child's mind. I've worked with children for over three decades; the more I talk with them, the less I know what they're thinking.

I'm reminded of a conversation I overheard in the playground a few years ago: A five-year-old girl discovers her goldfish floating upside down and asks her mother, "Is Rupert dead?" Thinking her daughter must be sad (after all, that's the way *she* felt when her first childhood pet died), Mom launches into a long and serious discussion of death. When she finishes, the girl looks up and says, "Well, if Rupert's dead, can we eat him tonight for supper?"

Psychologists Suzie Orbach and Louise Eichenbaum call this overidentification between women "merged attachment." Let's say your eight-year-old daughter Marissa approaches you with a problem concerning her best friend, Ariel. Without waiting for the details, you respond with a heartfelt "I know *exactly* how you feel. I had the same problem when I was in fifth grade. I lost my best friend and was ostracized by the group because I didn't fit in." Meanwhile Marissa is growing angrier by the minute. *Her* problem is that Ariel is too bossy. Marissa ends up feeling more dejected than before the conversation began and you feel thwarted. End of discussion.

If either parent "assumes," it's almost impossible to avoid trouble. But Mom's (even Stepmother's) assumptions carry a special "Mother knows best" weight that can make Dad feel out of it. As one father said, "Why should I even bother to talk to my daughter and come up with my own opinion? My wife is already convinced her view is the only right one. Anyway, she's a mother, so maybe she *does* know."

Such a situation occurred when eleven-year-old Kyra was about to go to her first "social." She felt extremely nervous and jittery about the event, but wouldn't explain her concerns. Stepmom assumed Kyra was shy about dancing with boys and made several attempts to discuss this with her. Dad countered, "Look, how do you *know* what her mood is about?"

Alice replied, "I just *know* these things. Remember, I was a girl once too."

If this were a TV sitcom about blended families, Alice and Kyra would settle into a cozy discussion and clear the air—within thirty minutes, no more. But in my experience with real families, it doesn't always turn out that way. The more Kyra stonewalled, the angrier Alice and Dad got—at each other.

"Leave her alone," Dad insisted. "You're making too big a deal out of this."

"You always minimize *everything emotional*. But I can tell she's anxious about dealing with those boys."

Mom and Dad spent the evening aggravated with each other. To add insult to injury, they later found out that Kyra had actually been nervous about something entirely different—the possibility that her best friend (who had a crush on Billy) would ignore her at the dance. What a wasted evening Kyra's parents spent! When it comes to kids, we're *never* safe when we assume.

Assuming . . . and the Boy in Your Life

With boys, mothers make a different kind of assumption. Worrying that reticence will surely lead to psychological problems, or fearful that their sons will become grown-up versions of their uncommunicative spouses, mothers try every possible tactic to pry boys open—especially if an upsetting event has occurred.

For example, suppose your preteenager Zachary has been hassled or mugged by some tough kids. You (understandably) assume that this is a traumatic experience. But you also *mistakenly* assume that it must be talked about so Zachary can "get his feelings off his chest." The more Zach says, "I'm okay. It's no big deal," the more you worry that burying his real feelings will lead to psychological problems—and that you're falling short in the Mrs. Huxtable department (*The Cosby Show*, still going strong in reruns).

Meanwhile, Dad jumps in with his own personal agenda about the "opening up" issue: "Leave the boy alone. You dig too deeply into everything." Before you know it, you and Dad are embroiled in the classic "men don't talk, women are intrusive" argument and. Zach, sensing an opening, escapes to his room—no more inclined to discuss his experience than before this hubbub erupted.

As a psychologist, it took me years to accept the fact that boys who remain stoical—even after an upsetting incident—don't always develop emotional problems down the road. I, too, assumed that they must be burying feelings to their own emotional detriment. But as Zach told me, he just wasn't that upset about being hassled. "A lot of kids have had trouble," he insisted. Aside from some temporary caution, he showed no emotional ill effects whatsoever. And without any further prompting, he began to casually mention the incident a few weeks later.

Zach's reaction is not unusual. We shouldn't assume anything about how boys or girls react to difficult experiences. But it's especially important not to pressure boys to open up. By school age, many boys experience pressure to reveal inner feelings as humiliating. They think their mothers are saying to them, "You must be *hiding* something shameful." And shucking clams is a snap compared to prying secrets out of a boy who's decided to "clam up."

What to Do

Remember, when you assume you know *exactly* how your child feels or that he must open up for his own good, that's exactly the time to prepare yourself for a surprise. Instead, try asking one or two specific, action-oriented questions. If he seems hesitant to share, *be patient*. Trust that if something is really upsetting him, the truth will eventually surface. If you're really worried, watch for the red-flag signals I described earlier in this chapter. In most cases, though, you won't have to wait for red flags to appear. One day, while raking leaves together, or in between activities, he'll turn to you and say, "Remember that time they found graffiti in the school bathroom? Well, I . . . "

When Negotiations Drag on Too Long

One of the most aggravating tensions on the parenting team results from the different ways mothers and fathers negotiate. Mothers complain about the endless negotiation that's a normal part of life with the kids. Fathers, though, often interpret it as a form of "spoiling." Mothers respond by accusing fathers of being impatient or arbitrary. Both are partially right. But the bottom line is that for kids' and parents' sakes, negotiation does need some limits. If negotiation has become the only way that Mom can gain a child's compliance, then you need to take Dad's concerns more seriously.

What to Do

Here are some guidelines, Mom, for effective negotiation.

First, don't negotiate when your child is upset. It will fall on deaf ears. At the same time, don't negotiate when *you're* upset. Instead, say, "I'm too upset to continue talking about this right now. I can't think straight anymore. We'll talk more about it later." Discontinue negotiations if you notice your child in "rejection mode." Each offer you make will only fuel another rejection. Always put a time limit on negotiations. Otherwise, your child will stall and try to wear you down. Say, "You have five minutes to convince me." With younger kids, use a kitchen timer.

If a decision must be made on the spot, it's best to make it immediately and live with the consequences rather than let frustration and anger build up—and *then* give in. Remember too that if you think of a better solution later, you can always change your mind.

If you lose it during negotiation, get your partner involved and let him take over if possible. The decision itself is usually less important than letting your kids see that parents help each other out when either one is at the end of his or her rope. However, remember to negotiate in private if the process unduly upsets your spouse.

And finally, try to avoid negotiation by anticipating hot spots. Help your child make choices ahead of time: "When your friends come over this afternoon, which of your toys will you be willing to share?" A moment of prevention wards off an hour of wrangling.

THE MISTAKES MOTHERS AND FATHERS BOTH MAKE

Don't Be Afraid of What You Feel

Today's mothers and fathers often believe—for different reasons—that they should keep spontaneous feelings to themselves.

Mothers have been influenced by the mental health establishment to not overpower children with emotions. "Don't impose feelings on your child's experience," experts warn—"it will only lead to false compliance or rebellion." Or, "Remember how much you hated your own domineering mother? Do you want your child to feel that way about *you?*"

Mothers are also advised that expressing their emotions will make their children feel guilty. For example, we're told that expressions of parental disappointment ("The way you behaved this morning ruined my day"), neediness ("I'm going through a hard time, and need you to help me"), anxiety ("I'm nervous about that job interview tomorrow"), or sadness ("I feel so blue today because it's a year since Grandpa died") contribute to a lifetime of emotional baggage. We so rarely associate these kinds of feelings with healthy childrearing that they seem "unparentlike" to modern mothers.

Statements like these, if used all the time, *do* leave children feeling unnecessarily guilty. But banishing them from your repertoire isn't human, nor is it effective parenting.

Fathers have different problems with spontaneous feelings. They distrust the strength of the bond that exists between them and their children. Dozens of fathers have told me that fear of losing the connection (usually expressed as "They'll think I'm falling apart," "They won't look up to me anymore," or "They'll hate me forever") inhibits spontaneity. Fathers often envy mothers for being able to have a wider emotional range with kids.

Laird, a dad I met at a parenting workshop, often criticized his wife Harriette's short temper. On the other hand, he also envied the way she and their two grade-school children routinely yelled at each other during the morning chaos. Laird described the following scene:

MOM:	Hurry up and get dressed. You're going to miss the bus.
BOBBY:	My toast is burnt. I don't want to eat it.
AMY:	Mom—Bobby took my hairbrush again!
MOM:	Will you both stop dawdling and get moving!
AMY:	I was only going to use it for five minutes.
MOM:	Amy, did you wash your face?
AMY:	*(Doesn't answer, staring at the TV)*
MOM:	Amy! I said, did you wash up? Bobby, I don't see you putting your socks on!
AMY:	Mom, stop screaming. I'm tired. I don't want to put my clothes on yet.
MOM:	*(yelling)* You two get downstairs immediately or . . . !

Yet five minutes after this series of miniexplosions, Bobby is contentedly sitting next to Mom munching Honey Nut Cheerios, and Amy is on Mom's lap getting her hair braided *as if nothing had happened.*

Laird is right to question these scenes. Harriette and the kids are probably embroiled in too many yelling matches. Yet at the same time, he can't understand this kind of emotional fluidity. He feels like a spectator watching another species in their natural habitat.

Other fathers worry that any spontaneous emotion is unmanly, even (or maybe *especially*) if it's expressed to children. I'm no different in this area. When my mom's closest friend, Lucy (who was really like a second mother to me), was dying of cancer, I frequently visited her in the hospital and returned home feeling very upset. I was determined, however, to keep a stiff upper lip in front of then six-year-old Leah. One evening as I was saying goodnight to her, Leah said, "Tell me the story of Lucy."

Though taken aback, I was also touched that she'd noticed my sadness. I brought out some old family pictures and described all the good times I'd had with Lucy as we were growing up. Suddenly tears began to well up in my eyes. Despite the fact that I'm a "childrearing expert," despite the fact that I endorse the expression of "unparentlike" emotions, my first thought was that I didn't want her to see me cry.

I tried to downplay my feelings, but a few tears got by anyway. Instead of looking overwhelmed or scared, Leah gave me a hug and loaned me her special teddy bear to sleep with. "This will make you feel better, Daddy," she tenderly assured me. "It will make you think of me." The next morning life went on. I saw no evidence in her eyes that she looked to me as any less of an authority figure.

It's ironic, isn't it? As parents, we express anger and frustration every single day, without so much as a second thought. Yet we designate many other human emotions as unparentlike. Mothers' and fathers' fear of showing children these strong feelings inadvertently contributes to tension and distance on the parenting team. We treat ourselves and one another like robots. We squelch natural reactions that are unavoidable in the ebb and flow of daily living, until they surface as angry explosions. No wonder parents often have a hard time feeling romantic toward each other. It's not simply that we're always tired or resentful; we also (supposedly for the kids' sake) forbid ourselves to be spontaneously vulnerable. And romance cannot exist without vulnerability.

During the next month, do something healthy for the kids and yourselves. Try to express an unparentlike emotion to your child—"I need," "I'm scared," "I'm anxious," "I'm tired," "I'm hurt." These expressions of vulnerability soften the robotic atmosphere and hectic pace of modern life. They lead to greater tenderness not only between parent and child, but also between mother and father.

Mr. and Ms. Fix-It

The final communicational error that *both* women and men make (again, for different reasons) is that we try to *fix* children's problems. Men often seek immediate relief from painful emotions and believe it is *helpful* to minimize them. "Come on, it's not so bad," Leon tells his four-year-old daughter Karen, who has just scraped her knee on the monkey bars. "Look. It's stopped bleeding already." At this point Karen screams so violently you'd think she'd been walking over hot coals. The more he attempts to minimize her pain, the louder she yells.

Mothers are also guilty of this attitude. In fact, the same mother who gets furious at her partner when he minimizes *her* feelings ("You don't listen to me; you just want to make it go away") is guilty of trying to "make it go away" with her own kids. A mother's desire to make things better is, of course, extremely difficult to give up. Since mothers are ultimately held responsible for a child's unhappiness, you can't help but try to immediately step in and assuage hurts, both physical and emotional.

Mothers often take children's negative feelings so personally that the moment they come back from work to a moody child, a whole checklist appears before their eyes. "Was I rushed this morning? Did I forget to pack lunch right? Am I away too much?" This personalization of children's day-to-day moods (which I've found practically nonexistent in fathers) makes moms an easy target for tuned-in, sophisticated kids. Within seconds, children pick up on your guilt and use it to gain special attention. This, in turn, may lead to a fight with Dad, who can't help but comment, "There you go again, spoiling the kids, and catering to them too much."

Many parental disagreements begin when we automatically try to fix children's pain. Think back to four-year-old Karen, who scraped her knee on the monkey bars. It's easy to see a fight brewing:

DAD: It's not so bad. It's stopped bleeding.

KAREN: No. It's bleeding worse.

MOM: (*picking Karen up*): Let's get some bacitracin on it right away.

KAREN: (*screaming*): No, I don't want that stuff! It stings!

MOM: How about some ice?

KAREN: Go away!

DAD: Look, it could be worse.

KAREN: OOOH, IT HURTS EVEN MORE!

DAD: Let's forget it. It's no big deal. Wanna go on the slide?

MOM: These things can get infected. You should have been watching her more closely.

DAD: Me? Where were *you*?

Now suppose Mom and Dad step back from their "fix-it" positions:

MOM: Ooh. I *hate* those things. They really hurt. I can't stand them!

DAD: I hate them, too.

MOM: Can you move it a little?

KAREN: No. It hurts too much!

DAD: I remember getting one right here. (*Points to his elbow*) I cried a lot.

KAREN: *You* cried!

DAD: Yeah.

KAREN: Did you get it on the slide?

DAD: No, on the seesaw. But yours looks worse.

MOM: It looks red already.

KAREN: Where did you get yours, Mommy? On the monkey bars, too? Did you cry a lot?

MOM: Yeah. Especially when they had to clean it. Can I put some bacitracin on it now?

KAREN: Okay. But go slow.

Remember, never try to talk children out of unhappiness by minimizing their pain or by rushing them to feel better too quickly. For if you do, they'll hang on to their hurt even more vehemently than before.

If you try some of these suggestions, you'll challenge one of the oldest and most tacit rules of family life—when things go wrong, *everyone* talks to Mom. If kids feel comfortable opening up to both Mom and Dad, they feel safer—and the parenting team has less friction—in other words, by making these small changes *everyone* can feel closer.

CHAPTER 9

NETWORKING
The Last Bastion of Women's Work

One day when Leah (and her babysitter) were sick, I canceled all my appointments and stayed home to take care of her. We lounged around most of the morning watching videos on TV, reading books, and playing with her Samantha doll. Stacey, who had gone to work, stopped in during lunchtime.

"Come sit with us for a couple of minutes?" I asked.

"Sorry, I can't," she said. "I have to make a few phone calls."

Here's a partial list of the "few" calls she made in a fifteen-minute period: the babysitter to see how she was feeling; the mother of Leah's classmate who would bring over Leah's homework assignments; Leah's gym class to arrange for a makeup session; Leah's school to let the "hotline" know why she was out; and the mother of Leah's best friend to reschedule a play-date for later in the week.

Fifteen minutes of watching her whirl around the apartment and I was ready for a nap.

Networking. That's something you do when you're looking for a job, trying to raise money, or organizing a class reunion, right? Well, partly. No discussion of women's and men's participation would be complete without including the enormous amount of networking between families that women do.

Networking is the web of communication that holds different families together and enables their day-to-day functioning in the world at large. Social networks are the Elmer's Glue-All of everyday life: families can't survive well without them, and yet because they're invisible, few of us are even conscious of the huge amount of effort that's involved in creating and maintaining them.

Most everyone takes networking for granted—even mothers who are masters at it. And there's something else we take for granted—that networking is still "women's work."

If you have any doubt about who's responsible for networking in your family, try the following quiz.

NETWORKING QUIZ

Answer each question quickly.

1. What's the babysitter's phone number?
2. What's the pediatrician's phone number?
3. Who would the school call in case of emergency? And if you're not available, who is the person they would contact?
4. What's the phone number of your child's school?
5. Who are your child's best friends? What are their parents' phone numbers? What are the names of *their* babysitters?
6. Whose appointment calendar lists birthdays, anniversaries, and special occasions for extended family members and friends?
7. Whose appointment book includes school events?

If you're like most families, the answer to just about all of the above questions is "Mom." Despite all the recent shifts in gender role expectations, networking—making connections with people and institutions outside of the family—is as much a woman's responsibility today as it was in the 1950s.

If anything, the burden on women has increased because there are several different *additional* networking areas that didn't even exist a generation ago. Donna Reed didn't have to think about "who has the kids this weekend" before making plans—but in this age of divorce, today's moms do. Today's moms also have to forge neighborhood connections without the help of the Welcome Wagon, because the Welcome Wagon driver has probably driven off to her own full-time job.

Unfortunately, I've found that trying to bring men into the networking loop is more difficult than in any other area related to participation. That's why I call it the "Last Bastion of Women's Work" in families. Whenever

I even *suggest* that men should pick up the phone and arrange play-dates for the kids or arrange for babysitting, they are often vehemently unsympathetic. "What are you, kidding?" they reply. "I don't get involved with other mothers in that way." Or, "That's *her* job." Or, "I'm much too busy."

RESISTANCE FROM WOMEN

But it's not just men who have a problem. When it comes to networking, many women are as resistant to change as their partners. In all my years of giving parenting workshops, I can count on the fingers of one hand the mothers who even *considered* that networking responsibilities could (or even should) be shared.

Mothers aren't willing to give up their position as family networker for a variety of reasons. Women recognize the importance of the social support network of which they're in control: belonging makes them feel less alone and more powerful. Having a supportive network to bolster one another is a perfect antidote to a society that devalues mothers' work. And, of course, many women simply feel obligated—it's their *job* to shoulder networking responsibilities.

But even those women who *want* to share some networking chores often can't find a way to accomplish this. Once a network is established, it acquires a momentum of its own that makes any change seem almost unthinkable. Women—and men—find themselves trapped in an insidious cycle: The more women network with each other, the closer their relationships become, the harder it is for men (even those who are so inclined) to find a way in—and the more mothers stand to lose (in the way of support, control, and involvement) if changes *do* occur.

WHY CHANGE IS NEEDED

Why, then, if change in this area is so difficult and both men and women resist it, should we devote energy toward making male inroads into this almost exclusively female domain? There are several good reasons.

1. Women are simply overburdened—enough is enough! Have you seen the woman's magazine advertisement: "I *run* to work just as fast as I *run* home"? Because most women are working two shifts—one outside the home and one within—networking has taken on a frenzied quality. Erma Bombeck remembers how it used to be years ago when "we could sit around until the kids got home from school eating cholesterol-rich foods and talk to each other about what was happening in our children's lives." Despite the serious, hidden troubles of that era, it was the heyday of *casual* networking, when women shared information and support at their leisure.

   But for today's mothers, having only two things to do at once is a luxury. Phone cradled on shoulders, they squeeze in frantic, three-minute phone calls to find out essential information and make necessary arrangements at the same time that they're preparing dinner, paying bills, or trying to explain to eight-year-old Scott why he can't rent a video game on a school night.

2. The less men participate in the family network, the more isolated they are from the fabric of everyday life. In this way the "Mom's responsible" paradigm becomes self-perpetuating—and parental tension is inevitable. Men *know* that they're out of the loop. "The phone rings all night," they tell me, "and ninety-nine percent of the calls are for *her!*"

   This observation is part complaint, part relief. Men are aware that most of what they know about their kids is obtained secondhand, but either they don't know how to gain access to the network or they feel uncomfortable entering this female world. They don't define themselves as part of the everyday, "making arrangements" network. Meanwhile the web of women's connections grows richer and more complex. Mothers and fathers then end up having yet another reason to live parallel lives—a surefire way for misunderstanding and resentment to develop and fester between them.

3. When one parent networks for the entire family and has all the crucial information, only that parent is qualified to make those on-the-spot decisions ("Can I sleep over at Tim's house tonight?" "Can I go to the mall with Jennifer and her stepmother?") that kids constantly demand.

Kids *need* their parents to network with the rest of the world. It's

where the emotional action is, and where much taken-for-granted
bonding occurs. Think about how complicated the details are for a
single play-date:

MOM:	Who do you want to play with—Rachel or Audrey?
JENNY:	Is Audrey's mom going to be there?
MOM:	No. Her aunt will be.
JENNY:	I don't like her aunt. She's too bossy.
MOM:	So you don't want to go there?
JENNY:	Can't Audrey come to our house?
MOM:	No, because nobody can be here to supervise you.
JENNY:	All right. I'll go. But can I bring my Baby Alive doll?
MOM:	I don't think so. What if you lose it? You'll be heartbroken. Take that old teddy instead.
JENNY:	Do I have to share it with Audrey?
MOM:	Doesn't she share her toys with you?
JENNY:	Not always.
MOM:	If you do bring it I think you might have to let her play with it for a while . . . so you decide.
JENNY:	I'll leave it at home.

Then there are a couple of calls—usually between mothers—to firm
up the logistics. Finally:

MOM:	She's going to have pizza there, so you'll eat dinner at Audrey's house. Also, I'm bringing a change of clothes because their backyard is still muddy from the rain yesterday.
JENNY:	Who's going to pick me up?
MOM:	Probably Dad will drive over and get you—but I'll call just to make sure.

Now remember, this is one play-date. Multiply this scenario several
hundred times (thousands if you have more than one child) and you begin to appreciate how intensely kids are bonded to the parent who
makes their social arrangements. You also begin to appreciate how disconnected your partner is if he does none of this. When Jenny
clutches her teddy at the play-date, eats pizza, struggles over sharing

with Audrey, or gets her check-in call from Mommy, who is she thinking of? To whom does she feel connected?

WHAT YOU CAN DO

For all these compelling reasons, we need to rethink how we divide networking responsibilities at home. Yet I also know from years of experience that it's simply not realistic to expect major changes in this area. Our beliefs about networking systems are too embedded to overhaul them easily or overnight.

But I do believe it's time to become aware of all the invisible ways that networking is imbalanced in families. It's also time to think of strategies that will slowly change the unhealthy situation we face today in which mothers are automatically expected to fill the role of family switchboard. If we don't, we ignore a crucial way that mothers and fathers could be in greater synchrony with each other.

So with modest expectations, here are the eight most powerful and taken-for-granted networking changes that can help your family.

1. Begin During Pregnancy

Both of you need to select the crucial members of your support network—pediatricians and babysitters—together. Despite the fact that fathers-to-be have become involved with the pregnancy and birth process, they tend to fade out of the picture as soon as decisions are made as to how life will proceed *after* the initial glow of birth. Even "liberated" couples tend to divide responsibilities à la Donna Reed. Is there any logical reason why mothers are still expected to find, interview, and hire babysitters and pediatricians?

Even the most sophisticated parents automatically make assumptions that unbalance the parenting team—before a baby is even born.

In my experience, men become more involved with networking during a first pregnancy than during any subsequent pregnancies. This is truly unfortunate because arguments inevitably develop when only one person makes important decisions. If problems arise with childcare (as they occasionally must), you, Mom, are vulnerable to criticism and self-

---

IS YOUR TEAM UNBALANCED BEFORE THE GAME BEGINS?

Here's what dads assume:

1. My wife should conduct the babysitter and pediatrician search because she's already hooked into a mothers' network.
2. It's ultimately my wife's decision. Since she'll be dealing with the babysitter and pediatrician, she has to be comfortable with them.
3. We both agree that her "judgment and intuition" about people is better than mine.

Here's what moms assume:

4. It's complicated enough to arrange interviews with pediatricians and babysitters—if we factor in *his* schedule, it'll never get done.
5. He'll have veto power, so why get him involved earlier?
6. He says he wants to be involved, but then when I want to discuss the details, he's not that interested.

---

blame. Dad, who is outside of the decision-making process, may then feel entitled to second-guess your decisions.

Being involved in the decision-making process *before* the baby is born is a powerful way of reducing the number of "Listen, *you* were the one who made the decision . . ." fights that can occur. If we ignore the need for equal participation here, we begin the childrearing process with the "Mom's responsible" paradigm already in place. No prospective parent can imagine how much trouble this will cause when the children actually arrive.

2. "I'd Like to Speak to the Doctor, Please"

Make those crucial phone numbers for caretakers and doctors available to *both* of you; otherwise, the assumption that "Mom deals with the doctor" becomes increasingly entrenched with each childhood illness (and we all know how often kids get sick). If a dad complains to me that he's worried about his son's fever that won't go down, I always suggest that he call the doctor himself.

"That's a good idea," many men reply, "but my wife has the number." Unfortunately, it's often hard for men to ask for information we don't already have. (How many of us will drive for miles, hopelessly lost, before approaching someone to ask for directions?) Now Dad is worried about Noah's health *and* the fact that he's got to ask his wife for help.

If Dad *has* the phone number at his fingertips, and has an ongoing relationship with the pediatrician, then calling for information is much easier. Few times are more stressful than when children run a 104-degree fever, and wake up at 3:00 A.M. It's especially important that the burden be shared so neither parent ends up feeling overwhelmed or panicked.

It's also true that sometimes mothers simply don't want their husband to call the doctor. You know what will happen: the doctor will start asking detailed questions about Noah's behavior and symptoms— "Has he been eating? Sleeping? Have his bathroom habits changed?"— and because your husband doesn't know the answers, you'll have to become involved in the discussion anyway. Why not save time and just call yourself?

The answer is simple. If you remain the sole liaison to the medical support network, you'll soon feel overwhelmed. You'll also open yourself up to second-guessing, which is the first step toward an avoidable fight. If, however, the responsibility is shared, the potential for conflict is significantly lessened.

It's not just Mom or Dad who perpetuates the stereotype of Mom as medical networker. More than we realize, babysitters and doctors don't always include fathers in discussions even if Dad attempts to be involved. Pediatricians and babysitters live in a world of women and children. Without thinking, they automatically speak to mothers. As Henry, father of eighteen-month-old Joey, described, "My wife and I get home from work at the same time. I'd often ask the babysitter how Joey was—what did he eat, when did he go to bed? But no matter how many questions I asked, the babysitter would answer my wife, looking right past me, as if I were the Invisible Man."

If your babysitter answers *you* even if your spouse just asked the question; if your pediatrician avoids Dad's questions and responds to you—then you and your partner need to instruct these professionals that Dad should be spoken to directly. Even though some men appear not to care in the slightest or profess relief to find themselves out of the babysitter–caregiver loop, many men feel angered when they're ignored. Others react by giving up and switching on SportsChannel, moving ever so slightly toward greater isolation.

If your babysitter cannot break the habit of only speaking "woman to woman," then Mom, *you* should leave the room, forcing Dad and caregiver to deal with each other directly.

3. "I'm Calling About Becky's Play-date"

Dads need to be more involved with their children's friends and their parents. Unfortunately, the role of social facilitator is still usually assumed by Mom. A friend told me, "My twelve-year-old son James asked a girl, Lindsay, on a roller-skating 'date,' so naturally I called Lindsay's parents to go over the arrangements: Where? When? Who will chaperon? How much money should they take with them? Lindsay's father answered the phone. As soon as I mentioned that I wanted to talk about the date, he said, 'Let me get my wife,' even though I know that *he* takes Lindsay roller-skating every Saturday. To be honest, though, I preferred talking to Lindsay's mom. There were a lot of details to arrange and this was James's 'first date'—I wanted to get everything *right*."

Women are expected and expect themselves to be social facilitators even when they're stepparents. For example, seven-year-old Kevin had trouble on a play-date—a big fight broke out over sharing toys. Yet somehow it fell to his stepmother, not his father, to make the necessary call to the girl's parents. She ironed things out with the other mom, and made arrangements for another play-date "to see if things could go better."

Sometimes men don't realize how "on the sidelines" we are until presented with dramatic evidence. Dan, father of one-and-a-half-year-old Jesse, told me the following story: "One day I saw a photo on the kitchen table of my son with a bunch of other toddlers. 'Who are these kids?' I asked my wife.

" 'Oh, they're his best friends from the play group,' she said—his *best* friends, and I didn't even know who they were."

This father (I'm not much different myself) could easily educate himself if he'd start arranging some of his son's activities. Yet many men would rather drive kids to the ends of the earth for a play-date than actually negotiate the details of one. Sure, it's true that most women prefer talking to other women. It's also true, Mom, that if you ask your spouse to work out the details, you'll *still* be pulled into the middle: "What time do you think Michael should come home?" he might call in from the next room.

But some battles are worth having, and dividing up the social networking responsibilities is one of them. Expecting that your partner also be a "social facilitator" fosters an independent relationship between him and the kids, allows you some much-needed free time, and cuts down on unnecessary friction.

4. "Hello, This Is the School Nurse"

Insist that the school have both parents' work numbers. *Insist* that the school alternate between reaching you and reaching your partner if your child becomes ill. I say "insist" because schools will rarely call Dad unless otherwise instructed.

Many mothers know this is reasonable advice but can't put it into practice. They worry about how upset or resentful Dad will get when he's disturbed at work. Even fathers who *ask* to be called find their requests ignored. "He'll secretly resent me," women think, or, "If it's an emergency, I better take care of it. I want it done right."

Obviously, these reasons shouldn't get in the way. Regardless of how important our work may seem, most men aren't in the midst of performing life-or-death brain surgery—even though we may present it this way. Yes, at first you will feel strange telling your boss, "I've got to pick up my son at school; he's got a fever." And yes, at first, you may be scared to appear "uncommitted" to the job. But lately I've noticed that the corporate world is slightly more accepting of men who take time off for their families. And there's also an unexpected reward. You won't quickly forget that look of surprise and gratitude on your kid's face—"Daddy, you came from *work* to get me?"

Fathers should also be involved in the everyday details of school life. Otherwise, children grow up believing that school and Mom form a tight alliance from which Dad is excluded. The intensity of this taken-for-granted connection reaches absurd proportions. For example, one morning Stacey didn't have time to write a note to Leah's school explaining that Leah would be going home with a friend. So I wrote it instead. On the way to school Leah asked to see the note. "This is *all wrong*," she said. "Mommy *always* writes it different." She then insisted that I tear it up and write another one. This wasn't just Leah being bossy—she was nervous: "Make it just like Mommy's; otherwise, Ms. Cruz won't understand."

The more we men learn to network with school, the more chances we have to develop a genuine bond to our children. What kind of specific questions can fathers ask if we don't know about the spelling bee, the fight yesterday in gym, or the fact that Ms. Cruz braided all the girls' hair? We need these crucial facts at our fingertips in order to ask our kids questions specific enough to engage them in conversation. If we don't—if we remove ourselves from this part of networking—the parenting team becomes increasingly fragmented.

5. "Let's See, It's Tuesday, So It's Soccer, Then Art"

Fathers also need to become more involved in the vast network of after-school activities that are part of kids' lives. Usually it's your wife who arranges for tutors, music lessons, religious school, and soccer practice. Your wife gets to know the tutors, and the music and Sunday school teachers. Yes, of course, we get involved, but mostly on weekends. Today, however, with children's schedules brimming over with after-school activities, the weekend (usually sports) connection isn't enough. Not only does it reinforce gender stereotypes, but it also perpetuates the imbalance of networking responsibility. The "Mom's in charge" paradigm remains intact. Think about it. Just how informed *are* you if you don't even know the name of your daughter's piano teacher? Oversights like these slowly add up, and the bottom line is that you'll become a bit of an observer in your own child's life.

6. One Weekend . . . Three Birthday Parties

This area is hopelessly imbalanced, and I haven't seen any significant change in over thirty years of working with families. Is there a synapse that doesn't fire in men's brains (including mine) when it comes to remembering and arranging "dates"? Sometimes, during counseling, I'll ask a man when his own birthday is, and he'll turn to his *wife*—just to be sure.

In your family, who keeps track of family occasions—birthdays, anniversaries, graduations, special celebrations? Who carries out the responsibilities for selecting, purchasing, wrapping, and sending or delivering gifts? Who makes sure there are enough birthday candles? What about thank-you notes?

Forget how much these chores inflate the Endless List. Consider for a moment how this astonishing imbalance affects the nature of connection within the family. When Mom and kids write out cards together and wrap presents, Mom is acting like a bridge to the rest of the world. A great deal of parent–child bonding goes on during these moments. This is "quality time" that no "Great Adventure Scream Machine" can replace. This is when values are taught, and generosity is modeled.

Just think of the poignant moment that unfolds at almost every birthday party when mother and child know what gift they've brought along. And then there's Dad on the sidelines, usually as surprised as the birthday boy or girl when the present is finally unwrapped. This familiar scenario makes it seem to children as if fathers care less than we really do. The truth is that getting more involved in the step-by-step process of commemorating special occasions is a *major* part of growing up.

7. "It's Ten P.M. Do You Know Where Your Children Are?"

A more balanced division of networking responsibilities is especially important as kids get older and the stakes get higher. Fathers need to feel as comfortable as mothers when it comes to picking up the phone and asking another parent whether an upcoming party will be supervised. If you hear thirteen-year-old Annie's sanitized version of a party, you'll be inclined to let her go—and get to look like the "good guy." Mom, meanwhile—who has spoken to other parents, grilled Annie, and knows more of the facts—comes off sounding like the "heavy."

This "nice guy" stance has its appeal, of course. But kids tell me there's a darker side—they think we're "fools" if we really don't know what's going on.

I've helped many parents decrease terrible fighting over preteen or early adolescent privileges simply by getting Dad directly involved by asking:

1. Which kids are coming?
2. What time is the party supposed to end?
3. Are her parents going to be home?
4. I'd like to call them.

When fathers hear *firsthand* the same set of facts as mothers—that beer will be smuggled into an eighth-grade basement party—it's astonishing how quickly men and women find themselves on the same wavelength.

8. Enlist Help from Institutions Outside the Family

The School

Impetus for change cannot come only from within the family. To strengthen the family–school network, you must demand that the school administration stress the need for both fathers and mothers to be involved.

For example, one night I attended a PTA meeting at Leah's school. I was initially impressed by the number of men who were in attendance. Sure, there were three times as many mothers as fathers, but certainly more men had shown up than would have several years ago. Then the chairperson began asking for volunteers to actually staff the school committees. All of a sudden I found myself sinking lower in my seat, busying myself with papers and inspecting my shoes. One of the mothers must have noticed other men employing the same tactic. She called out, "How come only women are raising their hands? We're not moving ahead until one of you men volunteers!"

Men need such "invitations" to participate more—especially from school authorities. For example, dads should be encouraged to go along on field trips. These provide an excellent opportunity for fathers to step into a child's world and make some important connections. Yet here too, if direct requests are not made, few fathers—even in these "liberated" times—show up. Recently, a full-time working mother told me that she had accompanied her son's fifth-grade class on an overnight trip to Washington, D.C. When I asked how many fathers came along, she replied, "Three—out of thirty." What I found interesting was that this thoroughly modern working mother had taken for granted this glaring imbalance.

When school administrators begin expecting dads to participate, the imbalance will begin to right itself. Here are some of the more successful school-initiated programs I've seen:

1. Establishing "Peer Groups for Parents"
2. Instituting "Fathers' Days"
3. Instituting "Career Day" during which parents teach kids what they do for a living
4. Requiring fathers and mothers to take turns serving as teachers' aides in nursery school
5. Requiring fathers to attend parent–teacher conferences
6. Requiring that fathers sign off on homework assignments
7. Requiring that the school send all notices to divorced fathers as well as to the custodial parent (usually Mom)
8. Sending information about school events to men's workplaces, so everything isn't routed through Mom
9. Asking fathers to volunteer on school committees in which they can use their professional expertise
10. Asking fathers to take girls *and boys* to their place of work—it's not just daughters who haven't seen Dad's workplace

Work

Cooperation is also needed from the business community. Men need to feel as if they won't be penalized for taking time off to attend to pressing family matters; otherwise, they'll be too fearful to make any changes at home. Women are also afraid to let their family concerns interfere too strongly at work for fear that they'll be labeled "not serious" or assigned to the "Mommy Track."

Yet many corporations, under pressure from their employees, are finding ingenious solutions to the problem. In addition to creating on-site day care, some companies have established emergency childcare centers for those times when regular babysitting arrangements fall through, and for sick-child day care. Some companies that are open around the clock have created nighttime childcare centers. Others maintain a referral network to help employees find reliable childcare. Flextime, which enables employees to create their own hours, and telecommuting, which enables employees to work at home, both help parents bridge the gap between work and family. Finally, many corporations have lunchtime parenting seminars.

These are all steps in the right direction, but more solutions need to be found.

"What Do You Do, Mommy and Daddy?"

Changes in the business environment won't happen overnight. In the meantime, you can begin to address the gap between family and job very simply, at home.

Many of the children I work with—including teenagers—can't explain to me what their fathers and mothers do for a living. This hurts the parenting team because kids tend to underestimate all the things Dad does around the house, and the responsibilities Mom may have to shoulder during the workday. Kids don't see parents as three-dimensional figures. We then get stuck being viewed by the children in narrow roles, which in turn makes parents view each other narrowly as well.

What can you do about this?

1. Sit down and explain to your child, in concrete, age-appropriate ways, exactly what you do for a living. You should begin these discussions when your child is as young as three.
2. Bring your child with you to your workplace, if possible (the annual "Take Your Daughter to Work Day" in late April is a good start). If you can't manage this during the work week, then make a trip on weekends. Just seeing the physical setting will help your child imagine you there.
3. Introduce your child to your coworkers so that she sees that you have relationships outside of the family. If your child can't actually meet them, identify your coworkers when they call on the phone.
4. Together with your partner, explain to your kids all the behind-the-scenes jobs that go on in order to keep the household running. Let them know that cars have to be taken to the gas station, plumbers have to be called, bank statements have to be reconciled. Be sure to teach them about the hidden responsibilities Dad has. Otherwise, kids see only Mom's contribution.

5. Whenever feasible, bring your kids along on maintenance errands to the auto mechanic or the bank and explain to them what you're doing.
6. Don't leave all your work-related problems behind when you come home. Kids are mystified when parents seem preoccupied or moody, and this creates more distance. Find a nonthreatening, age-appropriate way to explain: "My boss got really mad at all of us today," or "I had to finish an important job by five o'clock and I wasn't sure I'd make it. That's why I'm in a bad mood."

Religion

Affiliation with religious organizations is a natural way to bring men into the networking process. Though it's rarely mentioned, organized religion increases a man's contact with other families by ensuring that work is not his only reference group outside the family.

While gender expectations within certain religious denominations remain very traditional, the overriding sense of community increases the chance that fathers know more about what is going on in their children's lives. Regular religious services, rituals throughout the year, a support network that helps families in crisis—all bring men into contact with one another and with other children.

When fathers have more connection with neighboring families, the parenting team is likely to:

1. Have fewer battles over the definition of "normal" behavior at any given developmental stage—Dad sees for himself what the other kids are up to;
2. Experience less stress—because childcare can be shared between families. For example, Sabbath dinners are often communal events;
3. Focus less exclusively on work and career—a day of rest gives many "workaholic" men permission to disconnect from the job, and reconnect at home.

After more than three decades of being with families, I am continuously struck by the restorative potential of religious community. Not only does it address the spiritual void in modern life, but it also reminds families—especially men—that "life is with people." The community's rituals, customs, and communicational network become a bridge between families. Without this bridge, women end up having to forge these connections on their own.

Expecting modern mothers to continue to serve as the family's primary networker may simply be too much to ask. Working two to three shifts just to make ends meet, without the benefit of extended family members nearby, today's women feel that networking is just another Endless List chore to be tackled. With fathers on the sidelines in the networking department and mothers overwhelmed, neither men nor women experience networking as the life-affirming, nurturing activity it truly is.

Just one or two of these suggestions can make an enormous difference in terms of how connected your whole family feels—to each other, and to the world around you.

CHAPTER 10

LETTING GO

How to Survive
Life Transitions Together

The other day my wife said in a worried tone, "I can't tell you how overwhelmed I'm feeling about Sammy [our two-year-old] going to nursery school. Those applications, the new teachers, the scheduling changes—it's driving me crazy!"

"But that's a year away!" I said, a little exasperated. "What are you so worked up for already?"

She dropped the subject, but not before sending me one those "What do *you* know?" looks.

Parents have this kind of unsatisfying conversation about letting-go transitions all the time. After all, one fact about raising kids is certain—nothing *ever* stays "the same" for too long. No sooner do you feel comfortable with one developmental phase than your kids are on to the next.

Transitions can be so momentous that they're impossible to ignore—your child starting kindergarten or leaving for college—or not quite so earth-shattering—an infant beginning to crawl, or your pre-teen moving from utter disregard for personal hygiene to caring passionately about how he looks. Transitional periods are often sad—adjusting to a death in the family, divorce, or job loss—or happy—a sixteenth birthday or wedding.

But all these occasions, big or small, joyful or mournful, have several things in common. First, they all involve some kind of *letting go*. During these times, you feel the need to do two opposite, and therefore troublesome, things at once: say goodbye to the old and greet something new. Finally, they *all* increase the amount of tension on the parenting team.

LETTING GO IS HARD TO DO

Interestingly, despite the wealth of complex psychological research about why transitions are stressful, one of the most obvious reasons is rarely mentioned:

> Because most men and women have very different perceptions of who's *responsible* for family change during transitions, mothers and fathers are almost always out of synch with each other.

You could see this at work in my brief exchange with Stacey about nursery school. She was mentally preparing for a change that I hadn't yet spent one second thinking about. What could cause such discrepancy? Like most men and women today who work outside the home, we still both tacitly believed that while I certainly would be involved in the transition, Stacey would bear the brunt of the responsibility for managing it.

This is not unusual. Despite decades of social and political upheaval, mothers continue to be in charge of letting-go transitions. This taken-for-granted fact triggers many arguments on the parenting team. As Ellen, the mother of two school-aged children, said when discussing the family's upcoming relocation to Arizona, "I want my husband to start dealing with this move. It's only six months away, and I can see the kids are beginning to react. But no matter how hard I try or how much I ask, he just won't talk about it with me."

In response, her husband Rob answered, "What's with her? What's to talk about? We've got months! Why do we have to discuss and analyze every single little detail to death? Things will work themselves out!"

Ellen snapped back, "He can say that because he knows that *I'll* take care of the details. At the last minute, when the move is just around the comer, *then* he'll get more involved. Until then, I'll end up feeling as if I'm in this alone and responsible for everything."

LETTING GO AND THE ENDLESS LIST

When the Endless List is imbalanced, mothers and fathers can't help but be at odds—this holds true whether families are in the middle of transitions or not. During transitions, however, the Endless List grows exponentially, making it *seem* as if women are slower to accept letting go than men.

Here's a typical scene: "Why can't you just say 'Good night' and walk out the door?" Mark demands of his wife, Rhona. Their younger son, Adam, is six months old, and they are beginning to resume their customary Saturday-night dates. "It takes you an hour to get ready to leave the house—and we'll only be gone for two hours. By the time we get going I'm already in an aggravated mood. *You just can't let go.*"

But if we look at Rhona's behavior from the Endless List perspective, maybe she isn't just another overprotective, worried mother who can't "let go." Perhaps she's:

1. Checking to make sure there are enough diapers and new bottles for the baby.
2. Showing the sitter where the cookies and chips are stored.
3. Writing down emergency phone numbers, including the restaurant where they'll be.

And maybe, since this is a new babysitter, she's also:

4. Instructing the new babysitter about what time their four-year-old son should go to sleep, which television programs he can watch, and which snacks he can have.
5. Taking a little extra time to make sure she feels comfortable leaving the children with this relative stranger.

Sure, Mark's aggravated out there in the car. But as involved and as loving a father as he is, *he* doesn't feel responsible for this transition. Therefore, the details involved in letting go for the evening don't touch him the same way. In fact, he may not even realize all that's entailed.

As children grow, the specific items on the Letting Go Checklist change, but the details remain just as consuming. One woman, Annette, whose children are six and eight, tells me that when she and her husband go out together, she *still*:

1. Jots down the restaurant phone number on a pad near the refrigerator.
2. Reminds the babysitter how much Play Station each boy is allowed.
3. Reviews who can use the phone and for how long.
4. Goes over each boy's bedtime ritual with the babysitter.

True, her husband, Marty—a very involved dad—plays with the boys before leaving. But after these tasks he's ready to let go. In the end, *he's* not personally responsible for the babysitter. Annette *is;* and because of this, she still has about ten minutes' worth of work to finish.

Men have a hard time grasping how insidiously the Endless List affects letting go. Think of Ellen, whose family was going to relocate to Arizona, and whose husband, Rob, refused to participate in planning the move. The only way I finally got through to him was by comparing her worry about the kids to his worry about business.

"How long did you consider moving the company before deciding to go for it?" I asked him.

"At least three years," Rob replied.

"Tell me what occupied you during that time."

"Well, first we sent the scouting team. Then we hired a consulting firm, and then we approached various distributors. . . . " His painstaking explanation took a half-hour. I let him go on just to help make the point.

"Well," I said, "it sounds like you had to spend an enormous amount of time on thousands of details that you felt ultimate responsibility for. I wonder if this is the way Ellen feels about moving the family to Arizona.

As simple as this connection may seem, Rob had never made it before. Once he "got" it, though, his impatience with Ellen immediately lessened. For the first time, Rob saw that Ellen felt obligated to pay the same obsessive attention to the details of childrearing that he did to his business worries. He also began to understand how truly burdened she felt about the move.

Now, Rob and Ellen didn't immediately switch roles. There are no magical transformations when it comes to gender definitions. Ellen still did most of the childcare planning for Arizona. But Rob asked about it, and offered to become involved with some of the details. Because Ellen felt as if she was being taken a little more seriously, she was less upset. After all, at least she and Rob were in the same time zone about the upcoming move.

INTERWOVEN LIVES

When you look at transitions through the lens of Endless List responsibilities, you begin to appreciate just how complicated letting go is for many mothers. Because they tend to be more involved with the hands-on details of childcare, mothers' lives are deeply affected when children go through transitions. Each change in a child's routine precipitates losses and new beginnings that significantly alter how women actually *live their lives*. Yet we often take these changes for granted.

Joyce, a mom I met at a parenting workshop, described how she felt the year her daughter began kindergarten. "Janine had gone to the same preschool for three years. I knew all the teachers and many of the other parents. We had a certain routine; I knew which moms I could depend on. Now there are all new faces when I drop Janine off at kindergarten. I feel lost. I know it will pass, but I miss my old friends."

In other words, Joyce wasn't only letting Janine go, but letting go of an important reference group for herself as well. Her husband Les? He was elated by his daughter's beginning "real school." But because he wasn't saying goodbye to a whole network, he couldn't understand "what all the fuss was about." Typically, Les and Joyce were out of synch with each other at a point when emotional support could have made each feel less alone.

WOMEN INSIDE THE LOOP

Another reason women often take the rap for being reluctant to let go is because moms have more "inside information" than dads do about what's really going on. And with modern kids, there's plenty to worry about.

Here's an argument that took place between Cliff and Judy, parents of fourteen-year-old Marie, who absolutely *had* to attend her first basement party that Friday night. "*Everybody* will be there," she told he mother. I'll *die* if I'm the only one who can't go. Dad said I could go if you say it's okay," she challenged.

"Well, it's not okay!" Judy insisted.

"You *never* want me to have any fun!" Marie accused.

Cliff sided with his daughter. He was aggravated, and accused Judy of being overprotective. "It's just a simple party—you've got to let her grow up," he shouted at his wife.

"Maybe I do have a problem letting go," Judy said. "But did *you* speak with any of the other parents to find out what's happening at this party ?"

Of course, Cliff hadn't. The telephone network had been "manned" by women. Having questioned Marie and spoken with the other mothers involved, Judy knew a few details that Cliff wasn't aware of: The host parents would not be at home; elderly (and partially disabled) grandparents would be "in charge." She also heard talk that some kids from the fringe crowd of the high school were going to crash the party.

Cliff cared just as much as Judy about his daughter's welfare. As soon as he heard these details, he changed his position on a dime. "Forget it, Marie," he said. "Your mother is right. There isn't enough supervision for my taste either."

HEAD START ON CHANGE

In all these cases, Mom's ability to let go is affected by her:

1. Taken-for-granted responsibility to manage the transition.
2. Involvement with and dependence on the mothers' network.
3. More intimate knowledge of the kids' lives.

This imbalance not only leads to arguments about letting go, but contributes to a second phenomenon:

Mothers (whether or not they have jobs outside the home) become involved in transitions *earlier* than fathers do—often entering transitions at least six months before fathers.

Why six months? The Gesell Institute of Human Development (whose books on child development I highly recommend) has observed that children naturally go through transitional periods approximately every six months—which explains why once you finally get used to one stage, a new one immediately begins.

Given that most men and women have very different perceptions of who's responsible for family change, Mom is usually the first one to notice the twilight of an old era and the dawn of a new one. This just about guarantees that when it comes to letting go, Mom and Dad will feel out of step with each other. Obviously, this is not a recipe for a successful parenting team, but rather for conflict and parallel living.

For example, Diane, a mid-level corporate executive working full-time, came to counseling because she felt disconnected from her husband, Jay. Their son Nick was about to begin kindergarten. In discussing the past year, Diane reported the same "out of synch" quality to their relationship that so many couples report during times of transition. Here's how she'd spent the last year:

1. The September before Nick was scheduled to start, she began thinking about the change.
2. In December, she visited two schools in her area.
3. By January, she'd completed the necessary paperwork for the school.
4. In March, she formally registered Nick.
5. In April, she and Nick attended a series of orientation meetings.
6. In June, they began shopping—Nick picked out a knapsack and lunch box while Diane purchased his fall wardrobe.

By the time September rolled around and Nick showed up for his first day of kindergarten, Diane had been immersed in the change for a full year. Except for attending one or two orientation meetings, Jay hadn't become directly involved. There was no question about his interest—but that didn't seem to translate into actual engagement. In fact, he was annoyed that Diane was, in his view, having trouble "keeping things in perspective. What's so hard about registering a child for kindergarten? I can't understand it." Diane, meanwhile, felt alienated, as if she had no real partner in this enterprise for which so much work "had to be done." In typical fashion, Diane had entered the letting-go transition six months ahead of Jay.

WHEN MONTHS MAKE A WORLD OF DIFFERENCE

Even a couple of out-of-synch months can lead to tension between parents—especially if they have young kids. Paul, a friend of mine, can't get over the fact that his fourteen-month-old son Theo has begun to toddle around the apartment and rip it apart. "Here comes the masked marauder," he says to me, half-joking. "How could one little kid cause such destruction? He's like the Terminator. What time is it? Three o'clock? We've got five more hours before he goes down for the night. Pam doesn't agree, but we've got to put limits on him."

His wife Pam feels equally frazzled by Theo's capacity for mayhem, and also counts the minutes till bedtime; however, she's not as shell-shocked. When they both noticed Theo's first attempts at standing a few months ago, each reacted in fairly stereotypical ways: Paul, the proud papa, took pictures; and Pam, the proud mama, began *preparing*. She:

1. Babyproofed the house.
2. Put locks on the refrigerator and under the sink cabinets.
3. Read a few magazine articles on what to expect from todlers.
4. Talked to several other mothers.

Yet when she tried striking up a conversation with Paul about how Theo's walking would change the family, he objected on two fronts: "We'll deal with it when it happens," he said, adding, "You just have to face the fact that he's not going to be a baby forever." From these comments, Paul was obviously implying, to Pam's great displeasure, that she was having trouble letting go.

In fact, Pam *was* unhappy about how quickly the time was passing—"Theo's no longer my little baby," she said sadly. But she also knew that if anyone was going to manage the details of Theo's transition to toddlerhood, it was going to be *her*. The very act of preparing the house, reading, and talking helped Pam adjust emotionally. Paul, with no comparable preparation, experienced Theo's reign of terror like a resident of a low-lying coastal area during hurricane season.

If anything, being out of synch gains momentum as time passes.

While Paul was still reeling from the shock of discovering that a "miniature walking monster had suddenly moved into the house," Pam was already moving out of the babyproofing phase and gearing up for the "terrible twos." In other words, Pam was again several months ahead of Paul at a time when it would have been mutually beneficial to be on the same page.

There's a certain comic side to all of this—until you realize that parents who are out of synch during early transitions are at risk of remaining this way. As these subtle disconnections accumulate, the distance between parents grows and becomes chronic.

IT'S NOT IN THE GENES

Now, men don't *always* lag behind. I'm not suggesting a genetic difference. When Dad is responsible for managing a transition, *he'll* deal with letting go before Mom. Robert is a case in point. Because education is extremely important to him, Robert became very involved with his son John's college application process: he visited the schools with John, helped with the personal essays, and pushed him along during the application process.

Meanwhile, Robert's wife Arlene regarded this flurry of activity with a bemused and slightly resentful eye—"Why hadn't he been involved like this years ago?" Ultimately, she chalked it up to Robert realizing he had just one last chance at doing "the male-bonding thing." She was sad to think of John off at college, but given their two other kids and her full-time job, she also felt relieved that for once all the concrete work hadn't landed in her lap.

In short, Arlene didn't take her son's transition all that seriously until the day they deposited John in his dormitory room. "She spent the five-hour car trip home crying," Robert told me, "and then she went into a week-long depression."

In this case, stereotypical roles were reversed: Robert had been dealing with the work of letting go for over a year; Arlene, who'd been watching more than participating, was caught unprepared. But their out-of-synch experience was typical of couples who go about the process of letting go separately instead of together.

WHEN LETTING GO GETS STALLED

Because Arlene and Robert let go of their son at different times, they were unable to comfort each other during the inevitable mourning period that is part of every transition. When you look closely, letting-go transitions—happy or sad—contain an element of *loss:* We mourn what's left behind even as we greet what's ahead. Obviously, we all need support during times of loss. Yet neither parent can comfort the other if each grieves at a different time.

This mutual lack of support on the parenting team sometimes means that letting-go transitions get stalled. When this happens, and you don't pay attention to the growing disconnection on the team, kids begin to act out—often seriously enough that the guidance counselor or school psychologist becomes involved.

I am suggesting that the phenomenon of children having trouble during transitions is often not just a plea for attention, as many believe. Rather, it is a sign that Mom and Dad need help getting in synchrony with each other. In fact, the essential goal of *all* family therapy, family support groups, and parent counseling programs is precisely this: *to get parents back in synch so they can manage the letting-go transition together.*

For example, Marla, an overweight four-year-old girl, had been acting up in prekindergarten. She was babyish—whining so much that the other kids didn't want to play with her. Her father Jed thought that his wife, Rita, was at the root of Marla's problems.

"You're overly involved," Jed told Rita. "You worry too much and you don't set clear limits. Marla just has to grow up. Your problem is that you don't want to let go of her."

Rita didn't agree. "There is a lot to worry about," she countered. "We're in the midst of making a decision about whether to send Marla to a parochial or public school next year. And if she keeps up this behavior, I'm not sure any parochial school would want her."

Rita works full-time, as does Jed. They have another child, eighteen-month-old Eddie. Jed is a caring father who "pitches in" on a daily basis. Just like the classic father from the magazine surveys, he's involved—"when his schedule permits." But despite their twenty-first century profile, Rita was in charge of the hands-on details concerning *both* Eddie's transition to toddlerhood and Marla's transition to kindergarten. She had an approximately four to six months' jump on Jed in terms of trying to let go and move on.

When counseling began, neither of them noticed this arrangement. But it wasn't working. Jed was second-guessing Rita, Rita was second-guessing herself, and Marla was acting up. In my view, Marla was raising an unmistakable red flag signaling that Mom and Dad were out of synch. And they would have remained this way if the school psychologist hadn't called Rita to speak about Marla's behavior. *That's* what finally brought Jed into the transition process.

After just a few sessions, Jed and Rita began to see that their fighting was a *symptom* of how out of step they were during these two important transitions. No wonder they fought; no wonder they felt disconnected from each other. They needed to go through the transitions together. Concretely, this meant sharing information and responsibility for letting go and moving on. Once parents confront the same set of facts at the same time, they usually soften their opposing viewpoints and find themselves much more open to compromise.

I encouraged Rita and Jed to divide more equally the concrete work of deciding which school Marla would attend next year. I asked Rita to let go—not of her *daughter*, but of some of the daily tasks that arose during this transition. I asked Jed to take more responsibility for the impending changes, by doing more of the hands-on work. In short, I did everything I could to get them involved *together*.

As soon as Rita and Jed started sharing more of the nitty-gritty details, three things happened.

First, Rita felt less pressured and anxious. She eased off on Marla and Jed so that the fighting between all three of them lessened considerably.

Second, now that Rita was no longer implicitly managing the transition, Jed wasn't so quick to dismiss her concerns as fear of letting go. With his firsthand knowledge of all the complicated factors involved, he saw that nothing was black or white. Since he also felt responsible for the school decision, he didn't want to make a mistake, either.

Third, Jed and Rita found themselves on similar wavelengths, more in than out of step with each other. Of course, they didn't agree on every issue, but at least they were going through their family's transition *together*.

After a month, Marla settled down and her parents reached a decision about next year's school. Life went on.

WHEN THERE'S A CRISIS

Unfortunately, for many families, events don't always resolve so easily. Sometimes it takes a major crisis to express just how out of step we parents can let ourselves become. For example, Terri, a working mother found herself feeling overwhelmed. She was in the midst of two "stuck" transitions: Her thirteen-year-old daughter, Julie, was having a hard time adjusting to junior high and was beginning to cut classes; and eighteen-year-old Justin was sabotaging his own high school graduation by getting involved with drugs and alcohol. Her husband Matt shared Terri's concerns, but thought the problem was a "lack of discipline." Mom and Dad fought a lot about the need to set limits, but seemed unable to create a united front.

One day Justin was arrested for drunk driving. All four family members suddenly found themselves in a support group for families with chemically dependent kids, and in my office for family counseling.

After a few months, Terri and Matt began to realize that their problem was more than just "differences over discipline." In fact, the honest differences they *did* have were exaggerated to explosive proportions, because they'd automatically assumed that Mom would handle both these difficult transitions on her own, and Dad would enter later. As the manager of transitions, Terri had become so overloaded by constantly negotiating curfews, parties, and school grades that her own emotional circuits were going into meltdown.

When Justin got arrested, he was crying out for attention not only for himself, but also for his parents. He wanted them to become more connected, more in synch with each other. This is the unspoken message acting-out children telegraph to anyone who will listen: "I don't care what it takes, just get my parents working together. I'm too young to do it on my own."

Many times, parents don't realize how overburdened they are or just how out of synch the parenting team is. Here are some signals that a childrearing guide may not be enough, and that professional help is needed:

1. One of you always wins.
2. Your child views one of you as the villain and the other as the victim.
3. Bullying tactics—verbal or physical abuse, or the threat of physical abuse—are used.
4. You confide in your child instead of your spouse.
5. You talk more to someone outside the team than to your spouse, and say things you're afraid to say to your spouse.
6. Your kids can't stop fighting, and their fights mirror the fights between you and your spouse.
7. Your children begin asking you how come you argue so much, or why you don't spend any time talking to each other.
8. You are reluctant to spend time together without the kids around.
9. You lose interest in sex with your partner—not periodically, which is normal, but on a long-term basis.
10. Your children may get in trouble with outside authorities, or their mood or school performance is affected.

And remember, family counseling for difficulty with letting-go transitions is almost always short-term. Once you become involved together, you'll let go at a more compatible pace. Disagreements almost always become more negotiable when both of you feel equally responsible for and involved in managing transitions.

The secret to successful letting go is to redefine who's responsible for the transition and to get your pacing more in synchrony. The problem is less in letting go of our children than that we have, too often, let go of each other.

PART III

BEYOND GENDER . . . ALMOST

CHAPTER 11

HELP! HOW TO STOP "LOSING IT" WITH EACH OTHER

Time-out for Parents

It's dinnertime. You casually mention something—let's say about the next day's plan for the kids. You and your spouse disagree. Within seconds, the disagreement takes a nasty turn. Moments later, still sniping at each other, the two of you walk down the corridor to your bedroom. In her room, your six-year-old daughter is pretending to play with her Barbies, but you know she's been taking in every angry, harsh word you've said.

The sight of her downcast eyes is like a slap in the face. You secretly vow never to fight again over something so "stupid." Yet even as you make this resolution, you know that somewhere down the line another disagreement will arise and lead to another struggle. Fighting, you tell yourself with a sinking feeling, is an inevitable part of every parent's life.

Not necessarily. Or at least not as big a part as we're led to believe. My experience tells me it's possible to roll back the storm clouds of disagreement before the first thunderclaps of a real battle begin.

Fighting about the children is different from other types of fights couples typically have. On the one hand, all parents who have watched their children move on from nursery school to high school and off to college ask themselves the same question: "Where has the time gone? It was just yesterday when . . ." Kids grow up so quickly that you turn around and it seems like seconds, not decades, have passed by.

On the other hand, spending time with kids, even for as little as two hours, let's say between 6:00 and 8:00 P.M., can sometimes feel like an eternity. Every minute of organizing the details, paying attention to the "look at me" accomplishments, figuring out who "started it," helping with toothbrushing, and soothing hurt feelings (all this may add up to just five minutes during a typical evening) can stretch on endlessly.

So, even though parenting is over before you know it, you can feel completely *trapped in the moment* hundreds of times a week. This trapped-in-the-moment experience is at the heart of why minor parental disagreements quickly escalate into dead-serious fighting.

Understanding the experience of being trapped in the moment is crucial if you want to cut down on fighting with your spouse. Several factors come into play. First, we parents *are* trapped by our children to a certain extent. Childless couples are much freer to come and go as they please, even in the middle of a battle. If they disagree about which movie to see, how often to have sex, or how much "space" each needs, they can go their separate ways for hours—even days—and meet up when tempers have cooled.

But parents have no comparable trapdoor. If your child balks at getting dressed in the morning, for example, you can't say, "Oh well, let's just skip school today." When our one-year-old son Sammy recently put up a huge fuss over having to take the "bubble gum medicine" for his ear infection, Stacey and I didn't have the option of throwing our hands up and saying, "Let's just skip this dose and try again in four hours." Neither of us could walk away without taking some kind of action. Children *have* to attend school; medicine *has* to be dispensed; things *have* to get done. This overriding sense of necessity causes many parents to feel trapped in the moment.

There are also plenty of times when we're *physically* trapped in the moment. What parent doesn't have a story about a Car Trip from Hell? Robin, a woman I met at a parenting workshop, described her fantasy: she wished that the family car had an ejection seat. Then, whenever the backseat fighting and screaming reached a certain decibel level, she could simply push a button and catapult the kids into outer space. A rainy Saturday with a couple of cranky children can feel like a week in purgatory—which could actually be pleasant compared to a rustic, cabin-on-a-lake vacation dampened by three days of continuous rain. After the "morning rush" with everyone scrambling to get ready, we often end up feeling as if we've already put in a full day at the job and need a change of clothes. We've all sat at the table (or chased our toddler around the restaurant) for meals that seem to stretch on for stomach-wrenching hours. (Actually, I don't remember sitting down to a complete dinner until Leah was about two and a half.) And you could make a major motion picture out of just one shopping trip to a clothes store with your teenager.

The many misconceptions about childrearing I've tackled throughout the book also contribute to the sense of feeling trapped in the moment. You can't help but doubt yourself if you believe that there is an absolute "right" and "wrong" to childrearing that other parents and experts know about. All the accumulated "shoulds" of parenting—"I thought I should do it *this* way, but last week on TV they said you should do it *that* way"; "Didn't I read somewhere that you should *never* . . . "; "I'll ruin her for life. She'll be in a support group for 'Children of Incompetent Parents' somewhere down the line"—make us feel trapped in the moment, unable to act confidently and decisively.

Finally, children's insatiable needs trap us in the moment. Whether they want the breast, the answer to a question, a partner for a board game, or the keys to a car, they want it *NOW!* Parents often find themselves trapped within their child's urgency, acting in ways that go against their better judgment—and, of course, fighting with each other.

ANATOMY OF A FIGHT

If feeling trapped in the moment wasn't enough to make us get a little desperate with each other, there's a second reason why the cycle of parental fighting is so hard to break. After listening to thousands of couples rehash arguments about the kids, I've learned that the *real* problem with fighting is the *exact opposite* of what it feels like when you're in the midst of it. Let me explain.

"We're at our wits' end" is how most people introduce themselves to me. What do they mean?

- "We're on opposite ends of the spectrum about the kids."
- "We're light-years away from each other."
- "It's like we live on different planets."
- "We don't speak the same language."
- "We're not even close to seeing eye-to-eye."

In other words, everyone describes how *separate* and far apart they feel during a battle over the kids. However, when I ask for more details about the fight, the same pattern always unfolds—and the last thing the parents are is *separate*.

Tina and Elliott, for example, described their most recent fight to me. Elliott had become so engrossed in the ballgame on TV that he was a couple of minutes late taking their nine-year-old son Adam to Little League practice. Tina was furious at his "irresponsibility." For a few minutes they argued back and forth about the specifics of being late to practice.

And then suddenly the fight shifted into another gear. Everyone can relate to this change—suddenly you realize you're not just talking about a single incident anymore. The fight has widened. The issue you began fighting about is completely overshadowed by the frustrating and familiar pattern of *the way you fight*. You're both using practically the same words that you used during your last battle. You both know exactly how the fight will turn out. To quote Yogi Berra, "It's like déjà vu all over again," yet you can't get yourself to stop.

At moments like these we realize that *what* we're arguing over is secondary to *how* we're arguing, and that (once again) we're trapped in an interactional rut that we don't know how to get out of.

ENMESHED!

As I watch couples like Tina and Elliott (who are like most of us), I'm struck by a paradox: though we complain about being *miles apart* during a fight, the real problem is that we're *stuck together*. We're clinging to each other in what family therapists call a "dance," unable to step back and catch our breath. We're so hyperreactive that every word and gesture becomes fuel for the fire, yet neither one can stop the chain reaction.

The psychological term for what happens to couples at this stage of a fight is that they have become "enmeshed"—so intertwined that they can't let go of each other. In the middle of a fight, enmeshed mothers and fathers are like drowning people, clutching and thrashing about even though they know their chances of survival would improve if only they'd release each other and calm down. Here are five clear signs that you and your spouse have become enmeshed:

1. Your arguments ignite and spread like brushfire. "We seem to go from zero to sixty in a few seconds" is how one father described it.
2. You know you've fought this fight before and you know exactly how it will end, but you can't put on the brakes and extricate yourself.
3. You feel as if you're reading from a script: five minutes into the fight he brings up your mother, and a minute later you bring up his ex-wife.
4. You hear yourself fighting over the same issues that entangled your parents. The roles may be different—for example, you may be less strict than your mother was—yet you and your husband argue over discipline, just as your own parents did.
5. It's 10:00 P.M. Do you know where your children are? When you're enmeshed, not only can't you remember what started the fight, but you often lose sight of the kids altogether.

Any combination of these five signs means you've gone beyond the minor disagreement stage into self-destructive fighting. Now, what can you do about it?

TIME-OUT—FOR PARENTS!

In my years of work with tens of thousands of families, I've read just about all the books on childrearing and seen countless parenting fads come and go. But the most reliable, time-tested method is what I call "Time-out for Parents"—a technique I first learned from one of my family therapy teachers, Betty Carter.

The concept of a "time-out" is familiar to just about every mother and father. We've all tried it for children who are out of control. In our homes and schools we have time-out chairs, time-out corners, time-out rooms. But these are all for the kids. Why haven't we learned that parents need time-outs from each other?

This narrow focus on children's time-out would be laughable if it weren't such a critical childrearing error. The truth is, we *all* occasionally lose control. We *all* find ourselves entangled with each other in fights that are as intense as any child's tantrum.

Like time-out for children, time-out for parents sounds easy to implement, but the reality is always somewhat thornier. That's why I suggest that you faithfully follow the steps I've outlined below.

LEARN TO READ YOUR SIGNALS

The first step is to recognize the signs that you're feeling trapped in the moment and about to become enmeshed before, *before*, BEFORE the fight escalates out of control.

Work by numerous researchers, including John Gottman's studies on couples' interactions as well as interviews with "well-functioning" couples, has underscored the importance of interrupting escalations, heading off fights before physiological reactions intensify and hurtful words create residues of resentment. Because, as Gottman has found, the negative impact of intense arguments takes time to heal. We are far better off recognizing enmeshment before it gets out of hand. You can do this by familiarizing yourself with some of its "red light signals."

1. Body Language

Your body tells you that you're about to enter "hyper mode": "My stomach tightens like a knot," "My mind turns to scrambled eggs and I can't think," "My hands clench up into fists," "My mouth feels dry." We all have our early-warning signals. What are yours?

If you have trouble answering, you may need to think about what happens to you at an earlier stage of the approaching fight. Often, bodily signals register long before the dispute actually breaks out. For example, Ted, a dad I work with who was continually upset about his son Dwight's messy room—and his wife Corrine's defense that "he's just being a boy"—would start feeling tense as soon as he pulled up into his driveway. Merely approaching his house and imagining the latest "disaster" in Dwight's room—and the predictable fight with Corrine—tied his stomach in knots.

2. Going to the Brink

You're about to start generalizing. The words "never" and "always" are on the tip of your tongue, as in "You *never* think of me" or "Whenever I ask you to take care of something, you *always* disappoint me." Since this kind of exaggerated accusation is almost "never" correct, it's a sure sign that intense enmeshment is about to begin. It also invites an equally hyperbolic response from your partner, digging both of you deeper into the struggle.

3. Mud Slinging

You're about to stray from the content of the fight and attack your partner's character. As parents we're taught to criticize what a child *does* ("You left the towels on the bathroom floor again"), not who he *is* ("You're such a slob"). Unfortunately, we often forget this good advice when we fight with our spouses. Since character assassination will surely trigger a defensive or retaliatory response from your spouse, a two-minute disagreement easily escalates into a "war of the worlds" as soon as the mud starts to fly.

4. Emotional Bookkeeping

You're about to open your ledger of past grievances. This leads to enmeshment because it practically guarantees that you'll be stuck together fighting over a hopelessly expanding list of complaints. For example, Pat, a woman I work with, told me how her parents handled disputes. "When my mother was upset she'd cook totally inappropriate meals like soup, pork chops, gravy, and mashed potatoes in the middle of August. After two days of these unbearably heavy dinners my father would finally say, 'Is something bothering you?' And my mother would immediately present him with a list of grievances that she'd obviously been 'recording' for months without having breathed a word about them."

5. "Let's Get Away Together"

You feel a pressing need to get away from the kids, retreat behind closed doors, and settle the argument on the spot.

At first glance this may seem like a constructive idea—after all, we shouldn't fight in front of the kids, right? Unfortunately, more often than not, resorting to this strategy is a sure sign that you're enmeshed since these attempts to get away usually lead to hotter not cooler tempers. This is because what you really want, once you're behind closed doors, is to let off steam and blame your partner—without the restraint you feel if the kids were around.

6. "I'm Right, You're Not"

Finally your overriding goal in the disagreement is to get your spouse to admit that he or she is wrong. When this happens you're completely enmeshed: once you want your partner to admit something, you're totally dependent on him or her to say those magic words, "I'm wrong." For example, Ted, the father who hated his son Dwight's messy room, wasn't satisfied when his wife Corrine agreed that the room needed cleaning. Ted also needed Corrine to admit that she was "slovenly," that cleanliness was a virtue, and that she was wrong in allowing Dwight to live in such a "pigsty."

YOU'RE ON THE VERGE OF LOSING CONTROL IF:

1. Your body gives you early-warning stress signals.
2. You're about to use the words "always" and "never" during fights.
3. You're itching to criticize your spouse's character, not his or her behavior.
4. You're taking out your ledger-list of pent-up grievances.
5. You feel the urge to get away from the kids and resolve things with each other immediately.
6. Your goal is to get your spouse to admit that you're right—not merely to resolve the dispute.

KNOWING WHAT TO SAY

Once you've recognized these signs of enmeshment, the next step is to say out loud, "I'm *about to lose it.*"

As artificial as this may sound, you need to use exactly these words. Why? Because to say "*You're* losing it," or "I can see *you're* out of control," or "*You're* pushing my buttons" (which we're all tempted to blurt out) won't work for several reasons.

To focus on your spouse at this moment will only cause him or her to react defensively, to insist, "No, I'm not. *You* are." This kind of response will tighten the rope that is already enmeshing the two of you. It's also true that you're not the final expert on your spouse's emotional state—even though we often feel we know our partners better than they know themselves—only your *own*. That's why, in order to break the enmeshment, you've got to say, "I'm about to lose it."

Next say, "*I have to take a break for x amount of time.*" In other words, include how long it will take for you to regain your equilibrium. Sometimes simply saying these words and walking into the other room is enough to break the cycle. On other occasions you may have to go upstairs where you can be alone. Some people need to step outside or walk around the block. Anne, a woman I worked with, actually got over her fear of driving so she could leave the house at moments like these and take a cooling-down tour of her neighborhood.

Before you leave, though, it's *essential* to set a time when you'll be ready to talk about what happened. This is so your partner doesn't feel as if he or she has been left high and dry. Don't be vague, as in, "We'll talk about it later." Be *specific:* "Let's talk at seven-thirty tonight when the kids are finishing their homework."

I'M NOT TRYING TO PUT WORDS IN YOUR MOUTH, BUT . . .

Don't say:	"You're out of control."
Say:	"I'm about to lose it.."
Don't say:	"*You're* pushing my buttons."
Say:	"I can't discuss it now. *I'm* too upset."

Don't say: "We'll talk *later.*"

Say: "We'll talk about it at nine-thirty tonight after
                 the kids are in bed."

RUNNING WITH THE WOLVES

Once you're alone, the first order of business is to *calm yourself down.*
There's no universal way to do this. Some people, as I mentioned before, simply need to step into another room to regain their composure.
Others have told me that they talk to themselves, saying things like,
"No one is going to die. Nothing terrible is going to happen. We're
just having a fight." Another woman tries to remind herself that she
and her husband are fundamentally "on the same side—we both want
to do right by our kids" (sometimes it works, she says; other times, it
doesn't). Some people find mindless things to do, like watching television or folding laundry. One woman, who said she normally hated to
iron, found it very soothing when she was agitated—pressing the wrin-
kles out of clothes relieved her tension. A man I know takes an incredibly hot two-minute shower to "cool off."

Don't worry if you're not yet sure how you'll calm down, everyone
finds a technique that works best. To paraphrase that old song,
"Whatever gets you through the fight . . ."

How do you know when you've calmed down? Again, your body
will tell you. When the tension is gone from your hand, your throat,
your stomach; when your mind has stopped racing; when you aren't
compulsively rehashing the details of who said what to whom; when
the most important thing isn't being right or blaming your partner;
when you can breathe and think about other things—then you are no
longer trapped in the moment.

THE SECOND TIME AROUND

Before rejoining your spouse, remind yourself that:

1. It's very rare that one decision will traumatize or change your
   child's psychological development forever.

2. We don't have to present an artificially constructed "united front" for our kids.

3. It's okay for our children to see that we disagree as long as we don't consistently "lose it," and neither one wins every argument.

4. There's no one "right way" when it comes to childrearing.

5. Just about every decision can be reconsidered and changed afterward.

Some parents keep these five pointers plastered on the refrigerator, or write them on a notecard to keep in their pocket, as a constant reminder.

YES, BUT . . .

You're probably saying to yourself just about now, "Sure, this *sounds* easy, but it won't work in our situation." I understand your skepticism because I feel it myself. Every time Stacey and I fight over the kids, I hesitate and say to myself, "Forget it. A time-out will never work." But despite my own disbelief, *it does!* And the more you practice each step, the less enmeshed and trapped in the moment you'll feel.

Through the years, thousands of families who have heard me speak about this method have come up with many doubts and questions. I've included the most common—along with my responses—right here.

1. *We tend to have our worst fights either in the car or in a social situation where we can't get away from each other. How do we handle these situations?"*

   This is a perfectly reasonable question. The answer is simple: If you believe in your *right* to take a parents' time-out, you'll be amazed at how creative you become at separating from each other in even the closest quarters.

   Suppose you're in the car, arguing because you're lost on the way to visit friends. As soon as you realize that you're about to become enmeshed, try saying, "I'm about to lose it. I need a few minutes. Please pull over."

   Sometimes switching places—climbing in the back with one of the kids, for example—gives you the room you need away from your spouse to calm down. Rolanda, a mom I recently met at a parenting workshop, told me she keeps a "relaxation tape" in the glove compartment of the car. She turns the music on loud so no one can talk, and lets the tape soothe her. Other parents pull over or off the road: stopping at a gas station, going to the bathroom, buying everyone a soda, or pumping a tank of gas all give you some needed space.

Phyllis, a woman I work with, took what will sound like an extreme measure, but it proved very sensible. She and her husband Dan often fought terribly over the kids in the car especially if the kids weren't there (which could put quite a damper on the rare times they found themselves alone together). One afternoon in the midst of such a battle she told Dan to pull over and announced that she was getting out and taking a taxi home. "I couldn't even believe the words as they came out of my mouth," she reported. But her impulse was a good one. All of a sudden Dan took her commitment to breaking their enmeshment much more seriously. Now Phyllis routinely carries enough money in her purse so that at any time she can leave and get herself home. Interestingly, she's never had to resort to this again; simply having the money provides her with the escape hatch she needs. She knows she can pull herself out of the enmeshment no matter what.

2. *"What about those times when things have to get done, when you don't have the luxury of a time-out for parents?"*

As I described above, there's a natural enmeshment in many real-life situations that makes a time-out *impossible*. For example, when you have to get out of the house in the morning, or when a sick child has to take his medicine, the urgency of the moment takes over. You may spend the time bickering, steaming, or sniping at each other, but typically the nuts-and-bolts fighting gets saved for later. Don't use time-out for parents in moments like these; it won't work. Save it for later, when you get down to serious discussion (and possible enmeshment) about what happened when "Sam refused to take his medicine."

3. *"I've tried to take a time-out but my wife won't let me. I say, 'I'm about to lose it and I need a few minutes,' but she follows me and refuses to leave me alone. What then?"*

This is a very common problem. Mel, a father I work with, used to fight with his wife, Sue, over how much help to give their pre-teen son with his homework. If it escalated to the point that Mel felt himself losing control, he would say he needed to take a time-out away from his wife. But Sue wouldn't let him. She followed him from room to room. If he tried to leave the house for a walk around the block, she'd start screaming. Of course, when they were-n't embroiled in their arguments, she acknowledged that Mel was entitled to some time by himself to cool off.

What's the answer? Simple—install a lock on the door to one room in the house. I'm always amazed to learn how many homes don't have at least one room that can be locked. It may sound harsh, but locks were made for moments like these, when we need to be out of ear- and eyeshot of our partner in order to calm down. Sue agreed to try this strategy, *but only after* she voiced the follow-ing concern—one I hear from many other parents as well.

4. *"He says we'll talk about it later, after he's calmed down, but he doesn't follow through. If it were up to, him we'd never talk about the fight. I know I shouldn't follow him, but how else can I be sure we'll get around to discussing the issues?*

Sue's question is a crucial one. In fact, the main difficulty that many women have with parents' time-out is that they, like Sue, fear their husbands will never bring up the quarrel again, or that men are using the time-out "as an excuse" to withdraw.

If you can't trust that your spouse will keep his word and talk with you once he's cooled down, then you do have a problem. There is evidence that consistent refusal to talk about issues, *espe-cially by men,* is one of the most powerful indicators of potential di-vorce. It's one thing not to be able to discuss issues in the midst of a fight, but quite another to use time-out for parents as a way to avoid your spouse.

If this technique doesn't work because promises to speak together later are never kept, you need to consider taking radical action. Andrea, for example, a woman I met at a parenting workshop, de-cided that the only way to get her husband to take her seriously was to go on more of the business trips she had always turned down. By doing so she changed her stance from passively accepting his with-drawal to active assertion. And her husband, after a few rounds of having to deal with the kids alone, eventually got the message that she meant business. He, in turn, began keeping their post-time-out appointments.

Another woman, Helen, got quite a reaction from a large parenting group when she reported handing her husband the following ultimatum: "Either you keep your word and discuss how to handle the kids during mealtime or I stop cooking." "*That* got everyone's attention," she said. "I should have done it ten years ago."

For many other women, however, nothing seems to get him interested in talking later. If this is the case—if your spouse categorically refuses to discuss things—then you've got serious trouble that absolutely should not be ignored. This is one of the few instances in this book when I would suggest seeking family or marital counseling.

5. *"If I say I need a time-out for myself and bolt from the dinner table or the car, won't this set a bad example for my kids? Is this a healthy model of conflict resolution?*

If you carefully explain to your kids that you're taking time-out because you want to discuss disagreements when you're more in control of yourself, then you couldn't be setting a better model for your children. Remember, growing up means taking responsibility for oneself. If your kids see you making a greater commitment to self-control, they will, too. In fact, I often find that as parents institute a time-out policy for themselves, a whole range of out-of-control behaviors among the kids—sibling fights, tantrums, whining—"mysteriously" lessen.

But you can't wait for the last minute to explain this technique to the kids. Let them know beforehand: "If I get upset in the car I'm going to pull over, get out for a while until I calm down." Preparing the children for this possibility will leave them much less bewildered. And once they understand what's happening, they won't think that Mom or Dad is running away from the other, but rather the opposite—that their parents are trying to resolve their differences in a responsible, constructive way.

6. *"I'm afraid that if I say I'm about to lose it, I'll be the one who is capitulating."*

No one wants to "give in" in the middle of a fight. But actually, the first time you collect yourself enough to say, "I'm about to lose control," your partner will be thrown for such a loop that he or she will not get *any* pleasure from this "victory." Remember, one of the characteristics of enmeshed fights is their familiarity. By saying, "I'm losing control," you're announcing that this fight won't proceed as it normally does. Your spouse will probably feel so off balance at this unexpected course of events that he or she will be forced to act differently and to take what's happening more seriously. Rather than giving in, you're laying down a challenge.

For example, Julie and Hank used to stand in the doorway of their house during their worst fights (over disciplining their four-year-old daughter). Hank would threaten to leave the marriage "just to get away from the kids," a threat that compounded Julie's fury. I urged her to try taking a parent's time-out, but she refused, saying "I won't give him the satisfaction of giving in." Finally, because I promised that her initiative would make Hank much more uncomfortable than he'd be if the same old enmeshed interaction were to continue, Julie agreed: "If it will upset him, I'll try anything."

Here's what happened after Julie said, "I'm about to lose it." Hank walked out of the door in a huff, and made it halfway down the porch steps. Then he stopped, turned around, and came back into the house. He went into the den and sat, sulking by himself for fifteen minutes. Later that night he and Julie talked reasonably (for the first time since their daughter was born) about how handle their disagreements over discipline.

PARENTING FIGHTS THAT HELP KIDS GROW

As we all know, you can't always short-circuit a disagreement. In fact, children benefit from seeing their parents occasionally fight. This is how they learn not only that we all have different opinions, but that relationships can tolerate differences. Some fights, however, are more instructive than others.

Here's how to have a fair fight:

1. Stay sufficiently in control that you don't begin to call each other names, blame each other, or become physical with each other.
2. Don't drag your kids into the argument by asking them to take sides or to participate in any way.

3. Stick to "I" statements: "I feel angry," not "You're so stubborn." This helps move the fight away from blame.

4. Try to stay as specific as possible: "I hate it when you forget to do the laundry," not "You're so forgetful."

5. Make sure that neither of you "wins" all the time.

6. Resolve the fight enough to take action; forget about making the perfect decision. Kids have a harder time tolerating inaction than anger.

7. If possible, hammer out a fight-ending compromise in front of your kids. If you have to settle the argument privately, then tell your kids about the resolution. Even if they don't ask, they'll be wondering how it all turned out.

8. If at all possible, make up in front of your kids so they can see with their own eyes that the problem has been resolved. Seal your reconciliation with a hug or kiss. Children find physical gestures like these very reassuring.

9. Older kids can tolerate more tension between their parents than younger kids. If the fight is going to become fierce, wait until your toddlers and preschoolers are asleep or at a friend's house. As children grow, they can be exposed to higher levels of disagreement.

10. Finally, remember that even though you can't see your kids during a fight, if they're in the house, they're listening to you. The walls have ears!

Follow these guidelines and you might be able to turn fights into the sort of responsible human exchanges that can last our kids a lifetime. Not to mention, you'll certainly be happier with each other.

CHAPTER 12

TACTICS
AND TEMPERAMENT

*How Children Create Parental Conflict
and What You Can Do About It*

Though children's paramount strategy often seems to be "divide and conquer"—and they go to great lengths to succeed at this endeavor—don't ever believe that this is what they really want. Regardless of their actions, kids need (and secretly desire) parents to act as a coordinated team. In order for kids to grow up securely, they need to be "held" by parents who are strong and sure, who are not afraid to stand up for beliefs, express their feelings, and instill their values.

SO MUCH FOR THE THEORY

In the trenches of real life, however, children challenge practically every decision we make. They threaten to turn the tiniest detail of family life into a battle of wills. Whether the issue at hand relates to the "gimmes" ("I want that candy now!"), to ever-expanding privileges ("But, Ma, everybody will be there!"), or what to wear ("You're so cheap it's unbelievable!"), your children fight as if their lives depended on it. And they seem to want nothing more than to win. Before you know it you feel worn down—not simply because you are fighting your children, but also because somehow you become embroiled in a fight with your partner.

TEMPERAMENT: "HE'S BEEN THAT WAY SINCE DAY ONE"

Children create tension on the parenting team using two basic pressures that seem so powerful as to be forces of nature: temperament and tactics.

Temperament is a tricky term to pin down—except every parent knows exactly what it is. Temperament is the part of our personality we can't help being. It stays fairly stable. I've heard countless parents say things like "I knew right from the first week that my daughter would be a handful," or "He was always a quiet boy. He was like that as an infant and he's the same way now." A friend of mine swears she knew that her son would be a "dynamo" before he was even born, judging from his incredible activity while she was still carrying him. My neighbor's son Andrew slept twelve hours at a clip from the day he came home from the hospital, and was content to sit in his infant chair looking at his toes. This while my own children squirmed, wriggled, and ran their way through infancy and toddlerhood—and took years to sleep through the night. As I used to say to Andrew's mother, "If every kid had Andrew's temperament, you could have ten children, a career, win the Nobel Peace Prize, and not even notice them around." When it comes to temperament, we get dealt a hand and then we have to make the best of it.

TACTICS: "THE ENDS JUSTIFY THE MEANS"

But temperament isn't the whole picture. Kids are geniuses at discovering the specific tactics that are most effective at getting what they want. They will fight ruthlessly, say precisely what makes us feel guilty or unsure of ourselves, create tension so thick between us that you can cut it with a knife. And if you catch most children older than five during an uncharacteristically honest moment, they will admit to knowing which tactic they've just employed. I'll go one step further— most grade school-aged children not only are aware of their tactics but can do an absolutely perfect impression of how *we'll* react.

And yet, no matter intent they seem on winning, kids want parents who can, in the end, handle their temperament and match their tactics.

This chapter will focus on the most common ways children put pressure on the parenting team.

1. "I Need an Answer Now!"

Just as you're about to leave the house in the morning for work your twelve-year-old son Mark tells you that three of his best friends are getting together that afternoon at Jason's house. "Can I go, too?" he demands, one foot already out the door. You don't know what to do first. Should you make a decision yourself, ask your spouse? You know you want more information, but according to Mark there's *"no time to spare!"* You need to act decisively but instead you hem and haw, or simply give in.

Forcing parents to make split-second decisions like this is an especially effective tactic kids begin to use as early as elementary school. This is when they begin to "get" how preoccupied, rushed, and harried we are; they bet we won't have time even to see each other, let alone thoroughly discuss the matter. They figure that if our backs are up against the wall we'll take the path of least resistance.

This tactic obviously creates tension between parents. Split-second decisions like "Okay, you can go to Jason's" or "It's all right with me if it's all right with your mom" are often made in haste and ones we're usually sorry about.

What to Do

Reserve the right to say "no" *precisely* because you were given no time to discuss the decision with your partner. Tell your child, "If you'd asked me earlier I would have considered your request. But since you asked me so late my automatic answer has to be no. Next time you'll have to give me a chance to talk about it with Daddy." Since the aim of a good tactic is to win, your child will quickly learn that backing you into a corner won't always work to his advantage.

But what about those times when you *have* to make a split-second decision? Then you and your partner need to establish two ground rules. First, whoever was forced into making a rapid decision should do so without being open to second-guessing. If your partner can't resist criticizing, then say, "The next time I'll be sure to call you at the office—

and ask to speak to you no matter what kind of meeting you're in—so we can discuss it together." I think your spouse will get the point.

2. "But You Let Me Do It Last Time!"

By age four or five, just like the best TV attorneys, kids catch on to the idea of precedents: "You let me stay up late last Friday night, then I should be able to stay up late every Friday night!" or "But yesterday you let me have a chocolate wafer before dinner, so why can't I have one tonight?" This tactic is especially troublesome for the team when one parent allows a privilege that the other is strongly against.

What to Do

Reserve the right to make one-time-only decisions, and don't be afraid to admit you made a mistake. For instance, you can explain to your child, "Last night I let you have a chocolate wafer before dinner because Mom was held up at work. It was a mistake because it ruins your appetite. I'm changing my mind."

After going back on a "precedent," you must be prepared for the counterreaction. Four-year-olds will throw tantrums, seven-year-olds will cry "Unfair!", ten-year-olds will negotiate you to death, thirteen-year-olds will immediately spew out whatever threat comes to mind. In other words, any child worth her salt will be able to make you at least momentarily lose your resolve and begin sniping at your partner.

But if you stick to your right to make mistakes and change your mind after consulting with each other, kids will come back fifteen minutes later as peaceful as the country after a summer storm. Why? Because you've held firm—and despite their initial objections, this leaves children feeling secure. Remember, your child's sense of security is worth being a little inconsistent.

3. "The Walls Have Ears"

Even young children (from approximately four years and up) learn very early which "trigger" issues most frequently cause fights between their parents. If, for example, money has always been a sore spot in your relationship—let's say one partner is tighter or looser than the other—then the child who shouts in anger, "Dad, you're always so cheap!" is using her knowledge to create a wedge between the two of you. She knows that by saying this she's firing the opening shot in a war that routinely erupts between you and your spouse.

What will happen next, for example, is that you'll rush to her defense, saying, "You *are* cheap, Ralph. You always worry about every cent!" rekindling an argument that has been going on for years. Meanwhile, the issue that started the fight—whether or not to buy your daughter those designer sneakers—is conveniently forgotten. And by the time the parental fight is over you might be so worn down that you agree to buy the sneakers after all—even though both of you know how insane this is.

Five- and six-year-olds are no slouches in the divide-and-conquer department either. For example, Linda is always trying to get her husband Rod to open up and talk more instead of being so "inward" and preoccupied with work. It wasn't surprising that when six-year-old Cheryl was mad at Mom for pushing her to get ready for school (brushing teeth, combing hair, etc.) she screamed, "Get off my back!"—echoing exactly what she'd heard her father say so many times before. Rod, sensing a good opening in this ongoing marital battle, defended his daughter to the hilt. "Come on, Linda, you're always on top of every, one. She's right!" Meanwhile, Cheryl had accomplished her very modest goal—ten extra minutes of *Barney* while her parents turned their attention to each other.

What to Do

You need to become instantly aware of when your child is using sensitive relationship issues to her own purpose. Fortunately, there are easy-to-recognize warning signs:

1. You immediately forget the particular incident that sparked the disagreement with your child and begin fighting with each other.
2. You take out a ledger sheet of grievances and bring up instances that have no relationship to what's going on in the here and now.
3. A cross-generational triangle develops pitting parent and child against the other parent.

When you recognize any of these signals, try to stop the argument before it gains momentum: "Let's talk about this later and deal with

Kate now" is one way to throw water on the flames. Physically leaving each other and going to another room may also stop the cycle of blame.

Whatever works for you, the goal remains the same: let your child know that he or she can't derail the focus of your attention by seducing you into a fight with your spouse. This is important because when kids *are* successful at getting us really mad at each other, they feel guilty and scared. In this age of divorce, even five-year-olds know that parents separate—and kids of all ages tend to blame themselves anyway. Sometimes just remembering this fact may help you take whatever action is necessary to stop fighting with each other in the moment. No argument is worth making your child feel responsible for your relationship.

4. "But Mom Said I Could Have an Extra Cookie . . . "

Kindergartners begin to comprehend which parent is stricter on certain issues and carefully choose who to approach for any given request. Fudging the truth a little in the process, your child will exploit the inevitable differences between the two of you. For example, six-year-old Amy wants five more minutes of Game Boy and asks Mom, who's usually stricter about video game time, if it's okay. Except she leaves out one tiny detail—Dad's already given her a half-hour of Game Boy while Mom was driving her sister to soccer practice.

As children get older, they become specialists at knowing which issue plays better with which parent. A ten-year-old boy recently told me that he approaches his father when he needs permission for new privileges, like going home from school alone, but goes to his mother when he wants money. A thirteen-year-old girl told me that she lets only her mother in on the details about an upcoming party because if her father knew, "he'd go ballistic!"

What to Do
As soon as you "get" that you and your spouse are being fed different stories, compare notes with each other. Do this immediately and *in front of your child*. If your spouse isn't home and your intuition tells you something just doesn't add up, you're probably right. In that case, put off the decision until you've had a chance to go over it with your partner. Sometimes just saying that you and your spouse will compare

notes "miraculously" restores your child's memory. When Amy sees the two of you checking out her Game Boy stories, the triangle she put into play immediately breaks down.

No matter how busy or angry you are with your spouse, comparing notes is critical to restoring the power of the team. One of the most dramatic examples I've ever seen was when the messily divorced parents of eight-year-old Ethan came to see me because he was constantly lying at each house. The ex-spouses were still so angry with each other they couldn't sit in the same room, let alone compare notes. So I asked that they send postcards (this was in prefax days) describing exactly what Ethan was up to during his last visit, and how each had handled him.

Within two weeks of these exchanges, Ethan stopped lying and manipulating. When I asked him why he'd become such an honest citizen, he replied, "What can I do? They talk together more now than when they were married."

5. Public Humiliation

You've just sat down in a loud restaurant for a family lunch. Your youngest child, age five, starts banging his silverware loudly enough to be heard in the next state, dumping salt and ketchup into his water and crumpling his napkin into a ball to fling around the room. Your reprimands go unnoticed. Suddenly he's up on his chair yelling "butthead" and "penis breath" (have you watched TV lately?), defying your increasingly embarrassed threats.

The only thing more humiliating is the fight that's beginning to brew between you and your spouse. People at neighboring tables shake their heads over your inability to create a "united front" as they seem to move to different parts of the restaurant.

Who hasn't been in a similar situation? Children have radar when it comes to our sensitivity in public situations. They pick up on our nervousness and can provoke us until we lose it, embarrassing ourselves for all the world to see. This happened at a friend's wedding when a six-year-old girl whined so unrelentingly that her parents, unable to stand it, started screaming at each other during the dignified champagne reception. Ten years later, none of us has forgotten how thoroughly they lost it.

What to Do

When it comes to public humiliation, forget the "united front" business. The rule of thumb is for the less frazzled parent to immediately remove the child from the scene of potential humiliation. Take care of business out of everyone's—especially your spouse's—view. If you're even within earshot of each other, an argument can erupt.

If you're in a restaurant, take your son away to the lobby or an area near the phone booth or the restrooms. If you can't leave, then go as far away from everybody as you can manage. The goal is to get you and your spouse out of public focus. After an initial counterreaction, your child will almost automatically calm down. And without everyone's eyes glued on you, you'll be able to deal with the situation less self-consciously.

Personal experience has taught me how well this works. When Leah made a scene at the end of a play-date—whining, crying, kicking—my wife and I were growing tenser by the moment. Stacey kept feverishly negotiating and I wanted to make a public stand. Neither position was correct. We were reaching dangerous levels of potential humiliation. Conversation seemed to come to a halt as everyone waited to see how we were going to manage our out-of-control daughter.

Fortunately, I remembered my own advice. Since I was slightly less frazzled, I quickly took Leah's arm and marched her into the deserted kitchen away from her audience. Then I said in my most "I mean it" voice, "You can whine and cry all you want, but no matter what you do we'll have to leave anyway." No longer distracted by tensions on our parenting team, I felt very focused. After an initial burst of more whining, Leah suddenly quieted down and stomped into the bedroom to look for her shoes. It was such a quick turnaround that one of the other mothers commented to Stacey, "What did he do to her in there?"

Nothing special, really. It was simply a matter of lowering the public humiliation factor so that we could focus on our child—not each other.

6. "I Want Mommy!"

Temperamental Favoritism

It's common for children who are sick or exhausted or going through developmental transitions to prefer one parent over the other. Unfortunately, favoritism like this can cause many hurt feelings. What happens is that the rejected parent feels terrible while the in-favor parent feels overburdened. Both these feelings often remain unexpressed and bubble to the surface in that more typical parental emotion—anger.

I experienced this hurt when Sammy, my then one-and-a-half-year-old, was sick and refused to let me come to him. He only wanted Mommy. Karen, mother of three-year-old Max, admitted that beneath her criticism of her husband Steve she felt hurt and guilty ("Am I working at my job too much?") because Max would let only his father put him to bed each night.

What to Do

Except for obvious biological needs—nursing, high fevers, exhaustion—there's no reason you *must* go along with your child's choice of favorites. In fact, there are many reasons not to, since this can create a cycle that leads to a greater participation imbalance between you and your spouse. I can't begin to count how many mothers have come to me and said, "The one thing I'd *never* do again is be the only one who puts my kid to sleep. But now I'm trapped. He can't go down without me, and there I am a prisoner. What a mistake that was."

If you're the out-of-favor parent and want to break the cycle, spend small amounts of extra time with the child in order to wean him from your partner. At first, keep your contact short so your child doesn't have the opportunity to rebuff you. For example, stay for a few minutes at bedtime, and then let your wife take over. Each night increase the time a little. After a while you'll be able to be there almost until he's dropped off. Finally, one night, leave when he's asleep.

In almost all areas of temperamental favoritism, this gradual desensitization approach works. With more equal participation, both parents feel dramatically relieved. Randy, the father of four-year-old Casey, tried this method, and was astonished the first night Casey approached *him* to tuck her in and say goodnight. The only person happier was his wife Ellen, who found her Endless List responsibilities reduced by one half-hour every other night.

Tactical Favoritism

Often children will favor one parent simply because they're angry at the other. This creates a great deal of pressure on the parenting team, dividing you up into "good" and "bad" cops. The best approach is to act as if you don't notice. Keep your anger (as opposed to the hurt that usually arises in response to temperamental favoritism) in check and wait it out. Your child will usually come around.

For example, seven-year-old Lucy became furious at her mother, Sandra, when Mom wouldn't allow her out of the house to say good-bye to her grandparents at the car. "Don't touch me!" Lucy told her mother at dinner. "I only want my daddy!"

Now in this case Daddy sometimes feels like the family's fifth wheel. He may secretly relish Lucy's attention and even encourage it with a conspiratorial wink toward her. He's momentarily gratified, but this, as they used to say, "is no way to run a railroad"—and certainly no way to run a parenting team.

Instead of getting annoyed, Sandra kept a low profile until Lucy's bedtime. Then she explained to her daughter, "I didn't want you to go outside tonight because it was snowing. I know how excited you get when you go out in the snow, and it was almost time for bed. Maybe I made a mistake, but I wasn't trying to be mean. I only wanted you to be able to fall asleep tonight—there's school tomorrow.."

If waiting and reasonable explanations don't work, you may have to be "tactical" yourself. For example, try spending extra time with your other children. This usually gets the sibling-rivalry juices flowing enough to break the ice. A slightly dirty trick, perhaps, but one that almost always gives a child motivation to reestablish contact. And after your child begins approaching you, you'll find her more receptive to discussion.

7. "I'm Not in a Bad Mood and I Don't Want to Talk About It Anyway!"

Your eleven-year-old daughter Amelia comes home from school with a sour expression. During dinner you ask what's wrong and she says, "Nothing!"

MOM:	Are you sure?
AMELIA:	Yeah.
MOM:	Aren't you going to eat anything?
AMELIA:	Nah, I'm not hungry.
MOM:	Are you *sure* nothing's wrong?

DAD: Leave her alone, already. She's okay.

Unlike other tactics, this is not one children use on purpose. It's a natural law of family physics that difficult feelings spread from one person to the other. What's happening is that Amelia's bad mood is being transferred out of her and into her parents. During the rest of the evening, tension builds between Mom and Dad.

Hours later, Mom asks Amelia, "Did you finish your homework yet?"

AMELIA: *(staring at the TV)*: Last night you helped me with my homework and it was all wrong.

DAD: *(to his wife)*: Why are you being so compulsive? Let her relax.

MOM: She has four more pages of spelling and three more pages of math. Did you know that? You don't. How could you . . .

And within minutes Mom and Dad are at each other's throats while Amelia sullenly stares at the TV screen.

Later that night, as she's lying in bed, Amelia mentions that she'd had a fight in school with her best friend, Annie. "She told me that Jill is now her best friend," she cries. This, finally, is the source of Amelia's unhappiness. Unfortunately, her parents have wasted the night not speaking to each other over a fight that had absolutely nothing to do with them.

What to Do

Be alert to the signs that your child's bad mood is putting you adults at risk. To save yourselves, first recognize the "transfer of moods" phenomenon as soon as a fight develops between the two of you. If one starts, ask yourselves if you were mad at each other before your child arrived home. If not, chances are that he's getting you to take over his mood.

Next, don't chase him. If he won't talk about it, give him time. Hold back from getting into "pouncing" mode. Be patient—he'll talk when he's ready. Don't be afraid (or guilty) to go about your business with each other and even relax.

One couple I know became so good at spotting this pattern that they'd quietly retire to the den, or become engaged in their own separate activities. Sooner or later their daughter would plop down next to one of them, ready to talk. As Mom said, "By being careful like this we saved ourselves hours of useless bickering over her mood."

8. Just When You Thought It Was Safe to Go Back in the Water . . .

As all parents know, any child, no matter how old, is subject to sudden, almost violent regression.

- Your fifteen-year-old daughter who is too mature to have anything to do with "parents" and who out of embarrassment walks ten paces behind you at the mall all of a sudden sticks her feet in your face and says with the deadpan insistence of a two-year-old, "Mommy, take off my socks."
- Your preadolescent who won't allow his parents to come anywhere near his room without knocking and practically begging permission shows up in the doorway of your bedroom on Saturday morning and wants to snuggle with you.
- Your six-year-old daughter who has spent the past three months pressing you to get her ears pierced shows up for dinner on all fours, Cabbage Patch bottle dangling from her mouth.

Regressive behavior like this is not tactical. It's the way kids develop—two steps ahead, one step sideways, one step back. Unfortunately, the sudden swings create real tensions on the parenting team. For one thing, we'd all like child development to be linear—kids moving steadily forward instead of constantly looping back and forth. Out of frustration and worry, we tend to blame one another when these regressive episodes occur. A fifteen-year-old who shows up for dinner one night demanding soft food, "like when I was a baby," is unnerving and very provocative. In one family Mom may be sickened, thinking, "Oh, no, what's next?" while Dad growls, "Grow up!" In another family Mom may want to indulge the behavior for a little while, but Dad calls this spoiling and demands that the child be ignored.

What to Do
First, keep in mind that children almost always regress during times of transition. The most common times of transitional regression are just

before children make a developmental leap. You can save years of fighting with your partner by remembering that children seem most disorganized, clingy, and maddeningly regressed just when a scary new era is about to begin. Temperamental regressions are also more frequent when children feel vulnerable—if they're tired, sick, or hungry. These regressions are not tactical maneuvers to try to extort favors, but signs of fears that need to be soothed. Remember, they are usually also signals that development is on track—so don't despair or jump to blame each other. Again, that's easier said than done. Because parents often don't know how to tell whether regression is normal or a sign of trouble, here are some real danger signals to watch out for:

1. Regressive episodes go on for longer than several weeks in a row.
2. Regressions take place not just with you but with other people. This is a very important sign, because children normally save their worst for us.
3. Friends, relatives, and teachers notice the regression, and people are concerned enough to tell you.
4. Regression affects other areas of development (eating, speaking, sleep patterns, etc.) that have been stable for a long time.

Consider professional help when you notice any of these signs.

9. The "Gimmes"

If you need any proof that we live in a consumeristic age, just look at our children. Acquisition is in their blood. They walk around in a semistuporous daze induced by hypnotic advertising and the undying quest to "belong." The "gimmes" pull at everyone's purse strings and cause countless disagreements on the parenting team. It's probably one of the single biggest areas that comes up in my parenting workshops.

The urge to acquire is so powerful and kids will go to such great lengths when they set their sights on a particular item that we're usually dealing with a perfect blend of *both* tactics and temperament. Because of this, it sometimes feels as if we're fighting the force of the ocean.

But over the years, I've learned that certain measures can help you navigate these turbulent waters in a way that lessens conflict on the parenting team. First, decide that for any big purchase (and every family has its own definition of what constitutes a "big purchase") either parent can retain veto power—and the other one must agree to go along with his or her decision.

Second, when you start giving an allowance (early grade school is a good time to begin), distribute it on the same day each week. Otherwise children will purposely exploit our inevitable lapses in bookkeeping and approach each parent separately to increase fringe benefits or to finance impulse buying. We parents are vulnerable targets indeed. I worked with one boy, Richie, who routinely squeezed out an extra ten dollars each week thanks to his "creative accounting" of which parent had given him how much money when. Since there was no set schedule for allowance, nobody but Richie could keep track of the paper trail.

Third, watch what you say in front of children—it may be misconstrued and then used against you. "But you *promised* to get me Metal Head," your five-year-old son Randy cries. In reality, you didn't actually say those words. When the commercial appeared and Randy started getting hyped up, you grunted and said, "That looks like fun." To him, of course, this constituted an ironclad agreement. Likewise, saying to an eight-year-old, "Maybe one day we'll get the Super Soaker 200 for you" means that you've already signed on the dotted line.

But don't fall for these misinterpretations. Let your children know that mumbling or sighing doesn't add up to a promise. You may feel a little guilty because they misunderstood you, but you still don't have to purchase that game you absentmindedly nodded about two nights before.

Fourth, be on the lookout for certain trigger phrases that your children resort to when they desperately want something. Most kids (I've heard four-year-olds say things along these lines) draw comparisons evoking guilt and anger on the parenting team. "Molly has a computer in her room. How come I can't have one?" Other kids learn that by saying "You never want me to have fun, Mom!" their parents will become embroiled in an argument and forget about them. Older kids keep mental accounts of what *you* spend and then ask why you can't afford Play Station when the two of you just bought a new family car.

To combat these tactics, tell your children over and over that certain phrases will *always* fail. Parents I work with have actually drawn up lists of such phrases and have then given them to the kids. Insist that your kids figure out other ways to persuade you. Free enterprise works. If children know they can "earn" more by becoming more productive (and that they'll get less by ruthlessly negotiating) they'll start to have less faith in the power of empty argument. But you've got to earn respect too—and try to stick by your word.

Finally, money talks. Take turns paying for things. If Dad always pulls out the credit card after a family meal or routinely shells out the cash after a shopping trip, then your children will develop gender expectations about who actually controls the money. To our sophisticated kids, this says volumes about who pulls the purse strings in family life.

Taking turns also puts you and your partner on more equal terms about how much money is going out, and therefore on a similar wavelength about indulging your child's wishes. For this reason I recommend that both parents know exactly how the family's finances operate.

10. Tantrums

As every parent knows, tantrums don't disappear once your child outgrows the terrible twos—they simply become more sophisticated. In fact, parents often talk with more dread about their children's tantrums when kids are three or older. The problem, again, is that the child's anger is often contagious, spreading like wildfire as parents go up in smoke over how to handle the situation. There are some approaches, however, that safeguard both parents and children from tantrums that threaten to escalate out of control.

The first step is to distinguish between those tantrums that are tactical and those that are temperamental. Tactical tantrums (or "manipulative tantrums," as Stanley Turecki calls them in *The Difficult Child*) almost always follow saying "no" to a child's request. Unless your child is in physical danger, ignore them. Temperamental tantrums, on the other hand, are the result of feeling tired, hungry, or ill. These need to be soothed, for example by physically holding your child or tending to the underlying biological need. However, I've found that after a child reaches about four or five years, most tantrums are both tactical and temperamental in nature. If your soothing doesn't help, and you and your spouse are heading toward a collision course, then follow these guidelines.

First, recognize this simple, irrevocable fact: You cannot reason with a child (or for that matter with an adult) in the middle of a tantrum. Hundreds of fathers have told me how infuriating it is to watch their partners offer an ever-increasing menu of choices to a screaming child, or how aggravating it is to witness the endless negotiation that takes place when your child loses it and you keep pulling at straws for quick solutions.

Second, when these efforts don't work, start ignoring the tantrum with the following "practical consequences" kind of explanation: "I can't think when you're screaming like this. When you're less upset we'll talk about it." Or, "We're about to lose it with each other. We'll talk later."

Third, you and your spouse leave the room. Don't say to your child, "Go to your room." By about five or six kids start defying your order and you'll end up in another power struggle. Because your child will probably follow you, be prepared (if he's in grade school and there's no danger to his physical or psychological well-being) to close or even lock your door.

Fourth, if the two of you are upset, try not to talk with each other and solve things. You probably won't be able to get anywhere. Just try to calm yourselves down.

Fifth, wait for the first signs that the tantrum has reached a plateau or is decreasing. *This* is the time to knock on her door (if she's retreated to her room) or come out of your own refuge. Why intervene now? Because you shouldn't reward tantrums that are still on the rise. You want to approach only when she's started soothing herself. The message is "We'll try to solve this when we're all more reasonable."

Six, an ounce of prevention is worth a pound of cure. If you know that the super toy store at the mall induces emotional meltdown, then make your expectations clear ahead of time. Tell your child, "When we get to the store, you can pick out one toy. Ask for more than that, and you'll get nothing."

There's no way to banish tantrums in our kids (or in ourselves). But if you both agree to these guidelines, you will definitely have less trouble with each other. And you'll be doing your kids a huge favor. When they themselves are out of control, they need to see that you aren't.

11. Mom And Dad, Get Your Act Together

If the tensions kids create on the parenting team become chronic, it often serves a different purpose from those discussed above. Your kids may be trying to tell you something—that you need help for *yourselves*. A fourteen-year-old boy who got thrown out of boarding school because of his drinking problems started attending a substance abuse group with his parents. During one of these meetings he screamed out, "How can you expect me to deal with my drinking when you haven't ever dealt with yours?" A twelve-year-old girl who began shoplifting found herself with her parents in family therapy. After several sessions her mother realized that she had to address financial imbalances between her and her husband—she had absolutely no control over financial decisions. Because a third-grade boy was having trouble in school with his temper, Mom and Dad were asked to attend a meeting with the school psychologist. During the session, they talked for the first time about their own problems controlling their anger around the house.

In other words, if your child develops a chronic problem, don't interpret this as simply a cry for help. He may also be thinking of you! Consider whether this is a child's way of encouraging you to find the support you may have needed for years but were too afraid or too harried to ask for.

These, then, are the solutions to the special problems posed by tactics and temperament that thousands of parents have test-marketed and found to work best—for your kids and the parenting team.

CHAPTER 13

SIBLING RIVALRY AND THE PARENTING TEAM

No sooner do you become pregnant with your second child than other parents delight in saying, "Just wait. Two kids are ten times more work than one!" You smile patiently, confident that having another child won't prove all that difficult.

But then it turns out that you were wrong. The changes in your family—especially between you and your spouse—are more titanic than you could possibly have realized.

No wonder guides on coping with sibling rivalry fill entire bookstore shelves. Though they pay scant attention to parental disagreement, they are otherwise excellent, and I can't, in these pages, attempt to cover the extensive ground that they do.

Yet a short treatment on siblings is essential because of one simple fact: pressure from sibling quarrels not only creates general havoc in the household, but also places enormous pressure on the parenting team. In fact, the changes between partners are so enormous, and the potential for disagreement and disconnection so great, that it's one of the basic reasons parents find two children exponentially more difficult to handle than one. With the birth of the second child, the quality of life between Mom and Dad can easily begin to erode.

That's why I've decided to include a special section on sibling rivalry in which I will highlight only those techniques that meet two requirements:

- They have stood the test of time—meaning hundreds of parents have told me they work.

- They are the most effective in strengthening teamwork and connection between parents.

1. Learn to Recognize the Dance, or Predictable Interplay, Between Siblings

Never assume one child is always the victim and the other the aggressor. Remember, no matter how things appear, it takes two to tango. If you look closely enough, as I do every day in my professional (and personal) life, you will see how the victim subtly provokes the aggressor into attacking. It often works like this: Just as you enter the room, the "aggressive" older sibling smacks the "innocent" younger one. Predict, ably, you turn to your oldest child and reprimand him. "But, Mom," he protests, "she was breathing down my neck." Or, "She brushed up against my elbow." Or, "She was using that whiny voice I can't stand. Why do you always take her side?"

"Yeah," chimes in your husband, and before you know it, rigid lines have been drawn, with one parent and one child on each team.

In fact, the sibling battle was under way before you ever got into the room. In most cases, sibling sniping begins moments earlier, unobserved by either parent. Children as young as three learn how to be provocateurs. Their motives can be complex or simple—arising out of boredom, the need for attention, or their desire (as hundreds of kids have told me) "to see which side Mom and Dad take."

Here's how to stop the "dance":

Jot down on a piece of paper the subtle behaviors both children use to provoke the other. Then you'll have evidence in black and white that victim and aggressor constantly trade places.

Once you stop thinking of one child as "bad," you'll find yourself feeling sympathy for him. You'll probably want to spend more time with him. This will make everyone, including his overprotective father, feel better. Breaking stereotypes by learning your children's hidden dance is the first step toward ending reflexive parental battles over sibling rivalry.

2. Resist the Urge to Overidentify

It's astonishing how early parents and siblings break off into "sides." After no more than one or two months, many parents decide that "Jason is just like his father—they're cut from the exact same mold. Now Jennifer, on the other hand—she's a perfect clone of me!" This natural tendency to overidentify leads to many problems on the parenting team, creating two families within a household who can become antagonistic toward each other on a moment's notice.

Overidentification usually stems from one of two causes:

1. In some families, one parent is drawn to a particular child because of a strong physical resemblance or a temperamental match. For example, our second child, Sammy, was born blond, and everyone immediately likened him to my wife, who also was light-haired as a child. In another family, Robin remarks that her older son, Brett, is exactly like her husband. "Not only does he look like Clive right down to his finger- and toenails, but he's just as messy. And, just like his father, he walks to the beat of his own drummer." Robin identifies with their three-year-old son, Eddie. "He gets more easily hurt. He's overly sensitive to other people's feelings just like I am. In fact, I wish he was a little tougher, like Brett."

   Clive, of course, both loves and hates being lumped together with Brett. He loves it when they're admired for their spirit and determination. He hates it when they're called obstinate. Not that he doesn't do the same degree of overidentifying himself: "My wife and younger son are so sensitive. It's like walking on eggshells around here!"

2. Due to the pressure of caretaking a newborn, many families "split apart" after the birth of the second child. Often the older one finds himself paired off with Dad, while Mom tends to the all-consuming needs of an infant. Even after nursing is over—and sometimes forever—these two units remain rigidly intact, splitting the parenting team right down the middle. Each child has a champion and an antagonist, and before you know it you have two warring factions in the house.

   Both mothers and fathers have told me how unhappy they are about this configuration. Mothers feel as if they've lost a special relationship with the older child, while fathers feel cut out from getting really close to the younger one. Over time, of course, it may all even out, but the process can take several years during which many hurt feelings build up and erupt into struggles on the parenting team.

Whatever the cause, having two units in the house virtually assures parental fights. Here's what you can do:

- Stop yourself from remarking on how much one child looks or acts like your husband. Try to downplay the inevitable comparisons drawn by relatives and friends by at least not repeating them around the house. Think about who resembles whom all you want, but don't continuously emphasize it in front of the kids.
- Make a conscious effort to look for similarities between yourself and the child who seemingly isn't like you. Remember, they exist. Every child, no matter how much she may resemble one parent, has both parents' genes.
- Then, cultivate these similarities.

For example, Luisa and her partner, William, fought constantly over their two kids: Mom took Beth's side while William sided with Mark. Locked in a typical pairing-off syndrome, their house was like a battle zone. Recognizing overidentification in action, I asked Robin to look for traits she shared with her son, Mark. After initial objections, she actually helped identify a learning difficulty Mark had, which took a different form but was quite similar to a learning problem she had suffered with as a child. Her greater empathy toward Mark not only got him the tutoring he badly needed, but almost immediately stopped William from aggressively defending his son. The rigid battle lines became more fluid, and different pairings between parent and child began to naturally occur.

The fact that this turnaround happened within just a couple of months is not unusual. Remember, when children assume two-dimensional roles, as Mark had in his family, you're never seeing the entire picture. Your narrow view of your child and the inevitable parenting disagreements almost always hide something unexpected. This is especially true as children get older.

The most shocking example in my professional experience was with the Klein family. Seventeen-year-old "horrible" Leslie and her four-teen-year-old "perfect" sister Zoe were trapped in two-dimensional roles. For years (in fact, since kindergarten), Leslie had been identified by her father, Phil, as "just like her mother. She can be a real bitch, self-centered, materialistic, and capable of saying whatever mean thing comes into her head." His wife, Joan, actually agreed, and hated those parts of Leslie that "remind me of myself." Meanwhile, Zoe took after her mild-mannered dad and, except for continuous fighting with Leslie, was the ideal child—an excellent student, polite to a fault, and a pleasure to have around.

This deeply troubled family was almost at the point of divorce. Joan and Phil's anger rarely subsided, and the girls seemed to genuinely hate each other as well. If anything, both became more like their cari-catures as time went by—Leslie the "devil," Zoe the "angel." Only af-ter I began asking the parents to pay attention to the dance and to question the validity of their daughters' two-dimensional roles did the incredible truth emerge: perfect Zoe had been sleeping around promis-cuously and using drugs for two years; unfeeling, self-absorbed Leslie had developed an ulcer (she knew about Zoe, and the stress in the family had literally become too much for her to bear). As the truth became known (just as it always does), the immutable, inaccurate roles disappeared almost overnight—along with the constant parenting bat-tles, which up until that moment had seemed unavoidable. Leslie got the psychological and medical help she needed; Zoe was given both firmer limits and the acknowledgment that she was far more complex than she'd been given credit for.

In an equally astonishing case, I once asked eleven-year-old Damien, who caused his parents no end of trouble, why he was so bad all the time. "Well," he told me, point-blank, "I figure if they're going to scream, it's better that they scream at me because my younger brother—he can't take it. He's not as tough as me."

"What if they don't yell at either of you?" I asked.

"They'll still yell," he said thoughtfully, "only at each other, and that might lead to a divorce."

Out of the mouths of babes. And you know what? After I thought about it, I realized that Damien was absolutely correct in his diagnosis.

At the very least, he was certainly more complicated than his "bad" label would lead you to believe.

Remember, if your kids are too-neatly labeled, start asking yourself; "What's wrong with this picture?" You'll prevent many an unnecessary parenting battle if you do.

3. Spend Extra One-on-One Time with Each Child but in Different Combinations

Families in which Mom and Dad side with a different child fight because each parent has become an expert about one child and something of a stranger to the other. Here are some tips to break the deadlock:

- Spend time with the child you feel is least like you.

  For example, Andy found himself spending most of his spare time with his six-year-old daughter, Melinda, because she was quiet like he was. He then became her protector when she fought with her loud and bossy twelve-year-old sister, Iris. Iris's cause, not surprisingly, was championed by his wife, Cathy. Iris would pick on Melinda, calling her "fat and stupid," not exactly building blocks for healthy self-esteem. This enraged Andy and made him even more unwilling to learn about who his older daughter really was.

  The key to breaking this vicious cycle of anger was getting the family to spend time together in atypical combinations. I strongly encouraged Andy to go shopping with Iris for school supplies. He hesitated but eventually agreed, and ended up marveling at how many new things he learned about her life. After one short shopping expedition, Iris was beginning to outgrow her two-dimensional label. I also suggested that Cathy stop defending Iris and instead ask her younger daughter to be more accountable around the house. They began food-shopping together and doing other "grown-up" chores Melinda loved.

  Obviously, more balanced one-on-one time was what each daughter needed. As they continued doing activities in different combinations, Iris stopped baiting Melinda and Mom and Dad stopped picking on each other as well.

Several months later I asked Iris why she wasn't provoking her sister so much. "Well," she said, "I'm spending more time with my dad now. I don't feel like Melinda is his favorite. It feels like we have one family—not two."

- Break up alliances that form after the birth of a second child. Mothers need to spend special time with their firstborn children, and fathers need to get to know the baby in the family.

  Mary and Kevin saw an almost magical change when the typical older child/dad, younger child/mom combination broke up purely by circumstance. Kevin had to travel for business, and because of it Mary was forced to make time for firstborn Gilbert. Mary felt so relieved to be reconnected to her older son that even after Kevin stopped traveling she insisted that the family maintain its newfound fluidity. Mom and Dad began regularly trading off who spent time with whom and who defended whom during parental disagreements.

- Break down the gender stereotypes that exist in many families.

  If Mom is in the habit of shopping with daughter Sue, while Dad takes' Devon to Little League (along with a hundred other sex-stereotyped parent–child activities), you're laying the groundwork for dissension on the parenting team that can last a lifetime. Break through these gender biases. Dad can learn to make a French braid while Mom drives Devon to baseball practice or learns to play his favorite video game with him.

4. Stop Trying to Control Everything

A foreign newspaper reporter searching for her country's largest family found a woman who had twenty-two children. "Okay, what's your secret?" asked the incredulous reporter, herself the mother of four.

"I learned not to get involved so often, unless there was physical danger. Unfortunately, I finally realized this only after the eighth child. The biggest change with child number nine was that my husband and I fought much less. Maybe we were just too tired by then."

I'm sure she's right. I get tired just thinking about their situation. But not getting so embroiled as judge and mediator helps too. This works for parents as well as kids. Children actually tell me that they fight with each other more when we're around, often to simply see which "side" we'll take. (Have you ever noticed that things are quiet until you put the key into the front door?)

To help lessen fights around the house, stay out of the role of judge ...nd negotiator as much as you can possibly tolerate. Here are some ef- ...tive techniques to help:

- Let children come up with their own solutions to a dispute—but only if you know neither child is in actual physical danger.

  Even very young kids can participate in resolving a battle. Visiting friends a number of years ago, I observed four-year-old Clara fighting with two-and-a-half-year-old Rachel over who had rights to sit on a kitchen stool during dinner preparation. After ten minutes of listening to their screaming and crying, the adults in the room had reached their collective boiling point; the dinner party teetered on the brink of disaster.

  That's when the girls' mother, Naomi, said, "I'll give you girls ten minutes to come up with a solution to this problem" (or five minutes—let them have as much time as *you* can tolerate). "When we come back, if you don't have a plan we'll take the stool away and neither of you can use it."

  A few minutes later, Clara and Rachel told us their solution: Each of them would sit on the stool for two minutes, "and can we use the kitchen timer to make sure we share?" Naturally, midway through Clara's first turn the girls found something else to play with and the stool—a moment before the most important and desirable piece of property on the face of the earth—was entirely forgotten. Nonetheless, their solution was sound. They had hammered it out with no help from adults and no arguments between the adults.

- Isolate those few situations in which intervention is absolutely essential.

  As I said earlier, any time physical violence is threatened, parents, of course, need to become involved. But don't ignore verbal abuse between siblings. In one family I counseled, six-year-old Brad was experiencing trouble in school. The school psychologist, phoning Brad's parents, said that Brad seemed to lack confidence and assertiveness and was acting very babyish. Brad and his nine-year-old brother, Ike, fought relentlessly at home, and his parents were fighting too, each taking one boy's side. The squabbles were so bad that their dad, Paul, was beginning to fall into the familiar pattern of withdrawing and traveling whenever he could. So I suggested that Paul and mother Helen stop reacting to everything and isolate a few key situations. In this specific case, since words were used as swords, I told them to ask Brad which insults were especially hurtful to him. Brad was able to identify three: "sissy," "faggot," and "crybaby." To address both sides, I also suggested that the parents find out what annoyed Ike most about Brad. Ike quickly replied, "his whining."

Together the family drew up two contracts, which the warring brothers signed. The contracts clearly spelled out specific punishments that would follow Brad's whining, or Ike's using any of the three words Brad hated. In the matter of a few weeks the fighting between brothers—and between parents—markedly declined.

It didn't completely disappear, of course, but the school psychologist called me to report how much happier Brad seemed. And with destructive sibling behavior limited, there were significantly fewer opportunities for Helen and Paul to do battle with each other.

5. Spend Time Alone, Just You and Your Partner

Above all else, defend your right to spend at least small amounts of time alone with your spouse. Without question, the biggest complaint I hear from parents who have more than one child is that they see each other too little. Large-scale surveys such as the Child magazine study I cited earlier support this observation.

Less time together means that intimacy often drops to dangerously low levels. If that happens, it's almost impossible not to feel tense and angry when it comes to resolving differences over the kids. This increase in tension often accounts for the ominous tone veteran parents have when they warn parents who are expecting a second child: "Wait, two is ten times worse. . . ."

To better manage your time away from children, see Chapter 14, "Nourishing Each Other."

Th   .. are the five most important ways to cut down on parental
c   over siblings. Remember, having more than one child *is* a
t...   .dous challenge. But the suggestions I have just made will go a
long way toward protecting your relationship with your partner and
allowing you to savor the special joys that having a larger family can
bring.

CHAPTER 14

NOURISHING EACH OTHER

The Parenting Team Can't Live Without It

Though dinner is over, Larry and Jan try to steal a couple of minutes alone at the table. Very soon it will be time to start getting Danielle, their four-year-old, ready for bed. But these are the first seconds they've had to themselves all day, and they're not too eager to move on.

Suddenly a familiar refrain breaks into their quiet conversation. "Mommy, look at me! Look at this cartwheel!" sings Danielle, dancing into the kitchen. Larry stops talking in midsentence as they watch their daughter.

"That's great," Jan says, feigning enthusiasm. "Now, you know what? Go on upstairs and I'll be there in a minute. We'll play 'Beauty and the Beast' together."

"I'm going to color," Danielle says, finding her crayons and sketch pad. Larry and Jan resume their conversation where they left off.

"Look," Daddy! Look at this red sun I made!" Danielle snuggles up and sits on her daddy's lap.

"It's very colorful," Larry says, turning to Jan, who's struggling to finish her sentence.

"You know why I made it red?" Danielle continues. "Just a minute," he tells his daughter.

"No, but this is really funny!" Danielle insists.

Larry sighs. "Okay, okay, what's so funny?" He says to Jan, "We'll talk again later."

"HELLO, I MUST BE GOING"

Of course, they both know what "later" means. Unfinished conversations have a habit of disappearing in the rubble of everyday routine. But what can they do? Clearly Danielle needs attention right now. . . .

Sound familiar? Many studies have shown that married couples spend a tiny fraction of their day—a few short minutes *at best*—in conversation with each other. Of course, this shouldn't be surprising. When you consider how much time we spend working, commuting, tending to the kids, the house, our bodies, and watching TV, who has *time* for talking?

You'll notice that in the familiar list of what needs attention I didn't include one small detail—*your relationship*. That's because eventually most of us get so strung out in the push-and-pull of everyday life that we stop thinking of the parental relationship as something that actually needs attention. Working on automatic pilot, we assume that we can be an effective parenting team without investing any special energy in it.

Nothing could be further from the truth. Over the years, I've learned that all parents who manage to stay married, sane, *and* connected to each other share one basic characteristic: the ability to protect even small amounts of time together *no matter what else is going on in their lives.*

It's a simple rule. We can't nourish our children if we don't nourish ourselves. In this chapter, I'll discuss the ten most powerful ways you can protect your intimacy against the constant encroachment of kids, jobs, and outside obligations. As always I'll start with the smallest, most taken-for-granted aspects of family life and work toward the more difficult challenges.

1. You Need to Be Able to Finish Brief Conversations in Front of the Children

If your family is like mine, most dinnertime or "hanging out" conversation is child-focused. We talk to the kids about *their* day at school. We encourage the kids to tell us what *they* think about stories or current events. We are quick to praise their accomplishments when they seek recognition. This is an important part of growing up and of family life; kids need to be listened to. They thrive on attention.

But what's often overlooked in our child-centered world is that children also benefit from listening—to *us*. They need to feel that we are real, three-dimensional people who care enough about ourselves and each other to discuss our work, activities, feelings, and thoughts.

Yet can you remember the last time you and your partner found yourselves in a nonlogistical conversation that lasted more than two minutes when the kids were around?

Years ago, children couldn't believe that their own parents actually had sex. Today's younger generation, I can assure you, has little difficulty imagining parental sex (though the thought is still not very appetizing to them). What *is* difficult for them, however, is picturing their overscheduled, overworked parents spending time conversing with each other. How often do they see it? It's an activity seemingly on the verge of extinction.

PARENTS TALK . . . KIDS GROW

If you're like most modern parents, you'll find yourself abandoning "adult" talk when children interrupt, for the following reasons:

- "I need to build my child's self-esteem. Continuing our conversation may make him feel unimportant."
- "I want to know what's going on in his life. If I keep talking when he wants to talk, he'll think twice before opening up next time."
- "Nobody ever listened to me as a kid. I don't want my child to feel the way I did growing up."

Many of us worry about these bugaboos of modern childrearing. But here are five reasons why protecting brief conversations with your partner and ignoring kids is actually *healthy* for them.

First, children learn that when you become a parent, you don't stop being a person. Many of us grew up fearing that these two roles are mutually exclusive. In fact, most of the couples who see me for counseling during pregnancy are less frightened by the impending demands of infancy than they are terrified that baby's arrival will sound the death knell to intimacy. This is the message they received from their own parents—and even from their peers. Recent publications, Internet advice, chat rooms, radio and TV talk shows, as well as endless magazine articles address the belief that "after kids, you just don't have a life of your own." Changing this generations-old belief system requires that you *model* different behaviors for your own child. And this begins with that briefest moment of parental intimacy—adult conversation.

Second, children benefit immensely from hearing us talk about ourselves. They need to know us as people who have lives outside the home—in our other roles as workers, friends, and colleagues. Why? Because this helps them grow out of their normal childhood narcissism—their feeling that the world revolves around them. Ask yourself, "What does my child really know about me besides the fact that I'm her parent?" If you're honest, probably very little. Part of the problem is that today's service-economy jobs are pretty difficult to describe, and so many of us work far from home. Fifty years ago, the son of a farmer or the daughter of a family who owned a shoe store could have easily described how Daddy and Mommy earned a living; today, children of clerks, computer operators, consultants, and investment bankers need more help understanding the source of the family's economic livelihood.

A third important reason to talk together in front of the kids is that conversation between parents helps *kids* open up. If you ask your child, "So how was school today?" you know the answer you're likely to get—a clipped "Okay." But begin talking about *your* day and I can practically guarantee that your child will start telling you more than you ever knew to ask. Adult conversation greases the wheels of kids' conversation. When they don't feel the spotlight directly on them, children almost always talk more candidly.

For example, one couple I worked with had been very upset with their kindergartner, Paula, because she didn't tell them about "Big School." I suggested they talk more with each other during or after dinner rather than direct their questions at Paula. During one adult-to-adult dinnertime conversation, Mom began describing an upsetting incident at work. Suddenly, Paula chimed in, relating a story about some graffiti on the school's bathroom wall. "All the kids are sneaking in there to see it. We're not gonna tell the teacher. Do you think that's right?" Without adult conversation to loosen her tongue, who knows how long Paula would have kept this incident to herself?

Fourth, as old-fashioned as it may sound, teaching kids to tolerate adult conversation is part of teaching good manners. Children who feel free to interrupt conversations at home have no compunction about derailing other adult conversations, whether at Aunt Mary's, at a family birthday party, or during dinner out at a restaurant. Worse, these children grow up feeling as if they have the power to drive a wedge between parents. If a child knows that he can stop discussion dead in its tracks whenever he wants, he'll conclude that adults don't value their time together. This gives kids far more power than they feel comfortable with.

Finally, adults need time to share information about the kids *in front of the kids*. Children feel very secure hearing Mom and Dad dwell on even the mundane details of what happened at school or at the playground—that "all the girls are getting their ears pierced," or that "one of the boys got a bloody nose in the lunch room." Conversations like this reassure our children that we parents are actually in touch with each other and have their best interests at heart.

Five minutes of uninterrupted adult communication about your own workday or what happened with the kids helps Dad feel less peripheral, helps Mom feel less burdened, and helps children feel more secure.

2. You Have a Right to Have *Private* Conversations

This "right" is a difficult one for many parents to acknowledge. It's a powerful commentary on our times that many couples wait till they're at work to call each other and have private conversations. At the office, at least, they won't be interrupted by kids. But with word processors clicking, copying machines buzzing, and coworkers just a thin partition away, you can hardly describe these conversations as intimate.

Forget about phone conversations from the office. You're both entitled to private conversations at home. And I'm not only referring to those private conversations you can justify because they're inappropriate for kids' ears. I mean moments when you simply may want to talk about anything—without being interrupted by a child asking, "Guess how many pistachio nuts I've just eaten?"

If you don't establish this parental right, you'll probably find yourselves fighting with each other. Parents who are communication-deprived tend to become very jealous of any conversation that takes place between their child and their partner. To be sure, a mother watching her daughter and husband snuggle up to talk about what happened in preschool may smile, but she also can't help but remember that *she* rarely gets this kind of undivided attention from her spouse. Interestingly, one of the main reasons men tell me they get so infuriated with their wives for "spoiling" kids is "She hardly ever talks to me in that gentle tone of voice. All I get is the nagging."

What You Can Do

By the age of four or five, children are capable of comprehending that sometimes Mom and Dad need to have private conversations (though they're not happy about it). Here's how to make it happen, even over your kids' most urgent objections.

As with all changes I suggest, begin modestly. Young children about four and up understand and often like kitchen timers. Set one for five minutes or however long *you*, not your child, can tolerate. (If you try to enforce too long a separation, you'll be so anxious about your child's state of mind that you won't have an intimate conversation with your spouse anyway; in fact, you'll probably end up having a fight.) Say to your child, "When the bell rings, then you can talk to us." In my own family, we had to start *really* small—two minutes (actually, it might have been one) was all our child-centered consciences could tolerate.

If your child can't peel herself off of you, then say, "We need to talk together for a couple of minutes without being interrupted. So we're going into our bedroom and *closing the door*. When the kitchen timer goes off, we'll come out."

Then, of course, there's the counterreaction. Most children won't thank you profusely for your attempts at intimacy. In fact, they'll probably up the ante or bargain relentlessly: "Just one minute, Mom. I promise. Just thirty seconds and I'll be done. This is *really* important. . . ."

Don't be held hostage by any trigger phrases like "You *never* pay any attention to me." Go into your room, as planned. But even after you manage to settle in behind closed doors (and remember, I'm talking about just a few minutes), kids devote all their creative energy to trying to get you out. Sometimes they pitch a tantrum to get your attention or else they stage an especially ear-piercing sibling confrontation: "Mom, come quick! Timmy just broke my Lego city." These are not tantrums you should indulge. As long as you feel that your kids are in no physical danger, continue your conversation. Some parents have told me that they listen to music to help them focus on each other and off the kids.

After the time is up and you emerge, say very deliberately, "Now we're finished talking. Now you can tell us whatever you want." This way you're defining your right to have conversations and be with each other.

Remember, a few minutes of together time may be all that your relationship needs at that moment to be replenished. Along the way, your children will learn that adult communication is an essential part of parental life.

3. You Have a Right to a Private Place

According to one of the unwritten laws of childrearing, regardless of how much space you have in your house or apartment, only about one tenth is ever actually used; in fact, wherever you are is where the kids tend to be. That's why all parents need a place to even temporarily call their own—usually a bedroom or study. This is a room that is generally off limits to children unless you're there too, a room in which they learn to be respectful of your possessions and privacy. I've asked thousands of parents if they make use of such a haven; only a fraction of fathers do—and for practically every mother I've met, it's an exotic fantasy.

"I don't want to hurt my child's feelings" is what many parents (including some fathers) say. Yet children believe *they* have a right to privacy. Just look at the door of any modern kid's room and you'll find not-too-subtle reminders of his inalienable rights: ENTER AT RISK TO YOUR OWN LIFE or DANGER: TOXIC WASTE DUMP (which may be true).

Think about it. Having a room where you can go to talk means you will be more likely to resolve arguments with your spouse, and less likely to take out unresolved resentments on your kids. Once you believe that you are entitled to privacy, your children will slowly learn to accept it, whatever their initial reactions to the contrary. And when I say "slowly," that's exactly what I mean. One mother, Adelle, said during a parenting workshop, "It took me *a year and a half* to get my kids to understand that I need ten minutes alone in my room just to feel human on some nights."

4. You Have a Right to Lock Your Bedroom Door

Having a room of your own is important, but when it comes to children, a door without a lock is almost useless. Yet as I've mentioned earlier, many parents feel uncomfortable with this simple solution to the privacy problem. Countless parents buy a lock after hearing one of my talks and never get around to installing it. "Oh, we just can't find the time"—even though they've managed to squeeze in a dozen "taking care of others" activities that week. If only we would invest in our marital relationships as heroically as most of us try to be good parents!

In some families, a lock is installed and then rarely, if ever, used. I ask just about every couple I see, "Do you routinely lock your bedroom door on those nights you sense something sexual might develop?" A shocking number admit that they don't. We *know* how psychologically troublesome it is for kids to walk in on us during sex. We *know* how hard it is to stop and lock the door once things start heating up. We *know* how difficult it is to feel sexually uninhibited worrying that at any second little Adrienne may suddenly appear for a glass of water, teddy bear in hand.

"Well, the kids sleep soundly" is how we rationalize the sex-with-an-open-door policy. Or we ask, "What if something dangerous happens? Suppose my child calls for me and I don't hear? I feel nervous about having a locked door between us."

What we also need to ask ourselves, however, is whether a modern relationship, with all its stresses and strains, can withstand the loss of those relatively few moments of intimacy—sexual or otherwise—after parenthood arrives.

What You Can Do

A locked door doesn't make you totally inaccessible to your children, and will not necessarily hurt their feelings if they're adequately prepared. By the time children become preschoolers or kindergartners, you can offer them this explanation: "Sometimes Mommy and I want private time together. When we do, we'll lock our door. If you need us, this is what you should do."

Teach your child a special knock that he can use, a simple but distinctive pattern. All kids love codes—and making it a game takes away some of their anxiety. Practice it together a couple of times, and say, "When you knock this way we'll know it's you. Then Daddy or I will come out."

"But why do you want to be alone?" your child will probably ask.

"Everyone needs private time," you can explain. "Sometimes you don't want your brother or sister in your room, right?" Or, "I know you like to be left alone in the bathroom." These are experiences almost all grade-school kids can understand.

It's extremely important for your relationship and the kids' development to establish the right to privacy *when they're young*. This way, you not only nourish your relationship, but also teach children that intimacy (and as they get older, they'll understand that this includes sexual intimacy) is *part of family life*—not something that happens only before the kids are born, that takes place only on vacation, or that is illicitly done outside the marriage. If children don't learn this from the get-go, they'll automatically assume, when they're older, that having kids and being intimate are mutually exclusive.

5. You Need to Be Openly Affectionate with Each Other, Especially After the Two of You Have Had a Fight

Children often react dramatically when we adults attempt to be affectionate in public. Three- or four-year-olds squeeze in between us, looking very proud of themselves; preteens shove their fingers down their throats in the universal "I'm going to puke" sign; adolescents stomp out of rooms, morally offended when we show love toward each other. Yet despite these expressions of distaste, kids feel much more secure when we're affectionate in front of them.

Physical affection is never more important than after a fight. Think of it: How do you make up after an argument? More than likely, you probably move on to the next task that needs to be done. Very few of us realize how crucial it is for kids to see us hug or apologize after we've resolved an argument. Even nations end wartime hostilities with some sort of official ceremony. But in family life, we usually dispense with this final step, thinking that it's unnecessary.

Hundreds of children have told me otherwise. Remember, children are very *concrete*. They need to see us get physically back together after a fight. Even an "official" hug or apology staged for the kids' benefit satisfies them (in this area, I'm not such a stickler for authenticity).

"My parents had a fight," kids often tell me, sometimes as young as five. "Does this mean they're going to get divorced?" Today's children benefit from all the open displays of affection we can muster. A hug, a kiss, an apology—no more is necessary. And don't be surprised to discover that these end-of-fight expressions of affection—even those that are at first somewhat less than heartfelt—soothe you as much as they do your kids.

6. You Need Regular Time Away from the Children

Regardless of the problems that bring them to my office, many couples, within minutes, begin talking about the fact that an entire year (sometimes more) has passed since they've had a regular adult date. Countless couples ignore this fundamental way to nourish their relationship.

There are several reasons, all of which seem to have gotten worse over the three decades I've been practicing. The first is that *Mom* can't find reliable babysitting. (Unfortunately, as I've described, in over 95 percent of first, second, or even third marriages, arranging for the babysitter is *still* considered "women's work.")

Convenient, reliable babysitting is difficult to come by for several reasons. With the extended family a plane ride away, Grandma, aunts, or cousins can't usually drop over to help out. Finding a babysitter with whom you feel comfortable takes a long time. And if you do, it's often expensive. The contemporary teenage workforce has sophisticated tastes and habits to feed, and sometimes they charge so much that many families simply cannot afford regular childcare. Finally, by the time Friday or Saturday rolls around, many parents are just too exhausted to get themselves out of the house. Anyway, when you can watch movies on cable TV or rent a video and order a pizza, why bother leaving home? Being a couch potato doesn't sound all that bad, and it's a whole lot less expensive.

Yet despite the initial hassle, nothing is more nourishing than getting away together from the children and the Endless List. Here are the concrete steps successful couples take in order to enjoy time away.

1. Decide on a regular night out. If you can't afford a once-a-week date, then settle for every other week or once a month; frequency is less important than predictability—for both kids *and* parents. The earlier you establish this regular date, the more easily it's integrated into the pattern of family life. Parents make the mistake of waiting too long, assuming that separation is hardest on very young children. Except in special situations (usually having to do with a child's medical condition), exactly the *opposite* is true. Most young children may cry at first, but will settle down with a friendly and outgoing babysitter within a few minutes. Don't let an upsetting transition stop you.

   Again, young children need predictability. If possible, use the same babysitter, go out on the same night of the week (by around age three kids begin to grasp what "Saturday night" means), and spend approximately the same amount of time away. This way, both you and your children will more quickly adapt to the new routine.

2. If you can't afford babysitting or you can't find a sitter reliable enough to put your mind at ease, try cooperative babysitting arrangements with other families in your area. For example, John and Katherine, parents of five-year-old Michael and three-year-old Charlene, recently moved to their dream house in the suburbs. The dream, however, had its nightmarish side—six months had passed without a single Saturday-night date. I strongly encouraged them to call the other families at Michael's nursery school. Sure enough, they found a family willing to babysit for them every other Saturday night in exchange for the same favor. After a couple of months, the atmosphere in John and Katherine's house changed dramatically.

3. Once you're able to successfully establish a regular night out, make plans to go away *overnight* together. Remember, you can't be spontaneous and wait for the mood to hit or all the right circumstances to fall into place. After you have children, *you have to plan ahead.*

   To make the first trip away as painless as possible, start modestly, perhaps with a long day trip. Then you can gradually increase your time away as you feel more comfortable. For example, I suggested to one couple that instead of looking for a summer rental with kids in tow (a six-hour round trip; think of the possibilities for aggravation), they should go by themselves and make a day of it. The two had a wonderful time: "We're thinking about taking regular bus trips to-gether—anywhere—just to have some time sitting by ourselves talking or reading." After two more "practice" day trips, they were ready to go for the "big leagues"—an overnight.

4. As a rule of thumb, plan an overnight before your child's first birthday (unless your child has been sick or has recently suffered a major loss).

Why do couples so often return from an evening away raving about their sex lives? I believe it has something to do with getting away from not just the kids, but the Endless List as well. Around the house, everything we look at reminds us of something that needs to be done. Different surroundings simply don't have the power to trigger Endless List anxiety, which is a huge step toward making intimacy possible.

Stacey and I got away for the first time when Leah was about a year old. We left guilt-ridden and anxious at 5:00 P.M. on Saturday and came back rejuvenated and satisfied at 12:00 noon on Sunday, not exactly a trip around the world. But in the end we both have wonderful memories of that "steamy" night, as if it had been an ex-otic journey to a distant land. However, it took *a lot* of preparation:

HOW TO HAVE A GOOD TIME FOR TWO: FROM STEPPING OUT FOR A MOVIE TO PLANNING AN OVERNIGHT

1. Plan a moderate first date. Don't overdo things by going away for a weekend before you've been away for an afternoon.
2. The Endless List always swells with new items that need to be taken care of before going out. To avoid resentment toward each other, try to divide up these tasks as equitably as possible.
3. Give the babysitter detailed instructions and a full list of phone num-bers where you can be reached in case of an emergency. When possi-ble, make travel and hotel arrangements that can be canceled if the kids should get sick. Most airlines will grant refunds with a pediatri-cian's note.
4. Prepare young kids for your trip just a few days (a week at most) in advance. There's no reason to tell them months before and let their

anxieties build up over time. Older, school-aged children should be given a couple of weeks' notice.

5. Before leaving, give your child something of yours that has your smell, like a scarf or shirt, which they can take to bed with them. Or leave a tape of you singing a lullaby or reading a story if you'll be away overnight. Anything that will remind them of your presence will help.

6. Call home, but *not* at bedtime. Some kids who have settled down for the night become easily upset at this vulnerable moment. Don't be too concerned if your child starts crying when he or she hears your voice, or doesn't want to come to the phone. The upset usually lasts for just a few minutes.

7. Respect your partner's or your anxiety. Don't minimize or mock; instead, try to soothe it. You don't want to begin your time away with smoldering resentments. You want to make love, not war.

8. Don't expect intimacy immediately. It takes time to get used to being alone again.

9. Aim to relax—don't overschedule, especially during weekends away. Pencil in lots of down-time together and some shared activity, but keep these as easygoing as possible.

10. On your return, be prepared for kids who may act less than thrilled to see you. Kids tend either to ignore their parents or to act regressed, especially toward Mom. This is entirely normal and usually passes quickly. Don't interpret either behavior as a sign that your time away was harmful to them. Unless you can see serious physical or psychological problems resulting from your absence, try it again.

7. You Both Need Nonwork Time Away from Each Other

We don't immediately think of time *alone* as nourishing the relationship—after all, we hardly see each other as it is. Yet allowing each other a break without any responsibility for childcare, household chores, or even the necessity to "relate" is one of the most nourishing things you can do for the relationship. According to formal surveys and my own clinical experience, the thing mothers want most in life is "ten minutes alone with no one demanding anything from me." As fathers shoulder more Endless List responsibilities, they plead for the same thing.

What You Can Do

As always, begin modestly. Even a few minutes alone can change the way you feel about something as routine as nighttime chores. For example, Ken was useless around the house after his 8:00 A.M.–6:00 P.M. day at the job. This was not an insignificant issue to his wife Elizabeth since they have three children, ages five, eight, and eleven. I suggested that Ken take a ten-minute walk alone after dinner each night.

Elizabeth immediately blasted me: "But that's when I most need him around. This 'walk' will only let him off the hook even more!" She quickly saw, however, that these few minutes alone enabled Ken to participate more fully when he resumed playing with the kids, helping them with homework, and readying them for bed.

During a parenting workshop, Helen told the group how she started taking a fifteen-minute drive by herself after work before entering the house and relieving the babysitter: "It took me *years* to train myself and my family that I needed a little extra time to recharge my batteries."

Nancy, a friend of ours and a mother of two girls, ages eight and six, gets up before the family and meditates. If the kids unexpectedly come into the room, her husband takes them out to protect Nancy's time alone. This has become so accepted by the family that if anyone calls while she's meditating later in the day, the *kids* say, "Sorry, Mom's meditating. She can't talk now." If we're really serious about something, kids get it.

Another mother I met at a parenting workshop, Felicia, doesn't have such exotic tastes when it comes to solitude—she finds that ironing relaxes her mind and takes her away from moment-to-moment worries. "I know it sounds crazy," she says, "but I build into my weekly schedule at least half an hour of ironing. When 'Mommy is ironing,' my kids know not to bother me."

Remember, time alone and away from each other—whatever form it takes—must be planned. Don't expect that it will magically appear. In fact, if you don't consciously work it into the ritual of everyday life, you'll end up *fighting* to create an excuse to get away from each other. Then, time alone is identified with problems, rather than as an essential ingredient of all healthy relationships.

8. Use *Ordinary* Rituals to Nourish Your Relationship

Many experts talk about the need for rituals to bring families together. Who can argue with this prescription? However, in real life, it's a little more complicated. Rituals, viewed through the eyes of the person in charge of the Endless List, are a decidedly mixed blessing. Yes, they are times of renewal, but the necessary preparations add pages to the already swollen Endless List, causing Mom to feel as if she's drowning. This is the reason why big rituals often end up creating more, not less, stress on the parenting team.

Just think once again: Who does the present-buying, present-wrapping, and card-signing in your house? Who buys, writes out, and mails the thank-you notes! Who makes the telephone arrangements, buys the holiday tablecloth and placemats, and plans the menu? Who goes through your daughter's toys with her before company arrives, deciding which she wants to share?

Usually Mom. Then, by the time the holiday rolls around, she's too emotionally and physically exhausted to partake of the renewing, healing power of ritual. In fact, I have come to believe that this Endless List phenomenon is at least partially responsible for "holiday blues"—feeling overwhelmed (and alone) with a thousand details to take care of.

What You Can Do

In order for rituals to truly nourish, they must reduce stress and distance between parents. *Don't rely on the big holidays to bring you closer.* Start thinking of smaller, more modest rituals. The Sunday morning breakfast Phil instituted so his wife could have an hour to herself—and he could spend some time alone with the kids—is a perfect example. This tiny change in their routine helped them start Sundays out on a cooperative, nurturing note.

Another couple, Anne and Ron, carve out a few hours on a Saturday afternoon once a month—just to hang out with each other. If their three girls happen to be around the house, they've learned not to bother Mom and Dad except for emergencies. Often Anne and Ron just sit around listening to music, talking, or reading together; sometimes they make love. Whatever their plans, they look forward to this regular once-a-month holiday as if it were an official vacation.

Doug and Marlene have been taking a fifteen-minute walk around the block together every night for the last fifteen years. When their kids were young, the whole family went. As soon as the children hit preadolescence, Doug and Marlene began walking alone. Now, with one son in college, they still keep to this simple and very nurturing ritual. It gives them a chance to go over their day and to touch base with each other—a perfect example of the kind of *low-pressure ritual* that all couples need.

9. Doing Good Deeds Together Makes You Feel Closer

Doing nourishing things for *others* nourishes parents and brings us closer. We all need a sense of purpose beyond ourselves, whether we choose to fulfill a religious, political, or social calling. Too often these activities— serving on committees, fund-raising, volunteering—show up as items on Mom's Endless List. While she makes phone calls for the Sunday school picnic or helps organize a curriculum fair, Dad remains on the periphery and the distance between their parallel lives widens.

There are many ways for couples to undertake a joint commitment. Once a month, Barbara and Rick volunteer at a homeless shelter; twice a year Joanne and Rob take phone calls for a national telethon drive; Evette and Erland sponsor a biweekly church committee to feed shut-ins. These activities nourish the parents' relationship because they are done together; require small, realistic commitments of time; are built into ordinary life; help other people; and teach children about values—more than we could ever communicate in a hundred lectures. They also help combat the "I'm number one" mentality so pervasive today. It's almost impossible after doing a "good deed" not to feel kindlier toward each other.

10. Joining Together with Other Parents, on a Regular, Nonemergency Basis, Helps Strengthen the Bond Between You

Readers of *Parenting by Heart* and my column in *Parents* magazine know how much I value peer groups for parents. Life in the early twenty-first century can be pretty anonymous. We wave to neighbors over dashboards as we frantically head off to work, or nod to them in elevators. We get together with our extended family a couple of times a year, or during catch-as-catch-can phone calls. The average family moves once every five years. This leaves us with few naturally occurring opportunities to meet other parents and to discuss normal, ordinary childrearing issues.

Ironically, the only time most of us spend with peers is after a crisis occurs. If a child develops an eating disorder or drinking problem, we soon find ourselves thrust into a community—a peer group built around sickness. Twelve-step programs and sickness-oriented support groups have become the neighborhoods of our time.

But parents need to break through the isolation before a crisis develops, before we start feeling overwhelmed with the pressures of raising kids—and this is what peer groups for parents provide. Some sessions can be devoted to special topics: "How to Stay in Charge of the Kids," "How to Keep the Lines of Communication Open Between Parents and Children," "How to Deal with Violence in the Media," or "How to Create More Connection Between School and Home." The topics can vary, of course, but the goal remains the same: to provide parents with a regularly scheduled forum to get to know one another and to talk about what's going on in their kids' lives.

Peer groups for parents help mothers and fathers nourish each other because:

1. It's easier to stop "the blame game" after recognizing you're not the only parents going through a particularly difficult stage with your kids. Finding out that your child isn't the only one who's crawling into your bed at night can shave hours off the time you would otherwise have spent fighting over who was to blame.
2. Parents talk differently to each other in public than they do behind closed doors. Disagreements that occur during a peer group don't follow the same pattern they would at home. It's harder to slip into your more vicious arguments with ten or twenty other people looking on and listening in.
3. They bring dads into the parenting network. Fathers seem especially drawn to those groups that meet regularly and are long-standing. I've known several groups to remain in existence for ten years, way past the early days of childrearing. Obviously, they offer a community experience both fathers and mothers find nourishing.

4. They allow parents to develop their own fact-finding network. This frees them from having to extract information from kids, who are often notoriously close-lipped. For example, one couple found themselves arguing vehemently about why their five-year-old daughter had suddenly begun whining and talking like a two-year-old. During a peer group meeting, they discovered that the entire kindergarten class had reverted to baby talk. You could almost feel a collective sigh of relief spread through the room. What they all had assumed was a personal problem turned out to be a group phenomenon. Just think—one parent peer group meeting prevented a neighborhood of mothers and fathers from blaming each other unnecessarily about why "our kid" is the only whiner around.

5. Finally, peer groups for parents also allow mothers and fathers to marshal their forces—instead of fighting each other. This alliance becomes increasingly important as kids grow up and want ever-expanding privileges. For example, one couple called me, terribly upset, because their daughter Chrissie had been invited to an unchaperoned party at which alcohol would be smuggled in. Meanwhile, Chrissie was threatening, "I'll *never trust you* again if you tell *anybody* about the party." This lopsided power relationship—in which kids have peer support and parents feel alone—guarantees that mothers and fathers will end up battling with each other.

I encouraged Mom and Dad to forbid her from going and to call some of the parents involved. To their relief, they found that the other parents were as upset about the party as they were. Almost overnight, they mobilized themselves to establish guidelines for future parties. As for Chrissie, her predictable anger evaporated once she realized that she wasn't being singled out, and that her friends were in the same boat.

Kids appreciate it when they see us parents joining forces with other parents—no matter how vehemently they initially object. A friend of mine recalled that when she was in high school in the late sixties, experimenting with drugs, alcohol, and sex, she thought, "If only my parents would talk to my friends' parents they'd realize they're not alone and I'm not the only freak. I know they wouldn't fight so much about me." But because her parents were too embarrassed to contact anyone else, everyone—mother, father, and child—felt undernourished and alone.

Remember, the goal of parent peer groups is to have regular meetings so the process will be in place *before* a crisis erupts. For one thing, it's much easier to talk when everyone is calm. But more important, an ongoing group reinforces the idea that mothers and fathers need to talk with each other as much as kids do, to gain support in our difficult task of childrearing in this modern world.

These, then, are ten basic ways to create greater closeness in your relationship. Anyone of them can make a difference. A few will change the atmosphere of your entire home.

When we mothers and fathers are better able to nourish ourselves by protecting our ability to have even the shortest conversations, by going out together, by developing peer groups for parents—only then can we nourish our children as all children deserve to be.

INDEX

ABOUT THE AUTHORS

Ron Taffel, PhD, has supervised and written about working with children and families for over two decades. He is one of the country's most sought-after speakers for both professional and parent audiences. Dr. Taffel is the award-winning author of over 100 academic and popular articles, and has been a contributing editor to McCall's and Parents magazines for 12 years. His childrearing guides, translated into numerous languages, include the critically acclaimed Parenting by Heart and Nurturing Good Children Now as well as the professional handbook Getting Through to Difficult Kids and Parents: Uncommon Sense for Child Professionals. He is the founder of Family and Couples Treatment Services at the Institute for Contemporary Psychotherapy in New York City, where he lives with his wife and two children.

Roberta Israeloff is the author of four books of personal nonfiction—Kindling the Flame: Reflections on Ritual, Faith and Family; Lost and Found: A Woman Revisits Eighth Grade; In Confidence: Four Years of Therapy; and Coming to Terms—as well as What to Do About Your Child's Moods and Emotions. She is the coauthor of Your Competent Child: Toward New Basic Values for the Family and Raising a Thinking Preteen; has written dozens of feature articles, book reviews, and essays for numerous magazines and newspapers; and has published short stories in various journals and anthologies. She taught writing for ten years at Hunter College and New York University, and currently leads a writing workshop. She lives in East Northport, New York, with her husband, David, a psychologist, and her two sons, Jake and Ben.